SALMAN RUSHDIE IN THE CULTURAL MARKETPLACE

To Rafael

Salman Rushdie in the Cultural Marketplace

ANA CRISTINA MENDES
University of Lisbon, Portugal

LONDON AND NEW YORK

First Published 2013 by Ashgate Publisher

Published 2016 by Routledge
2 Park Square, Milton Park, Abingdon, Oxfordshire OX14 4RN
711 Third Avenue, New York, NY 10017, USA

First issued in paperback 2016

Routledge is an imprint of the Taylor & Francis Group, an informa business

Copyright © Ana Cristina Mendes 2013

Ana Cristina Mendes has asserted her right under the Copyright, Designs and Patents Act, 1988, to be identified as the author of this work.

All rights reserved. No part of this book may be reprinted or reproduced or utilised in any form or by any electronic, mechanical, or other means, now known or hereafter invented, including photocopying and recording, or in any information storage or retrieval system, without permission in writing from the publishers.

Notice:
Product or corporate names may be trademarks or registered trademarks, and are used only for identification and explanation without intent to infringe.

British Library Cataloguing in Publication Data
A catalogue record for this book is available from the British Library

The Library of Congress has cataloged the printed edition as follows:
Mendes, Ana Cristina.
  Salman Rushdie in the Cultural Marketplace / by Ana Cristina Mendes.
    pages cm
  Includes index.
  ISBN 978-1-4094-4673-6 (hardcover: alk. paper)
  1. Rushdie, Salman—Criticism and interpretation. I. Title.
  PR6068.U757Z766 2013
  823'.914—dc23
                                                                    2013011281

ISBN 13: 978-1-138-25347-6 (pbk)
ISBN 13: 978-1-4094-4673-6 (hbk)

Contents

Acknowledgements	*vii*
Introduction	1
1 Rushdie as Gatekeeper	37
2 Exploding the Canon	77
3 Film and Television: Showcasing Pictures of India	103
4 Music and the Brown Culture Industry	127
5 Rushdie, the Public Intellectual	145
Conclusion	169
Works Cited	*175*
Index	*197*

Acknowledgements

Valuable support at different stages of this project was provided by the Portuguese Fundação para a Ciência e Tecnologia (FCT). A special acknowledgement goes to the University of Lisbon Centre for English Studies (CEAUL-ULICES) which generously gave me the opportunity to share my research with others and contact with different perspectives. My gratitude also goes out to Professors Teresa Malafaia and Luisa Leal de Faria, supervisors of the PhD out of which this book came to life. I would also like to express my appreciation to Lisa Lau and Christopher Rollason for their helpful comments. At Ashgate Ann Donahue was always very supportive and patient. My gratitude goes also to the anonymous reviewer of my original manuscript, who provided many suggestions that helped enrich this work.

Lastly, my greatest debt is to Rui for his never-ending faith in me, especially for his unfailing support. I dedicate this work to Rafael, our most accomplished joint project.

Introduction

From Dante to Bob Dylan

> I don't deliberately set out to create this melange of form, this high-low, east and west, north and south, jumble sale of literature. Given that every book is an attempt to understand the world, I use the stuff that lodges in my memory. I have a magpie tendency. I remember fragments of everything from Dante to the lyrics of Bob Dylan.
>
> —Salman Rushdie qtd. in Michael Silverblatt 206

> Thanks to my unusual, and (by conventional standards) hopelessly inadequate education, I had become a kind of information magpie, gathering to myself all manner of shiny scraps of fact and hokum and books and art-history and politics and music and film, and developing, too, a certain skill in manipulating and arranging these pitiful shards so that they glittered, and caught the light. Fool's gold or priceless nuggets mined from my singular childhood's rich bohemian seam? I leave it to others to decide.
>
> —Rushdie, *The Moor's Last Sigh* 240

A magpie, literally a long-tailed black-and-white bird of the crow family, is figuratively an individual who collects or hoards objects that have been discarded by others as worthless. This study deals with Salman Rushdie's self-professed magpie tendency as displayed in both his literary writings and critical pronouncements. Rushdie, a compulsive cultural magpie, avowedly draws inspiration from multiple sources, thieving and reconfiguring disparate elements from "high" and "low" cultures[1] to reflect them back to his reader. Through this creative plundering, various elements are cobbled together in narratives where new relations develop, and the fracturing of high and low is bypassed. Because, as Rushdie sees it in the essay "In Good Faith" (1990), "[m]*élange*, hotchpotch, a bit of this and a bit of that is *how newness enters the world*," he feels free to repudiate that criticism of his work – notably of the controversial novel *The Satanic Verses* (1988) – that would base itself on "the absolutism of the Pure" (394). In keeping with such "rejoic[ing] in mongrelisation" and celebration of "hybridity, impurity, intermingling, the transformation that comes of new and unexpected combinations of human beings, cultures, ideas, politics, movies, songs" (394), he writes elsewhere: "[m]eaning is a shaky edifice we build out of scraps, dogmas, childhood injuries, newspaper articles, chance remarks, old films, small victories, people hated, people loved" ("Imaginary" 12).

---

[1] For the sake of readability, quotation marks have been elided when referring to "high" and "low" cultures hereinafter.

One of the main purposes of this work is to draw attention to a dimension of Rushdie's oeuvre that has often been mentioned, but has not been subjected to consistent scrutiny – the transgression of the high/low cultural divide and, beyond that, the actual debunking of the artificiality of that divide through parody and pastiche. Linda Hutcheon draws attention to the centrality of parody to postmodernism, arguing: "through a double process of installing and ironizing, parody signals how present representations come from past ones and what ideological consequences derive from both continuity and difference" (93), an understanding of parody that finds resonance in Rushdie's writings. Most relevantly, this book addresses the roles assumed by the writer as cultural broker, both as a gatekeeper and a mediator, in various spheres of public production. It looks at the roles performed across various creative platforms including, besides those of novelist and short story writer, those of public intellectual, reviewer, and film critic. His is a representative voice, whether he intended it or not. Examining the issue of cultural brokerism in Rushdie's life and work, this study positions itself in a line of a growing body of scholarship which has been situating the contemporary production, circulation, and consumption of postcolonial texts within the sinuous workings of the cultural industries. The need to assess such processes taking place in a market strictly regulated by a few multinational corporations proves essential when approaching a postcolonial author personally and professionally enmeshed in the dealings of the cultural industries. In such critical assessment rests the wished-for relevance of this study for contemporary cultural studies. One of the key points this work seeks to address is, on the one hand, the extent to which Rushdie's novels and miscellaneous writings exhibit a self-ironic acceptance and questioning of an instantaneous cut-and-paste contemporary culture, in particular regarding the changes that have taken place in the cultural industries since the 1980s. On the other hand, the characteristics of self-irony and self-reflexivity, compounded by strategies of re-orientalisation, are conversely clear sources of the marketability of his works, finding as they do particular purchase with a metropolitan readership.

Recent research on postcolonial cultural production within the increasingly complex dynamics of global exchange has been sparked off by John Hutnyk's 2000 *Critique of Exotica*, Graham Huggan's 2001 *The Postcolonial Exotic*, and Sarah Brouillette's 2007 *Postcolonial Writers in the Global Literary Marketplace*, to name but three. Their complementary critical allegiances – in particular Huggan's and Brouillette's Bourdieu-derived field perspective and their conceptual reliance on the market – had a visible impact on this monograph. The field of cultural production, in Pierre Bourdieu's theorisation, is "a *field of forces*, but it is also a *field of struggles* tending to transform or conserve this field of forces" (30) and concerns the creation and dissemination of cultural capital within "the cultural value stock exchange" (137). Hutnyk's work was likewise crucial in helping to develop a critical perspective of the intersection between postcoloniality and Theodor W. Adorno's Freudo-Marxist-based approach to the political economy of the culture industry. The intersecting debates generated by those three works were instrumental, from the very beginning, in setting up the present theoretical framework.

This study aims to situate itself within the reconfiguration of modes of cultural analysis that examine the operations of the industries of exotica (Hutnyk 5), alterity (Huggan *Postcolonial Exotic* x), and postcoloniality (Brouillette 20) in the construction and negotiation of cultural difference at large. A critical approach to the mainstreaming of postcolonial literature involves, as Huggan and Brouillette persuasively argue, besides resistance to neo-colonial power structures, issues of marketability and commodification of difference. As Mustapha Marrouchi puts it in regards to exoticism:

> In the global culture environment of late capitalism, exoticism is turned into an activity not of foreignness but, on the contrary, of familiarity. Goods from other cultures expand and circulate domestically and internationally within the global economy, housed in the Western Mall where Nescafe, virgin olive oil, Kodak, pampers, samosas, Colgate, couscous, Channel [sic] No. 5, Evian water, Coca-Cola and the post-colonial novel, say, *Midnight's Children*, get tossed into the cart .... It is precisely the novel's accessibility side by side with these other goods that makes it exotic. (42)

Marrouchi's words introduce two questions: Does postcolonial literature ultimately resist or reproduce the logic of the global literary marketplace? To what extent are market forces guiding practices of canon-formation involving postcolonial authors? The present critical project aims to offer tentative answers to these, and other, thorny questions by focusing on the manoeuvres played within the space of South Asian diasporic cultural formations and textual practices, an unsettled and porous "diaspora space" which Avtar Brah defines as "'inhabited,' not only by those who have migrated and their descendants, but equally by those who are constructed and represented as indigenous" (209).

The critical engagements Hutnyk, Huggan, and Brouillette pursue rest on the materialist premise that postcolonial cultural production needs to be examined through its economic mediations. The emphasis of these critiques remains overwhelmingly on the processes of commodification of difference within transnational public spheres, specifically on the anxieties surrounding a perceived neutralising of the political eruptions and subversive potential allocated to postcolonial expression, and also on the strategies involved in capitalising on the "exotic" in an increasingly globalized cultural scene. These strategies include those employed by artists themselves under the guise of staged self-commodification, re-orientalism, or strategic exoticism, the latter defined by Huggan as "the means by which postcolonial writers/thinkers, working from within exoticist codes of representation, either manage to subvert those codes ..., or succeed in redeploying them for the purposes of uncovering differential relations of power" (*Postcolonial Exotic* 32). Strategic exoticism in particular should not be understood as necessarily a way out of the conundrum posed by the incorporation of postcolonial cultural production into globalized networks of consumption (32), which makes its political impact of resistance at times ambiguous. In the case of Rushdie's work, as with V.S. Naipaul's and Hanif Kureishi's, Huggan contends that staging exoticism is indeed part of an operation of resistance. In these works, exoticism "is effectively *repoliticised*, redeployed both to unsettle metropolitan expectations of cultural otherness[2] and to effect a grounded critique of differential relations of power" (ix–x). The fact that Rushdie, Naipaul, and Kureishi are perceived as coming from the cultural margins, Huggan notes, is taken to their own advantage "by *staging* marginality in their works" (xii). Rushdie thus performs marginality, actively foregrounding in his oeuvre – in particular *Midnight's Children* (1981) – its own entanglement in the process of commodity production, undermining the cultural commodification of the margins *from within*. However, this seems to presuppose that postcolonial writers are located in the margins and hence outside the centre, as if centre and margin were clear-cut opposing forces, an understanding which fails to accommodate Rushdie's multiple roles as cultural broker and his canonical status as in all probability "Britain's only global writer" (Todd 11).

After the theorising of Homi Bhabha, postcolonial resistance is time and again regarded in terms of ambivalence or hybridity disrupting the binary oppositions on which the operations of power lie. What the present study contends is that marginality should not be construed exclusively as the basis for understanding Rushdie's work, as a critical grounding in marginality would predictably involve a reproduction of the traditional postcolonial binaries of oppressor/oppressed and colonizer/colonized the writer subverts altogether. This study does not dispute that, however wholly contained by "hybridity-talk," terms such as "hybridity," "ambivalence," and "mimicry" must be engaged with. Suggesting a way beyond the confines of "hybridity-talk" (Hutnyk 33) as the cipher for understanding Rushdie's work, this book endeavours to be part of a much needed renaissance of Rushdie criticism. It attempts to add new critical itineraries and frameworks of interpretation of the writer's work today, itineraries and frameworks that take into account the actual conditions of postcolonial cultural production and circulation within a marketplace which is global in both orientation and effects. The release in 2012 of Rushdie's memoir, *Joseph Anton* (alias adopted while under a fatwa that sentenced him to death in 1989) and its immediate inclusion in the longlist of the 2012 Samuel Johnson Prize, Britain's leading non-fiction prize, further verifies the importance of surveying the relevance of the life and work of such a prolific author in the twenty-first century. The impact Rushdie has had, since the 1970s, on various aspects – cultural, literary, ideological, political, and even theoretical – deserves the critical scrutiny that this book aims at contributing to.

Since the 1980s, the field of Rushdie studies has offered far too many outputs to account for here. A sense of the field before 2000 can be drawn from M.D. Fletcher's "An Annotated Bibliography" (1991) and Joel Kuortti's 241-pages-long *The Salman Rushdie Bibliography* (1997). While most of the bibliography recorded by Kuortti was motivated by the fatwa, the Rushdie critical industry has not failed to continue production. At the turn of the twenty-first century,

---

[2] According to Homi Bhabha, we may locate the other as "something else besides," as a "countervailing image" based on a "negotiation" or "translation" (*Location* 64).

David Smale attested to this thriving industry and to the plethora of new material that continued to be published: "[t]he sheer volume of criticism surrounding Rushdie's work is astounding if one considers that it is just over 25 years since the 1975 publication of his first novel *Grimus*" (7). As in earlier decades, the post-2000 monographs and volumes of essays on the Rushdie corpus have largely followed a literary-based trajectory and adopted postcolonial and/or postmodern readings, with the result that the critical methods employed have often remained narrowly inscribed in a particular disciplinary field and that the lion's share of this research has focused on themes of globalisation, migrancy, and cultural hybridity. An incomplete list of studies which have situated Rushdie's work among these interpretative frameworks includes Jaina C. Sanga's 2001 *Salman Rushdie's Postcolonial Metaphors: Migration, Translation, Hybridity, Blasphemy, and Globalization*, Sabrina Hassumani's 2002 *Salman Rushdie: A Postmodern Reading of His Major Works*, John Clement Ball's 2003 *Satire and the Postcolonial Novel: V.S. Naipaul, Chinua Achebe, Salman Rushdie*, Rajeshwar Mittapalli's and Joel Kuortti's 2003 edited volume *Salman Rushdie: New Critical Insights*, Neil ten Kortenaar's 2004 *Self, Nation, Text in Salman Rushdie's* Midnight's Children, and Madelena Gonzalez's 2005 *Fiction After the Fatwa: Salman Rushdie and the Charm of Catastrophe*.[3]

While the present study focuses on a predominantly literary author, its critical approach is in keeping with Huggan's observation that "the status of literature and the literary has shifted with the move to a more culturally oriented analysis" (*Interdisciplinary* 12). If one is to continue to insist on the above-mentioned themes, other possible conjunctions and readings of Rushdie's work can run the risk of being prematurely closed down. In line with "a more culturally oriented analysis," Andrew Blake's 2001 "beginner's guide" *Salman Rushdie* dedicates its last three chapters to the Rushdie critical industry and to the many guises under which Rushdie makes his presence felt as a twenty-first-century author in a "new literary world" (70–71). David Smale's *Salman Rushdie:* Midnight's Children/The Satanic Verses*: A Reader's Guide to Essential Criticism* (2001)[4] surveys not only Rushdie's novels, but also his essays and his critical reception, as well as examines reviews from a variety of sources in a welcome effort for cross-referencing; this much is attested by the back cover description: "[a]s a novelist and icon, Rushdie has embraced both 'popular' and 'high' culture; reflecting this, the Guide brings together both academic criticism and journalism to investigate the passions and preoccupations of Rushdie's many critics." Other noteworthy studies are Andrew Teverson's critical study of 2007 *Salman Rushdie*, which includes a chapter on the political and intellectual sources from which Rushdie's fiction springs, and

---

[3] For comprehensive overviews of Rushdie criticism, see Teverson (195–216) and Morton (163–174).

[4] Reader's guides such as Blake's and Smale's are the most popular forms of academic publishing in the area of Rushdie studies, which confirms the institutionalisation of the writer's work in academia.

Stephen Morton's *Salman Rushdie: Fictions of Postcolonial Modernity* (2008), which places the writer's work in a broad historical, critical, and theoretical context and for that purpose productively draws on Rushdie's non-fiction.

Though these academics have addressed Rushdie's work from a cultural studies perspective, none of their critical assessments has offered a substantial, sustained, and systematic engagement with the writer's self-declared cultural magpie tendency or, relatedly, with his role as cultural broker, nor posed these issues as central problematics. This book attempts to fill that gap in Rushdie criticism – it challenges the analysis of the author's oeuvre to move beyond a concentration on questions of cultural hybridity, migrancy, and postcolonial "writing back" to a critique of these analytical categories themselves, while simultaneously considering the vital significance of the questioning of the high/low cultural divide in the development of those questions. To reframe Rushdie's work thus will allow this study to attend to the transgression of boundaries at its core and also apprehend the transformative possibilities coiled within the contact between high culture, traditionally elitist, and low culture, traditionally pertaining to the masses. In an oeuvre open to multiple readings, the selection of a focus inevitably leaves some material unexamined and interpretations from other positions unheard. Still, this book hopes to reawaken a field which, saturated by the constant retreading of the same themes over time, has for too long remained uninventive.

It will hence attempt to push forward Rushdie studies into new areas of enquiry that accommodate, for instance: the Rushdie who, in line with his many collaborations with visual artists, wrote a foreword to photographer Taryn Simon's collection *An American Index of the Hidden and Unfamiliar* (2007); the Rushdie who, as cultural critic, contributed an essay on the "hijra" entitled "The Half-Woman God" to *Aids Sutra*, a 2008 volume edited by Negar Akhavi focussing on HIV infection in India; the Rushdie who, as a celebrity, was a sitter in a portrait by Richard Avedon, best known for his early success in fashion photography; the Rushdie who, as a media pundit, commented on the verbal abuse of Bollywood star Shilpa Shetty in a British reality TV show; the Rushdie who, as a renowned postcolonial writer, had his portrait painted by the Indian artist Bhupen Khakhar in 1995 (entitled *Salman Rushdie: The Moor*) and then purchased by the National Portrait Gallery in London; the Rushdie who, as part of his self-described "lifelong film addict[ion]" (qtd. in Dube 9), wrote the screenplay of *Midnight's Children* for Deepa Mehta's cinematic adaptation of the novel, as well as the plays for *Haroun and the Sea of Stories* with Tim Supple and David Tushingham[5] (with a stage premiere in 1998 at the Royal National Theatre, London), and for *Midnight's Children* with Tim Supple and Simon Reade (with a stage premiere in 2003, produced by the Royal Shakespeare Company); the Rushdie who, as a film critic, was involved in an intense critical debate with Stuart Hall and Darcus Howe surrounding the Black Audio Film Collective's film *Handsworth Songs* (Procter,

---

[5] An adaptation by Charles Wuorinen of *Haroun and the Sea of Stories* for the opera stage premiered at the New York City Opera in 2004.

Dwelling Places 7); the Rushdie who, as a polemicist, features as a villain in the banned Pakistani action film *International Guerrillas* (dir. Jan Mohammed, 1990), and as Salman "the Face" Rushdie in a YouTube spoof of the television series *The A-Team* entitled "The AL-Q Team"; the Rushdie who created a sci-fi television drama series entitled *The Next People* for Showtime, a US cable TV network, in 2012; the Rushdie who, as literary anthologist, both co-edited *The Vintage Book of Indian Writing: 1947–1997* and guest-edited *The Best American Short Stories* a decade later; the Rushdie who, through seminal works such as *The Satanic Verses*, was one of the muses of novels such as Hanif Kureishi's *The Black Album* (1995) and Zadie Smith's *White Teeth* (2000); the Rushdie who, as power brand, endorses upcoming authors, such as Kiran Desai, through book cover blurbs; and many more "Rushdies." In sum, the overarching thesis of this work is that Rushdie is a cultural magpie whose creative output borrows from a multitude of cultural forms in his literature and, indeed, himself maintains influence in a number of cultural arenas in his multifarious role of cultural broker.

Rushdie and Cultural Brokerism

> Trying to suggest that Homer and Homer Simpson are the same kind of thing... there are still people who really resist that stuff, but for me it just seems natural. If I like *The Simpsons* and I like *The Iliad*, why shouldn't I talk about them in the same sentence?
>
> —Rushdie, qtd. in Dave Weich

Randy Boyagoda regards the undercutting of the high/low divide in Rushdie's work as a curse: "as engaged by Dorothy in Oz as by destruction in lower Manhattan, he is willing and able to pass between cultural registers and diverse subjects with an insouciant disregard for the relative value of the insights offered, the consistency of his arguments, or the durability of his commitments" (47). To Rushdie, though, placing Homer next to Homer Simpson in a sentence is not a sign of the "dumbing down" of high culture, but instead an affirmation that, for him, the split between "highbrow" and "lowbrow" does not exist. In this respect, John Seabrook (2000) contends that the distinction between "lowbrow" (e.g. *Vogue* magazine) and "highbrow" culture (e.g. *The New Yorker*) has been eradicated and substituted by the category "nobrow." This testifies to the increasing intertwining of marketing and culture that Theodor Adorno and Max Horkheimer had identified many decades before with specific reference to the North American apparatus of cultural production and marketing in the essay "The Culture Industry: Enlightenment as Mass Deception" (1944), a classic of cultural studies' readers. Reading "highbrow" and "lowbrow" together is expressive of a dialectical complexity, as high art as well as more popular forms of cultural expression are crucial to the process of meaning-making in Rushdie's oeuvre. Here, the distinction between elite and popular cultures is replaced by the constant use of intermingling and hybridity. Rushdie, whose father hired a painter to decorate his nursery with pictures of

Disney animal characters (Brennan 73), straddles aesthetic boundaries through his magpie inclinations.[6] More than illustrating his characteristically provocative and polemical tone, putting *The Simpsons* and *The Iliad* on equal terms is a refutation of the patronising condescension narrative that opposes "serious" art to "frivolous" and disposable popular culture.

An illustrative example of Rushdie's inclusive processing of texts, cultural practices, structures of power, and artistic forms can be found in the short story "Chekov and Zulu" (1994), where the "old Doon School[7] nicknames" (150) of the story's protagonists draw inspiration from the cult US television series *Star Trek*. Even though neither the main characters nor their Indian classmates could have seen any episode of the series back when they were at school, *Star Trek* was "a legend wafting its way from the US and UK to [their] lovely hill-station of Dehra Dun"; "just like Laurel and Hardy," they "were Chekov and Zulu" (165). Attesting to Rushdie's belief in the emancipatory potential of popular culture, it is noteworthy that his characters are not fashioned after Captain Kirk and First Officer Spock, but are instead based on two of *Star Trek*'s subaltern characters. Zulu is named after the helmsman Hikaru Sulu[8] of Japanese and Filipino descent, whereas Chekov is fashioned after the character of the Russian Starfleet officer Pavel Chekov.[9] When Chekov visits Zulu's home, he distinctively identifies their alter egos with *Star Trek* memorabilia assembled on top of the television set, namely "the Asiatic-looking Russky and the Chink"; these are "not the leaders … but the ultimate professional servants" (151).

In the story's present, the protagonists are self-described "diplonauts" (151) (a fusion of "diplomats" and "astronauts") stationed at India House in London at the time of Indira Gandhi's assassination by her Sikh bodyguards in 1984. As a security specialist strongly opposed to Sikh fundamentalism, Zulu, himself a Sikh, ardently believes he is a soldier in a war "between Good and Evil" (162). Rushdie uses imagery from J.R.R. Tolkien's *The Lord of the Rings*, a popular epic fantasy novel to which he was introduced as a student at Rugby School by his history teacher J.B. Hope-Simpson. Tolkien's images, which, in the early 1960s, "entered his consciousness like a disease, an infection he never managed to shake off" (*Joseph Anton* 27), are deployed to simultaneously disparage Chekov's unwillingness to take a moral stand against terrorism and to debunk the utopian idea of "Merry England" (a nostalgic longing that, ironically, the idyllic and pastoral settings of *The Lord of the Rings* might be interpreted as nurturing):

---

[6] One of Rushdie's narrators describes himself and his mother as "language's magpies by nature stealing whatever sounded bright and shiny" (*Ground* 56–57).

[7] Doon School is an elite boys-only boarding school in India, located in the Himalayas at Dehra Dun and founded in 1935. Its first headmaster was Arthur E. Foot, a former teacher at Eton College.

[8] Zulu's wife resents being called Mrs Zulu because it "sounds like a blackie" (150).

[9] Interestingly, there is also a character named Chekov in the science fiction television show *Stargate SG-1*.

"while this great war is being fought there is one part of the world, the Shire,[10] in which nobody even knows it's going on. The hobbits who live there work and squabble and make merry and they have no fucking clue about the forces that threaten them, and those that save their tiny skins" (162).

In the appropriation of *Star Trek* as the narrative framework for "Chekov and Zulu," the villainous Klingons stand not for the demonized Soviets of the original TV series, but for Sikh separatists, and Klingon territory is located in Birmingham, the stronghold of pro-Khalistani militants[11] in the English Midlands at the time. Political turmoil in India, in particular the Tamil uprising in the early 1990s, is likewise seen through the lenses of a product of US pop culture. Against the backdrop of an actual political event – the assassination of Rajiv Gandhi in 1991 by a Tamil suicide bomber – Chekov's fantasies about *Star Trek* exploratory missions materialize as he faces death by Rajiv's side: "[t]he scene around him vanished, dissolving in a pool of light, and was replaced by the bridge of the Starship *Enterprise*" (170). When the bomber, smiling, approached the then Indian Prime Minister, Chekov "could see the Klingon Bird of Prey uncloaking, preparing to strike" (170–171), once the explosive concealed under her garment was detonated, "the speeding balls of deadly light approached" (171).

Further evidence of a fictional manifesto wherein the dichotomies of high and low cultures are eroded abounds in the work of a "child of popular culture," in Timothy Brennan's description (73). Edward Said – to whom Rushdie himself dedicates an eponymous essay in *Step Across This Line*, his non-fiction compilation published in 2002 – saw the novel as "an incorporative quasi-encyclopaedic cultural form" (*Culture and Imperialism* 84). Rushdie's novels are all the more appropriate for illustrating such inclusion of encyclopaedic, seemingly random, information. To name but two examples: he weaves names of TV series, Bollywood actors, newspaper headlines, advertisements, magazine stories, and film clips into the narrative of *The Satanic Verses* to depict Bombay; and, describing the process of conjuring *Midnight's Children*, he mobilizes a sprawling array of pictures and delves back to popular songs from both Hindi cinema (*Shree 420*, dir. Raj Kapoor, 1955) and Broadway theatre (*The Music Man*, dir. Morton DaCosta, 1957)[12] to recover the Bombay of his childhood:

> I even remembered advertisements, film-posters, the neon Jeep sign on Marine Drive, toothpaste ads for Binaca and for Kolynos, and a footbridge over the local railway line which bore, on one side, the legend 'Esso puts a tiger in your tank' and, on the other, the curiously contradictory admonition: 'Drive like Hell

---

[10] In Tolkien's legendarium, the Shire is a region of the continent of Middle-earth which is inhabited by hobbits, a fictional race. The Shire is sometimes seen as resembling the British countryside – as Zulu observes, "the map of Tolkien's Middle-earth fits quite well over Central England and Wales" (163).

[11] "Khalistan" is a would-be independent Sikh state in the Punjab.

[12] *The Music Man* was made into a film in 1962; the film too was directed by Morton DaCosta.

and you will get there.' Old songs came back to me from nowhere: a street entertainer's version of 'Good Night, Ladies', and, from the film *Mr 420* (a very appropriate source for my narrator to have used), the hit number 'Mera Joota Hai Japani', which could almost be Saleem's theme song. ("Imaginary" 11)

Rushdie's magpie inclinations are equally discernible in later novels such as *The Ground Beneath Her Feet* (1999) which, in a nutshell, recasts the mythical figures of Orpheus and Eurydice as the Indian rock-and-roll superstars Vina Apsara and Ormus Cama, with this retelling of the Greek myth set in the context of the glittering world of twentieth-century stardom. Likewise, in *Fury* (2001), the fictional narrative built by the protagonist Malik Solanka, an ex-Cambridge history professor working under the alias of Professor Akasz Kronos, "fed on every scrap it could find: its creator's personal history, scraps of gossip, deep learning, current affairs, high and low culture" (190). In an interview in which Rushdie discussed the latter novel, he notes how, throughout his career, his work has been consistently, though not intentionally, following this magpie approach:

> I'd started with a slightly different project, which was not to find these fast slides between, as you say, high and low culture. … [I]n *Fury* and in what comes after it, I'm sure, I'm very interested in this kind of intensity of contact between all kinds of culture, between the most arcane and the most everyday. To see where they join, or if they don't join to make them. (qtd. in Weich)

Another case in point of this magpie tendency is "The Courter" (1994) where, because of an Indian character's inability to pronounce English accurately, an apartment building porter becomes a "courter." In this short story, the character Certainly-Mary suffers from an unidentified illness which the first-person narrator comes to discover results from her unsuccessful attempts at trying to adapt to British culture. That internal struggle is compared to scenes from John Huston's film *The Misfits* (1961), where the three main characters, performed by Clark Gable, Montgomery Clift, and Marilyn Monroe, are each at a crossroads in their lives:

> So it was England that was breaking her heart, breaking it by not being India. … Or was it that her heart, roped by two different loves, was being pulled both East and West, whinnying and rearing, like those movie horses being yanked this way by Clark Gable and that way by Montgomery Clift, and she knew that to live she would have to choose. (209)

For the purpose of exploring Rushdie's magpie tendency and the writer's interrelated roles as cultural broker, this study is theoretically grounded in a complex and nuanced Adorno-based critique of postcolonial cultural practices. As originally theorized by Adorno and Horkheimer in the early 1940s, the "culture industry" is an all-pervasive structure driven by capitalist imperatives of profit which manipulates mass audiences into passivity through the factory-style production of standardized cultural commodities. The concern here is not so much to focus on what critics have perceived as a bourgeois tendency to unify the culture industry, as rehearsed in countless studies. Likewise, it is not this book's intention to endorse a simplistic reading of popular culture based on the subjection and powerlessness of cultural producers and audiences which allegedly resulted from the flattening effect of a Fordist rationalisation of cultural practices. Rather, an analysis of Rushdie's life and work should rely on an understanding of the dynamic and conflictual make-up of the "cultural industries," a potentially more constructive concept than the one originally coined by theorists associated with the Frankfurt School, or at least a concept better attuned to a cultural landscape dominated by global media corporations and their systemic circuits of cross-cultural exchange.[13] Opting for the term "cultural industries" resulted from the desire to retain the visibility granted to the concept by Adorno and Horkheimer, while wanting to endow the analytical category with the idea of diversity and complexity that those critical theorists could not have anticipated. Whereas in its original formulation Hollywood was seen as a cultural Detroit and became the model for mass production applied to the cultural sphere, "cultural industries" highlights the diversity inherent to cultural production today. Such foregrounding bears out the transition from a Fordist model of mass production and consumption during the 1940s to 1960s to a post-Fordist system of flexible production and dissemination. This system has emerged since the 1970s and has been witness to an aggressive transnational co-optation of cultural practices for economic purposes.

In this context, Scott Lash's and John Urry's research in the 1990s constituted a groundbreaking effort to integrate the concept of the cultural industries into a more general analysis of post-Fordist and postmodern consumer capitalism. Lash and Urry argue that economies are increasingly ones of signs, either with a primarily cognitive content – information – or chiefly an aesthetic content – "postmodern goods," instead of material objects (4). Within this "economy of signs and space" – or what they coin "disorganized capitalism" (2) – there is a significant change at the levels of production and consumption of commodities, and both signs and reflexive social subjects – tourists, migrants, and so forth – travel at much greater speeds than during the earlier period of "organized capitalism." Even though Lash and Urry do not explicitly attempt to engage with Adorno's and Horkheimer's theses, references to them are numerous in *Economies of Signs and Space* (1994). In fact, they contribute to rehabilitate Adorno's crucial contribution to cultural studies when they recognize that the German critic "has often been castigated in the culture studies literature for a one-sided pessimism" (142).

Against a reading of Adorno's theses on popular culture as inadequate, sweeping generalisations, and in an attempt to recoup the theorist's arguments in a time of transition, other critics have revisited them over the years and argued that the culture industry thesis is more counterbalanced and less pessimistic than it

---

[13] Notwithstanding Adorno's warnings about the "iron grip of rigidity despite the ostentatious appearance of dynamism" in the culture industry ("Schema" 72), a feature of present-day cultural industries is undeniably their resilience and dynamism.

appears at first sight.[14] An acknowledgment of the double-edged nature of Adorno's scathing critique of the encroachment of market values on to cultural production might well be pivotal when engaging today with the effects of commodification upon cultural practices and, specifically, in grounding a theoretical basis for a broader understanding of postcolonial cultural production. Because Freudo-Marxist critical theory relies heavily on the analytical potential of the concept of commodification for a dialectic reconstitution of contemporary culture, it is productive to return to this theorisation as a way to reconnect global capital, cultural hybridity, and postcolonial resistance within a context of shifting politics of representation. To enhance the understanding of the workings of postcolonial cultural production, and particularly how cultural difference is entangled within the circuits of commodity culture, the theoretical set-up of this book stresses, in relation to Adorno's critique of the political economy of the culture industry, the undercutting of the traditional high/low culture distinction and the commodification of culture, namely, standardisation, pseudo-individualism, and schematisation of the cultural industries' products, in particular postcolonial cultural products.

High culture, John Frow holds, should be regarded as "a *pocket* within commodity culture" (*Cultural Studies* 86). Moreover, as maintained in Adornian thought – to which Rushdie might be seen in certain respects in close alignment with – the relationship between high and mass culture is dialectical, not oppositional. For Adorno the issues that the culture industry raises ensue from the potential for social transformation that it contains, even if under capitalism. Having construed culture, along with Horkheimer, as a "paradoxical commodity" (Horkheimer and Adorno 161), his critique of cultural formations was, above all, dialectical, being as it was interested in their critical possibilities for both control and emancipation from reification and alienation. Besides, the high/low culture distinction does not correspond to a divide, but is, rather, an acknowledgement of a convergence of two cultural spheres which cannot be pulled apart.

In an 18 March 1936 letter to Walter Benjamin, Adorno explicitly withheld, as Rushdie has consistently done throughout his career, from drawing a stark discrepancy between high culture and industrially produced popular culture, famously describing them as "bear[ing] the stigmata of capitalism, both contain[ing] elements of change," and as "torn halves of an integral freedom, to which however they do not add up" ("Letter" 123). Adorno had already applied this holistic image when contrasting "light" and "serious" music in the 1932 essay "On the Social Situation of Music," viewing them "as halves of a totality which could never be reconstructed through the addition of the two halves" (395). He later recuperates

---

[14] In spite of somewhat one-sided accusations against Adorno, of both elitism and distrust regarding postmodernist cultural makeovers on Adorno's part, and directly against such accusations by contemporary critics, positive revaluations of his cultural critique have been made by J.M. Bernstein, Peter Hohendahl, Deborah Cook, Robert Witkin, Shane Gunster, and Alex Thomson, to name but a few that were published in the last decades.

this trope in "On the Fetish Character of Music and the Regression of Listening" (1938):

> Light and serious music do not hang together in such a way that the lower could serve as a sort of popular introduction to the higher, or the higher could renew its lost collective strength by borrowing from the lower. The whole cannot be put together by adding the separated halves, but in both there appear, however distantly, the changes of the whole, which only moves in contradiction. (35)

As such, a wider understanding of works of literature is one that acknowledges their endowment with an aura of high culture, but also their circulation within the exchange mechanisms of the publishing industry. Books are like any other cultural product in the sense that they acquire meanings within the complex circuits of commodity culture. In this sense, this study is interested in the materiality of books as objects with covers, blurbs, reviewers' praise in the media, and so on, but also as artefacts endowed with a "social life," to borrow anthropologist Arjun Appadurai's notion of a "social life of things" (1986). This social life is made up of a tangled web of readers' expectations, sanction or disapproval by the critical industry, publishing houses' marketing agendas, the author's media aura, intertextual relations with other books, among other aspects. Viewing books from this perspective makes it possible to analyse how these commodities increasingly circulate as signifiers within a chain of production, circulation, and consumption of signs. Such approach is thus able to contribute to a broader examination of the ways all the above levels of signification have been involved in the creation and maintenance of an international market for Indian Writing in English (IWE), in its indisputable metropolitan readership appeal fostered, including, but not limited to, marketing campaigns and literary prizes, as well as in the entry of IWE into the canon.

*****

Providing illustrations of Rushdie's multifarious role as cultural magpie and cultural broker is the purpose of the two case studies that follow. Focusing on the short story "At the Auction of the Ruby Slippers" (1992), the next subsection features a case study of the author's subjection of the idea of "home(land)" to critical scrutiny. Along with the strategies of re-orientalism that figure prominently in Rushdie's fiction (and which are the subject of the ensuing subsection entitled "Offering a taste of the spicy continent"), this is one of the specific – and most noticeable – instances of Rushdie's cultural brokerism in its simultaneous thwarting, reinforcement, and challenging of postcolonial theory. The longing for an irretrievable imaginary homeland has indeed been highly valued for its currency in the postcolonial literary marketplace (significantly, *Imaginary Homelands* was the title selected for Rushdie's first collection of non-fictional writings published in 1991). In the last few years, the ever-growing Rushdie critical industry has been more attentive to the author's reception and location as postcolonial celebrity within diasporic South Asian culture. Nonetheless, this critical industry has not yet fully accounted for the subversion of categories such as "home(land)" in texts which, constituting a sort of metacommentary on the politics of cultural translation, comprise a vital part of the political ends of his writing. Being his aspect crucial to an appreciation of the writer's subversion of and complicity with the rules of postcolonial literary marketplace, the case study that follows is well deserving of an inaugural status.

Bidding for Home

> What if all of it – home, kinship, the whole enchilada – is just the biggest, most truly global, and centuries-oldest piece of brainwashing?
> —Rushdie, *Ground* 176–177

In light of Rushdie's position in relation to a postcolonial literary economy, the following reading of "At the Auction of the Ruby Slippers" serves as the perfect starting point to introduce the key assumptions and concerns of this book. The focus is on Rushdie's self-consciousness about his positioning as a writer working within a global economy of postcolonial cultural goods. This subsection, acting as a case study, looks into the process by which the author self-consciously engages with the cultural politics of postcoloniality, deploying the tropes of migrancy and exile, but also undermining their authority through self-referentiality. The emphasis rests on the writer's foregrounding of the ambivalence of "home" through his interpellation of the myth of Ozian magical slippers. In sum, this short story satirizes the commodification of "home," for it is not just that Dorothy's ruby slippers are negotiated within the terms of metropolitan commodity exchange, but that the discourse of homelessness and displacement itself is found to circulate as a commodity in postcolonial texts.

*****

As Rushdie discloses in his review of Said's *Out of Place: A Memoir* (1999), "out-of-place experiences lie at or near the heart of what it is to be alive in our jumbled, chaotic times" ("Edward Said" 317). He sees the creative ground on which the migrant walks as abundantly fertile ("Imaginary" 15), in line with recent developments in travel theory that posit that the experiences of diasporic people deconstruct power relations between the periphery and the metropolitan centre, namely through a deterritorialisation of culture (Loshitzky 323).

Before addressing the issue of the current commodification of spatial and cultural unmoorings in the postcolonial marketplace, it is imperious to highlight that the relevance of "home" for Rushdie's fiction is an expected after-effect of enforced and wished-for exiles. The writer's first migration was at the age of thirteen when he was sent from Bombay to Rugby School in England. He later left England for Pakistan, where his family had moved in the aftermath of Partition. Rushdie then went to Cambridge University in 1965 and became a British citizen afterwards. To this date, he resides in New York in a self-chosen exile which began in 2000. Compounded with all the voluntary migrations the author has undertaken over the years, the 1989 fatwa has inevitably resulted in his troubled connection to "home." Rushdie does not blindly celebrate the unconstrained and unencumbered subject and reflects the diasporic subject's search for constituency and origin. In his case, Bombay remains a strong locus of identification for the diasporic subject, who is *by definition* displaced. The writer recounts as one of his most painful memories his father's selling of his childhood home in Bombay: "I felt an abyss open beneath my feet" ("Dream" 195). In the essay "A Short Tale About Magic" (1992), the first part of his British Film Institute monograph which acts as a companion to the short story "At the Auction of the Ruby Slippers,"[15] he describes his connection to "home" as "problematic" (19). This short story was first published in 1992, at a time of Rushdie's imposed exile due to the fatwa issued three years earlier. The writer would in all probability have liked to have had the possibility of returning home during that period of enforced homelessness when, over much of the 1990s, he was refused entrance into his native country. As he confesses: "I've done a good deal of thinking, these past three years, about the advantages of a good pair of ruby slippers" ("Short Tale" 19).

"At the Auction of the Ruby Slippers," published originally as part of Rushdie's monograph on Victor Fleming's classic Hollywood film *The Wizard of Oz* (1939), centres on the actual auction in 1970 of a pair of red slippers supposed to have been worn by Judy Garland, who played Dorothy Gale, the leading role in Fleming's film. The chronological setting of the 1970s is displaced and, taking on a dystopian view of an affluence-driven West, Rushdie depicts a futuristic sale of the ruby-sequined shoes, regarded by then as much more than a souvenir of the shooting of the film, indeed as full-fledged magical items reputed to have qualities of crossing space and reversing time. At the beginning of the story, the narrator stands in the "Grand Saleroom of the Auctioneers" amid exiles, political refugees, outcasts, deposed monarchs, orphans, and untouchables (90–93), in short, amid a range of disenfranchised figures embodying the condition of rootlessness. Those who attend the auction-turned-celebrity event include "displaced persons of all sorts" (90), "memorabilia junkies" (88), and even fictional characters out of popular culture like E.T. (94) who have come to bid for Dorothy's slippers, reputed to hold magical qualities of traversing spatial and temporal boundaries, while offering the reassurance of a safe return home. The collective hope of these anonymous characters is that the all-powerful shoes will allow them to experience a "reverse metamorphosis" (92) and go home again as the protagonist in *The Wizard of Oz* did in her transit from sepia-coloured Kansas to kaleidoscopic Oz. Religious fundamentalists have also gathered at the auction to bid for the slippers. They regard them disapprovingly as fetishized magical icons and openly declare to be "interested in buying the magic footwear only in order to burn it" ("At the

---

[15] "A Short Tale About Magic" was later reprinted with the title "Out of Kansas" and included in *Step Across This Line*.

Auction" 92), echoing the events that followed the fatwa. Maybe because of this suggestion, the narrator is cynical about the prospect that the ruby footwear can indeed return the homeless home. Highlighting the ways in which "home" is crossed by a plurality of meanings that challenge a one-dimensional discourse, and underscoring the imprecise and unstable location of "home," he notes how it "has become such a scattered, damaged, various concept in our present travails" and despondently adds: "There are so few rainbows any more. How hard can we expect even a pair of magic shoes to work?" (93).

As already noted, Rushdie's critical musings on the idea of "home" should be complemented by his life experiences. According to Anshuman Mondal, establishing connections between Rushdie's biography and his work elucidates the transmutation of the writer's conceptualisation of "home." Mondal points up the changes in the broader interrelated idea of geopolitical space which have occurred – albeit subtly – over the course of his career (178), arguing that the writer's discourse on migration has "shifted from an earlier affiliation with postcolonial theories of transnationalism and diaspora, both of which complicate and dismantle nationalist perspectives on belonging, home and identity, to a species of cosmopolitanism" (181). For instance, in *The Ground Beneath Her Feet*, the narrator Rai reflects on the conflicting "fantasy of Home" and its counterpart "fantasy of Away," or "the dream of roots and the mirage of the journey" (55). Rushdie believes that a tendency to migrate lies at the heart of every individual: "In our deepest natures, we are frontier-crossing beings" ("Step Across" 408). Still, it is possible to refute Mondal's argument according to which the novels *The Ground Beneath Her Feet* and *Fury* signal a reinvention of location in Rushdie's fictional universe. As the writer declares in an interview with Vijaya Nagarajan on the occasion of the publication of the first-named novel, his search for new geographical coordinates for his fiction began with the "migration novel" *The Satanic Verses*, written well before those two novels: "*Midnight's Children* had been, broadly speaking, about India, although some part of it was set in Pakistan. And after all those books, I thought, 'Well, it's time that my writing did the thing that I did,' which is to migrate. And so I began to design a novel of migration."

Certainly one of the most prominent issues to haunt present debates in the area of postcolonial studies is the relationship of diasporic subjects to the slippery and fluid concept of "home." To quote Appadurai, the "seductiveness of a plural belonging" and of an "attachment to an unbounded fantasy space" (*Modernity* 170) that migrant individuals experience, and time and again celebrate, seems to account for the recurrence of the trope of "home" that traverses postcolonial cultural production. Simon Gikandi observed a decade ago that "migrancy," "exile," and "hybridity" were becoming stock terms in postcolonial literary criticism (213). To those, one now might add, to a necessarily incomplete list, "diaspora," "displacement," "uprootedness," "deterritorialisation," and "disaffiliation." Gikandi further stressed Rushdie's creative representation and simultaneous critical puncturing of these tropes related to the migrant experience; with reference to *The Satanic Verses*, he critiqued this work as "self-consciously performative in its engagement with the cultural politics of postcoloniality, spaciously deploying many [postcolonial] tropes but also undermining [their] authority in its many self-referential moments" (208). Elsewhere, in the essay "Imaginary Homelands" (1982), Rushdie exposes the discourse of a static, mythical home, showing that it can never be the same as that which was imagined. In looking back, a part of home is nowhere to be found and it is impossible to recover precisely what used to be: "if we [exiles, emigrants or expatriates] do look back, we must also do so in the knowledge – which gives rise to profound uncertainties – that our physical alienation from India almost inevitably means that we will not be capable of reclaiming precisely the thing that was lost"; in looking back, what is recovered – the memories of the India that has been left behind – is a nostalgic fantasy, nothing but a fictional construct, "not actual cities or villages, but invisible ones, imaginary homelands, Indias of the mind" (10).

"At the Auction of the Ruby Slippers" both underscores the ambivalence of "home" as a concept and satirizes its commodification in the context of postcolonial cultural production. As Rushdie states in his monograph on *The Wizard of Oz*, he was spellbound by the film as a child to the point of it being his "very first literary influence" at the age of ten ("Short Tale" 9). While the most obvious tribute he pays to *The Wizard of Oz* is this short story, the impact the film had on him extends, for example, to a reference in *The Ground Beneath Her Feet* when the character Sir Darius Cama, "drunk, opium-addled, filled with self-hatred" orders the tail-coated string quartet at the exclusive Malabar Hill Masonic Lodge in Bombay "to 'have a bash' at the movie tune 'We're Off to See the Wizard (The Wonderful Wizard of Oz)'" (48).[16] The entanglements of the plot of Fleming's film fascinated Rushdie: Dorothy is a resourceful orphan in Kansas, snatched up by a tornado and deposited in Oz, amid witches, a tin man, a talking scarecrow, and a lion. Her cinematic adventures end when she returns home with the help of a pair of magic red slippers. Although watching the film "made a writer of [him]" (18), he detested the finale because Dorothy's unwavering desire to go home did not make sense to him. On the basis of Gikandi's reading of Rushdie's work as a "metacommentary of the postcolonial condition" (213), what is noteworthy here is the author's foregrounding of the ambiguity of "home" through the play on Dorothy's magical ruby slippers, undisputedly revered as the quintessence of

---

[16] Another example is the following description in the novel: "The boutique has famous painted windows, featuring the Wicked Witch of the West from the land of Oz. She flies over Emerald City, cackling. Her smoking broom does sign writing in the sky. *Surrender Dorothy*. (The ignorant and unfashionable mistake this for the name of the shop. Such persons are invariably refused admission. Antoinette Corinth loathes Dorothy Gale, her dog and all inhabitants of Kansas, Kansas-as-metaphor, flat, empty, uncool. Antoinette Corinth is Miss Gulch.)" (283).

unrestrained movement. It is not just that the ruby slippers, which enable Dorothy to return home, are negotiated at the auction within the terms of metropolitan commodity exchange, but that the discourse of homelessness and displacement *itself* is traded in postcolonial texts.

Accounting for the success of the Mickey Mouse films in the 1930s, Benjamin argues that their "huge popularity" is not based on mechanisation, nor on their form, but instead on "the fact that the public recognizes its own life in them" as they "are founded on the motif of leaving home in order to learn what fear is" ("Mickey Mouse" 545). Rushdie similarly posits: "in the case of a beloved film, *we are all the stars' doubles*. Our imagination puts us in the Lion's skin, places the sparkling slippers on our feet, and sends us cackling through the air on a broomstick. ... The world of *The Wizard of Oz* has possessed us. We are the stand-ins now" ("Short Tale" 46). As the writer recounts, at the end of the film, the protagonist asks the good witch Glinda: "If I ever go looking for my heart's desire again, I won't look further than my own back yard. And if it isn't there, I never really lost it to begin with. Is that right?" (56). For Rushdie, this "conservative little homily" (56) is "the least convincing idea in the film" for, as he argues, "it's one thing for Dorothy to want to get home, quite another that she can only do so by eulogizing the ideal state which Kansas so obviously is not" (14). Even if this nostalgic evocation of a film he watched as a child growing up in Bombay might suggest an attempt to bring to mind the security of "home," Rushdie defied the view that the protagonist's successful return to the triviality of her life in black-and-white Kansas could lead to the conclusion that "there's no place like home." He further comments: "Are we to believe that Dorothy has learned no more on her journey than that she didn't need to make such a journey in the first place? Must we accept that she now accepts the limitations of her home life, and agrees that the things that she doesn't have there are no loss to her? '*Is that right?*' Well, excuse *me*, Glinda but is it hell" (56–57).

Rushdie's analysis of the film's narrative progression in the essay "A Short Text About Magic" charts the protagonist and her house being displaced from the "monochrome 'real' world of Kansas" (19), "shaped into 'home' by the use of simple, uncomplicated shapes" (21). Then, a "twisty, irregular and misshapen" tornado, described as "an untrustworthy, sinuous, shifting shape" (21), displaces Dorothy to the oppositional space of kaleidoscopic Oz. At that location, she becomes an uprooted migrant, and, although she attempts to get back to her home, the film's visuals, with its landscape of vivid Technicolor, make Oz seem, according to Rushdie, much more appealing and exciting than the world Dorothy left behind. In his words, "'Over the Rainbow' is, or ought to be, the anthem of all the world's migrants, all those who go in search of the place where 'the dreams that you dare to dream really do come true'. It is a celebration of Escape, a grand paean to the Uprooted Self, a hymn – *the* hymn – to Elsewhere" (23). Regardless of the plurality of meanings associated with the concept of "home," the yearning for home often involves a nostalgic desire for equilibrium even if, the writer concludes, life teaches that you cannot actually go home:

Oz finally *became* home; the imagined world became the actual world, as it does for all of us, because the truth is that once we have left our childhood places and started out to make up our lives, armed only with what we have and are, we understand that the real secret of ruby slippers is not that 'there's no place like home' but rather that there is no longer any such place *as* home: except, of course for the home we make, or the homes that are made for us, in Oz: which is anywhere, and everywhere, except the place from which we began. (57)

Rushdie had already used the contrast between greyness and Technicolor when he chronicled in the essay "Imaginary Homelands" the impact that revisiting his birthplace had on him. He describes how an old black-and-white photograph of his childhood home in Bombay turned his early years monochromatic by association. This picture dates from 1946, months before his birth on 19 June 1947, yet the writer's memory, "feeding on such images as this, had begun to see [his] childhood in the same way, monochromatically" (9). The opening paragraphs of this essay detail precisely how, shortly after finishing his poorly-received first novel *Grimus* (1975), Rushdie returned to his childhood home and discovered to his amazement that, while the "colours of [his] history had seeped out of [his] mind's eye," in that moment his "other two eyes were assaulted by colours, by the vividness of the red tiles, the yellow-edged green of cactus-leaves, the brilliance of bougainvillaea creeper" (9). This eye-opening experience marks the inception of *Midnight's Children* – it was on this occasion that he "realized how much [he] wanted to restore the past to [himself], not in the faded greys of old family-album snapshots, but whole, in CinemaScope and glorious Technicolor" (9–10).

The futuristic setting of "At the Auction of the Ruby Slippers" provides a heightened version of contemporary continuous movement, migrancy, and exile. Rushdie's memoir *Joseph Anton* recounts how he decided "too easily, even a little ruthlessly," as a teenager, to go to boarding school in England and "follow the dream of 'away', breaking away from the lure, which was also, of course, the tedium, of 'home'" (28). Diasporic subjects are, in the writer's formulation, caught between "the human dream of *leaving*" and the "countervailing dream of roots" ("Short Tale" 23). The disenfranchised characters inhabiting "At the Auction of the Ruby Slippers" search for the normalcy of "home" as a sort of counterpoint to "the moral decay of our post-millennial culture" ("At the Auction" 94). The yearning for home results in the collapsing of the barrier between reality and fiction, as characters from sci-fi films, literature, and paintings participate in the auction. For Rushdie's characters, the slippers represent "a lost state of normalcy in which we have almost ceased to believe and to which [they] promise us we can return" (92). The nameless narrator wants to purchase the red pair of slippers as a gift to regain the love of his cousin Gale, whose name mirrors that of the protagonist of *The Wizard of Oz* and who has a tendency to cry out during lovemaking: "Home, boy! Home, baby, yes – you've come home!" (95). When he notices her in a bar, grieving over "an astronaut stranded on Mars without hope of rescue, and with diminishing supplies of food and breathable air" (96), but still shown on television singing a medley of *The Wizard of Oz* songs, he takes upon himself to purchase

Dorothy's slippers to allow her to salvage the spaceman and bring him back to Earth. "Perhaps," the narrator considers, "I might even click the heels together three times, and win back her heart by murmuring, in soft reminder of our wasted love, *There's no place like home*" (98).

Just when the bidding reaches its climax, the narrator unexpectedly drops out. At the end, he crosses a "delirious frontier" and recognizes that his yearning for both Gale and Dorothy's slippers – and their correlate "home" – is a "dangerous" fiction (102). Even after Gale abandons him for "a hairy escapee from a caveman movie" (95), he continues to long for her. Only by renouncing such fictions, or at least acknowledging them, does the narrator become unfettered from this nostalgic longing for a fixed and stable "home." "In fiction's grip," he comments, "we may mortgage our homes, sell our children, to have whatever it is we crave. Alternatively, in that miasmal ocean, we may simply float away from our desires, and see them anew, from a distance, so that they seem weightless, trivial" (102). The slippers are highly desirable because they (misleadingly) promise to take the wearer home. According to an anecdote about *The Wizard of Oz* memorabilia, a "pair of ruby slippers, found in a bin in the MGM basement, was sold at auction in May 1970 for the amazing sum of $15,000" ("Short Tale" 46), but later "it was suggested that the ... slippers were too large to have fitted Judy Garland's feet. They had, in all probability, been made for her double, Bobbie Koshay, whose feet were two sizes larger" (46–47). This anecdote further suggests that, like Dorothy's ruby slippers, "home" is ineradicably a cultural construct – a fundamental idea in Rushdie's work.

Rushdie's critical analysis takes in the discourse of a never-changing home(land) which enables the migrant in her fantasies to return home as it was before. The writer produces a counterdiscourse out of the inner instability of the "mythical homeland" discourse itself. Home *does* change; moreover, the ideas that there is a home left to go back and that "there's no place like home" are questionable. Dorothy's absurd longing for home, in Rushdie's perspective, exposes the impossibility to recuperate exactly what such a place used to be. In these times of constant movement, "home" has ceased to exist. The narrator's relationship with his cousin Gale – in particular, the fact that he caught her betraying him with "a hairy escapee from a cave movie," thus annihilating any chance of returning home – seems to act as a stand-in for the connection between the migrant and her homeland, when the reality of displacement intrudes into the fiction of "home" (96). "At the Auction of the Ruby Slippers" engages critically with this relationship with a homeland, one that all migrants have to negotiate. The narrator questions the ability of the slippers to return the homeless home: "They promised to take us *home*, but are metaphors of homeliness comprehensible to them, are abstractions permissible? Are they literalists, or will they permit us to redefine the blessed word?" (93). Given such recognition of the constructed nature of discourses about "home," in Rushdie's writing this becomes a slippery notion. Furthermore, the story satirizes the commodification of "home" as a conceptual category that traverses postcolonial texts. Postcolonial cultural production and the academic field of postcolonial studies have capitalized on the notion of "home" while helping turn exile itself into a commodity. According to Huggan, the expression "staged marginality" designates "the process by which marginalised individuals or minority groups dramatize their 'subordinate' status for the imagined benefit of a majority audience" (*Postcolonial Exotic* xii). Rushdie has effectively staged homelessness in "At the Auction of the Ruby Slippers" and, in the context of a public sale, the longing for home, represented by the rich and mythic image of the ruby slippers, is in effect repoliticized. The short story hence makes its readers aware of the constructedness of postcolonial categories such as home, exile, and migrancy, in the same way as the ruby slippers are themselves a fictional construction.

"At the Auction of the Ruby Slippers" paints the current market-based culture as an unruly futuristic dystopia and offers a cynical commentary on the extremes of a commodity-fetishist society, the product of the West's market-oriented capitalism. "These are uncompromising times," the narrator declares (91). Similarly to the auctioning of the ruby slippers, the postcolonial longing for home is displayed as a reified item, even if not irredeemably so, in the global market of cultural exchange. "How is value ascribed to, and regulated within, the cultural margins?" asks Huggan, positing this as one of the central questions of postcolonial cultural politics (20). The auction of the ruby slippers, taking place against the backdrop of a dystopian post-millennial society, stands in general for the cultural commodification of postcolonial writing and in particular for the exotic appeal attributed to the postcolonial longing for the homeland and for the allocation of value to the margins by the centre. In this short story, Rushdie sets out to "work within, while also seeking to challenge, institutional structures and dominant systems of representation" (32). Assuming that the West, as the author argued in "In Good Faith," has moved into a post-religious age, its fetishes are now the market, where everything – literally everything – can be turned into a commodity. The auction room itself is described as "the beating heart of the earth" (98), where wives, husbands, state secrets, and "all the wonders of the world," including the Taj Mahal, the Statue of Liberty, the Alps and the Sphinx are up for sale (98), in short, where the "vast complexity of life" is "packaged into lots" (99) by the action of commodity fetishism.

To conclude, Rushdie self-consciously traffics in commodified images drawn from an identifiable postcolonial repertoire, viewing them from the edge. He uses the category of "home" as a provisional working term as he defines his own analytical coordinates. Using the trope of a global auction house where the promise to return the exile back home is up for sale, the writer subjects the yearning for "home," the main driving force in this story, to a dual politics of resistance. Staging the longing for a homeland, the author not only strategically redeploys postcolonial displacement by juxtaposing nostalgic discourses of "home," centred on the ruby slippers, with a range of contemporary diasporic alternatives, but also exposes the commodification of narratives of "home" arising from the marketing of postcolonial literary texts.

*****

Rushdie builds on the discursive nature of the categories West and East on numerous occasions – for instance, the narrator of *The Ground Beneath Her Feet* offers a "variant version of history" that implies the refashioning of a West that is "exotic, fabulous, unreal" (260). Commodification in the postcolonial literary marketplace remains a topical issue in the next case study, particularly the commodification of selected, ethnically-identified authors and works that conform to specified imagery. A critical issue for this study, and as such deserving a thorough discussion at this introductory stage, emerges from what is a perceived process of self-exoticisation, or re-orientalisation, of South Asian-origin authors and their works.[17] Indeed, this book attempts to explore the ways in which the Rushdie's texts, like other recent works springing from the South Asian diaspora, reconstruct, manipulate, and subvert re-orientalist representations. As this next case study will argue, the commodification of the diasporic experience of space in Chitra Banerjee Divakaruni's novel *The Mistress of Spices* (1997), through the notion of a "vertigo of homelessness" (137), and the foregrounding of the migrant's longing for home in the novel echo Rushdie's anxieties concerning the commodification of "home" voiced in "At the Auction of the Ruby Slippers." In sum, in the succeeding subsection, attention will be directed at 1) the disruption and renegotiation of subversive representations within shifting notions of orientalism and re-orientalism, and 2) the resulting anxieties spelled out by postcolonial cultural producers, not least of which by Rushdie himself.

Offering a Taste of the Spicy Subcontinent

> [I]f it had not been for peppercorns, then what is ending now in East and West might never have begun.
> —Rushdie, *The Moor's Last Sigh* 4

The present inquiry into processes of re-orientalism was initially motivated by *Midnight's Children*, with its self-conscious juggling with re-orientalist elements and its self-reflexive implication of the postcolonial writer's status as exotic commodity in the global literary market. This case study of Rushdie's cultural brokerism considers how this novel, through its self-deployment as cultural commodity, staged, in the early 1980s, the writer's challenge to its anticipated commercial appeal and accommodation within a metropolitan publishing industry. The main argument is that *Midnight's Children* subverts re-orientalist representations of India as the exotic other by repoliticising orientalist imagery. Thematically, via the narrator Saleem Sinai, the novel satirizes western notions about India and

---

[17] Admittedly, the concept of "re-orientalism" can be applied to other contexts; in the present case, though, its use involves South Asia and/or South-Asian diasporic cultural formations. For more on re-orientalism, see the collection *Re-Orientalism and South Asian Identity Politics: The Oriental Other Within* (2011), edited by Lisa Lau and Ana Mendes.

exposes the metropolitan consumer-reader's complicitous desire for exoticism. On a related level, the figure of the cosmopolitan reader is central to the success of the deconstruction and subversion of orientalist codifications. The novel's recourse to food imagery – the "chutnification of history" (459) propounded by the narrator, which Tobias Wachinger reads as "a meta-commentary on the production and consumption of 'postcolonial' literature from the subcontinent" (73) – is the starting point for scrutinising the "taste of the subcontinent" proffered by Divakaruni's bestseller *The Mistress of Spices*. Proceeding to a short examination of Divakaruni's novel, this subsection surveys its re-orientalist strategies, under the guise of culinary fiction and postcolonial magical realism. Of relevance here is the text's deployment as some sort of a "Rough Guide" to India, which visibly invites its western readers to have a taste of the "spicy subcontinent."

*****

Sex sells, and so does exotica. As the advertising industry has extensively demonstrated, sex gets consumers' attention, so what better promotion for a film than displaying in the teaser poster a scantily clad couple lying down on a sea of red chillies? The brandishing of erotic exotica seemed to be the promotion strategy behind the poster for the film *The Mistress of Spices*, directed by Paul Mayeda Berges in 2005 and adapted from Divakaruni's 1997 novel. The couple on display in the poster is made up of the Hollywood hunk Dylan McDermott and the Bollywood stunner and former Miss World Aishwarya Rai, the latter the most visible leader of the so-called Bollywood invasion as she had been making inroads into Hollywood.[18] Should the dazzling couple and the supply of red chillies in the teaser poster prove not to be spicy, that is, exotic and erotic enough, the prospective consumers of this film are expected to notice on Rai's upper body an extra trace of the exotic: the henna painting ("mehndi"). This temporary skin decoration, most often applied on the palms and feet (not on the shoulders as seen in the poster), is traditionally worn by brides before wedding ceremonies and its status as cultural marker resulted in its incorporation, along with the "bindi," into western fashion in the late 1990s.

The association between food and sex is a recurring motif in literature and cinema – one need only recall the novel and film *Like Water for Chocolate* (the novel by the Mexican writer Laura Esquivel, 1989; the film by Alfonso Arau, 1993). Exotica is a complementary hook to draw western audiences in, and cookbook authors such as Rushdie's ex-wife Padma Lakshmi and their editors have not failed to draw on that. In 1999 Lakshmi published the cookbook *Easy Exotic*, which displays photographs of her preparing food, such as of her kneading dough dressed in a lacy nighty, in a silk slip cooking a recipe, and going to the market in a low-cut dress. Bearing out Appadurai's argument that cookbooks

---

[18] Interestingly, Rai's first feature film in English was Gurinder Chadha's *Bride & Prejudice* (2004), whose tagline read "Bollywood meets Hollywood ... And it's a perfect match."

"tell unusual cultural tales" and that they feed on "the vicarious pleasures of the literature of the senses" ("National Cuisine" 3), *Easy Exotic* conflates food with eroticism and peppers it with expectations of consumption of the exotic, seeking to provoke a full sensory response from its readership.

These representational strategies clearly draw on re-orientalist practices. Moreover, the photographs by Priscilla Benedetti included in *Easy Exotic* literally illustrate Frank Chin's concept of "food pornography" (1981), which, as delineated by Sau-ling Cynthia Wong in her 1993 study of Asian American literature, refers to the process of "making a living by exploiting the 'exotic' aspects of one's ethnic foodways" (55). Wong credits the Chinese American author Chin with the first use of the concept in the plays *The Chickencoop Chinaman* and *The Year of the Dragon* (1981). "Like exchanging sexual services for food," Wong contends, "food pornography is also a kind of prostitution, but with an important difference: superficially, food pornography appears to be a promotion, rather than a vitiation or devaluation, of one's ethnic identity" (55). In a way that resonates in Divakaruni's novel, Wong adds that food pornography "translates to reifying perceived cultural differences and exaggerating one's otherness in order to gain a foothold in a white-dominated social system" (55), and that, as a consequence, food pornographers "wrench cultural practices out of their context and display them for gain to the curious gaze of 'outsiders'" (56). It was Lakshmi's successful performance as food pornographer that earned her the title of "Mistress of Spice" granted by *Cosmopolitan* magazine in its January 2002 issue, three years before she was cast as the character Geeta, the young woman who wants to marry a Chicano against the wishes of her family, in the almost eponymous film by Berges. If the idea of food pornography finds echo in Divakaruni's narrative, given its use of re-orientalist strategies through culinary imagery, the same is true of its cinematic adaptation. The film's photography, directed by the Indian cinematographer Santosh Sivan, consistently takes the appearance of a tantalising food-magazine layout, with the Indian spice shop, the central setting in both novel and film, constructed and presented as a magical and alluring territory.

Divakaruni's assimilation from the margins to mainstream discourses of cross-cultural representation, proffering a version of what Anita Mannur calls "palatable multiculturalism" (61), will be the focus here. Specifically, the focus will rest on the ways her novel capitalizes on the crossover appeal of the exotic and on the increasing visibility of India within globalized cultural industries, sustained through the circulation of highly marketable commodities such as the film adaptation directed by Berges. Of interest also is the interrelated issue of the burden of representation, influentially characterized by Kobena Mercer as the predicament "whereby the artistic discourse of hitherto marginalized subjects is circumscribed by the assumption that such artists speak as 'representatives' of the communities from which they come" (214). Such burden, recurrently placed upon diasporic artists, has led to an incidental grieving over the lack of communal and ethnic advocacy. As Zadie Smith relates: "Do you go to Don DeLillo and say, 'He doesn't represent middle-class white people enough'? ... No. You give him complete freedom. Why would you limit writers of any ethnicity or gender to be a sex or class politician and give freedom to white writers to write about absolutely anybody?" (qtd. in Procter, "New Ethnicities" 102).

In Divakaruni's *The Mistress of Spices*, the ruler and ever-present figure in the space of the Indian spice shop is Tilo, a woman in possession of supernatural talents and trained in the art of healing with spices. Divakaruni, an Indian immigrant to the US herself, elects as the narrative engine for the novel the arrival of this spice-Mistress in America. Tilo has had different provisional homes before travelling to the US: a small village in India while growing up, the sea as pirate queen, and the fantastic world of "the island of spice" as Mistress of Spices. Being "at home" is, for this female character, an intangible condition and she is thus afflicted by an unwavering sense of spatial unmooring. The assumption that "home" only resides in the memory of the migrant, echoed in *The Mistress of Spices*, is a crucial and inescapable question when addressing Rushdie's creative project. Furthermore, the previous case study, devoted to the short story "At the Auction of the Ruby Slippers," assists in framing Divakaruni's narrative within a generalized commodification of postcolonial displacement. While the island of spice is the first diasporic place Tilo inhabits, her journey does not end in Oakland, California – this location is to remain her home only momentarily, insofar as her duty is to act as spice-Mistress. Initial steps outside the physical boundaries of her work-place to explore the world outside (according to one of the strict rules of the spices, she is not allowed to leave the store as long as she is acting as spice-healer) bring a "sudden vertigo of homelessness" (137). Upon coming to her newest home, Tilo becomes the "architect of the immigrant dream," she "who can make it all happen, green cards and promotions and girls with lotus eyes" (28), she who has in her hands – when she splits "*kalo jire* seeds for all who have suffered from America" (173) – the ability to curtail other difficulties that immigrants might experience.

Tilo's exceptional powers allow her to help diasporic Indians that enter her shop, while the remaining others "must go elsewhere for their need" (68). Some of the characters in necessity are Haroun, a Kashmiri Muslim taxi-driver who is beaten in a racially-motivated incident; Ramu, Geeta's grandfather, an elderly Gujarati immigrant, who performs the role of the stock character trapped between (eastern) tradition and (western) modernity; and Jagjit, an alienated Punjabi teenager who is bullied at school and so decides to join a gang (145). For instance, to ease Jagjit's troubles, the spice-Mistress administers cardamom, "to open [his] teacher's unseeing," and "[c]innamon friend-maker, cinnamon *dalchini* warm-brown as skin, to find [him] someone who will take [him] by the hand, who will run with [him] and laugh with [him] and say See this is America, it's not so bad" (39–40). The underlying premise here is that the problems these characters face – "their suffe[ring] from America" – can be solved by the "spiritual" power of the spices Tilo willingly prepares and dispenses. Consuming fennel or turmeric in the prescribed doses, so the story goes, can shield Indian immigrants in the US from racist verbal and physical assaults. Divakaruni's deployment of the healing energy of her protagonist's Indian spices capitalizes on the commodity value of eastern mysticism in the global cultural marketplace. It is, in this respect, consistent with what Vijay Prashad labels "New Age orientalism" (53–54), that is, the quest for the spirituality of the Indian subcontinent as a remedy for the alienation induced by western materialism. Interestingly, Tilo's characterisation is evocative of Deepak Chopra (Mannur 60), the celebrity Indian medical doctor and guru who, according to Prashad, is the hip precursor of New Age orientalism (53).

In *Midnight's Children*, the character Aadam Aziz, while studying medicine in Europe, had "learned that India – like radium – had been 'discovered' by the Europeans," and felt that he himself was an "invention" of his colleagues' ancestors (11). Even long after the period of the so-called "discovery" of India – "but how could we be discovered if we were not covered before?" asks the narrator of *The Moor's Last Sigh* in an early passage in the novel (4) – the country remains "not so much sub-continent as sub-condiment," as the mother of that narrator, Aurora da Gama, puts it (5).[19] Aurora, who traces her family lineage back nearly four generations to Vasco da Gama – in fact, she is a Catholic who is of the "wrong-side-of-the-blanket descent from the great Vasco de Gama himself" (6) – elaborates on the profit motivations at the heart of the colonial enterprise and construes the spice trade thus: "From the beginning, what the world wanted from bloody mother India was daylight-clear .... They came for the hot stuff, just like any man calling on a tart" (5). In *The Mistress of Spices*, spices are deemed to "hold magic, even the American spices you toss unthinking into your cooking pot"; yet, "the spices of true power are from [the Mistress's] birthland, land of ardent poetry, aquamarine feathers. Sunset skies brilliant as blood" (3). Even if disparaged by the critics (Mannur 63), Divakaruni's text was a bestseller, received as some sort of a "Rough Guide" to India, under the guise of an increasingly commodified and formulaic postcolonial culinary fiction, allowing its metropolitan readers to have a taste of the spicy subcontinent. Besides, magical realism is here turned into an exotic device: it is feasible for the metropolitan reader-consumer to embark on a tour of the subcontinent without leaving the comfort of her home through the aid of a magic realist text sprinkled with Indian spices. Divakaruni narrates India not as polyvalent cultural sign, and confirms an orientalist association of the East with the wondrous, mysterious other. In this particular respect, postcolonial culinary fiction such as *The Mistress of Spices* can be seen, similarly to travel writing, as performing the purpose of exhibiting the "rest of the world" for a metropolitan audience.

Consumer items need to be recognisable in order to guarantee commercial success, and being categorized as postcolonial culinary fiction serves a merchandising apparatus. Numerous Indian authors based in the West have surrendered themselves to a characteristic food imagery and, in this sense, the deployment of a recognisable food trope in Divakaruni's novel illustrates the

---

[19] In *The Satanic Verses*, the narrator notes that Cochin was the harbour to which "Vasco da Gama had come in search of spices and so set in motion the whole ambiguous history of east-and-west" (76).

"predominance of the effect," "the technical detail over the work itself," that Adorno and Horkheimer identify as one of the features of the culture industry. Postcolonial culinary fiction bears, at times, a striking resemblance to the workings of what the German critics call "art for the masses": "There is nothing left for the consumer to classify" as "[p]roducers have done it for him" (125). As the journalist and novelist Anis Shivani trenchantly remarks about what might be construed as a form of ethnic self-exploitation, "[s]ince western audiences are best acquainted with Indian food, a typical Indo-Anglian novel will deal obsessively with exotic, spicy food, as if Indians spent the greater part of their lives pondering the taste and timing of their food intake" (2). By the same token that *Midnight's Children*, the novel which established the food trope used so recurrently by diasporic Indian authors, displays chutney jars on the cover of the 2008 Vintage Classics edition, *The Mistress of Spices* was sold with a packet of spices when it was first released. Besides drawing attention to the fact that the novel itself is as much a marketable commodity as the packet of spices, this promotional campaign, one suspects, was devised to cash in, as the *Midnight's Children*'s Vintage Classic cover design does, on the exotic lure of postcolonial culinary fiction. Thus, the inscription of an orientalist codification such as the persistent theme of spices, even if deconstructed by Rushdie within the covers of the novel, resurfaces in the marketing design of the cover.

The recurrence of imitation of successful products in the culture industry – a case in point being what Pankaj Mishra has dubbed the spreading of "Rushdie-itis" in recent novels by postcolonial writers, i.e. the crystallising of standardized writing techniques and leitmotifs – was denounced by Adorno mostly with reference to popular music: "As one particular song scored a great success, hundreds of others sprang up imitating the successful one. The most successful hits, types, and 'ratios' between elements were imitated, and the process culminated in the crystallization of standards. ... [T]hese standards have become 'frozen' ... and rigidly enforced upon material to be promoted" ("Popular Music" 23). In connection with jazz, Adorno further illustrates the issue of pseudo-individualism in the culture industry:

> while it must constantly promise its listeners something different, excite their attention and keep itself from becoming run-of-the-mill, it is not allowed to leave the beaten path; it must be always new and always the same. Hence, the deviations are just as standardized as the standards and in effect revoke themselves the instant they appear. Jazz, like everything else in the culture industry, gratifies desires only to frustrate them at the same time. ("Perennial Fashion" 273)

The German theorist, referring to the "two spheres of music" (what he calls "serious" and "light" music), writes that "[t]he advanced product has renounced consumption," whereas "[t]he rest of serious music is delivered over to consumption for the price of its wages" and thus "succumbs to commodity listening" ("Fetish Character" 35). Admittedly, Rushdie's works have not renounced consumption in the global literary field. The author does not actively downplay nor disclaim his involvement in the inevitable commodification of postcolonial cultural production. His primary cultural products – his novels – are consumer items themselves and their financial viability relies on their mainstream success.

The publication of *Midnight's Children* made Rushdie's literary name in the early 1980s. In that novel, via the main character and narrator Saleem Sinai, the author critically mobilizes discourses of the exotic and self-ironically engages with orientalist essentialisations, and does so by exposing the metropolitan consumer-reader's complicitous desire for exoticism. Saleem is a skilful merchant of narratives – he knows how to put his stories on the market, hawking their exotic trimmings such as snakecharmers and fakirs to satisfy the exoticist appetites of his imagined audience. *Midnight's Children* uses meta-exoticism, that is, a strategic redeployment of the exotic: it plays on re-orientalist representations of India as the exotic other and hence repoliticizes identifiable orientalist imagery. In this sense, the novel introduces alternative modes of resistance to the western appropriation of India – its exotic appeal is undercut by the text's self-reflection on the process of cultural consumption it fosters. Rushdie embarks then on a critique of exotica by appropriating exoticist codes of cultural representation: the exotic here is reinvented as an empowering decolonising category because a reconfiguration of discursive power has been generated. Nonetheless, fiction that involves re-orientalist representation risks replaying to the reader orientalist stereotypes by reinscribing them. In fact, authorial intent is only one of the meanings included in the field of meanings already attached to diasporic cultural products in the global cultural economy. A question remains, to which is difficult to offer a clear-cut answer: Through a re-orientalist frame, are orientalist stereotypes questioned or also unwittingly reinscribed in *Midnight's Children*?

Rushdie's self-consciousness about his books' position in a globalized literary marketplace, in particular in the context of their authorized and academically-promoted circulation, frames *Midnight's Children*. While such self-consciousness is one of the trademark features of his works, self-consciousness being a "constitutive feature of the postcolonial field" (Brouillette 1), the figure of the cosmopolitan consumer-reader is central to the success of the strategies involved in the novel's reliance on representations of a marketable exotic India and on the subversion of exoticist and orientalist codifications. In addition to Rushdie's staging of his novel's own imbrications with the marketing of cultural difference, *Midnight's Children* posits the admittedly controversial question as to whether postcolonial literature posits an "ideal reader," a reader who is cosmopolitan and an active consumer of re-orientalised cultural products in the sense that she is expected to negotiate the instabilities of re-orientalism. In other words, does the difference which the novel self-ironically builds on hold up to scrutiny in the eye of a cosmopolitan beholder? As observed previously, spices signal the "Indianness" of novels in the context of the western publishing markets because, despite globalising fluxes, the local element remains a central reference point in marketing and identifying images of, or from, "authentic" or "traditional" India. As a commodity, Divakaruni's novel drew on the constructed and contested signifier of "Indianness" and was hence marketed as an item of postcolonial exotica. If this bestseller was initially promoted by using a packet of spices, the cookbook *Spice: Recipes to Delight the Senses* (2007) used the opening paragraphs of *The Mistress of Spices* as the epigraph for one of its introductory texts, aptly titled "The Sensuous World of Spices" (9). Through interconnected actions such as these, the western publishing industry further contributes to the commodification of India as spicy and sensuous.

In an inquiry into postcolonial culinary fiction as exotic commodity, but drawing primarily on South-East Asian diasporic fiction, Tamara S. Wagner argues that a recent trend in literature set in Malaysia, Singapore, and Australia has begun to self-reflexively comment on its own standing as a trademarked consumer item, by articulating consumption and nausea as outcomes of the same process (31). If food metaphors "help to promote the marketability of the multicultural," Wagner asserts, "their renegotiation in more self-reflective [and self-ironic] writing has recently begun to engender new food fictions that capitalize on repulsion as a form of resistance to this demand for self-Orientalization" (31). Divakaruni complies with such expectations for self-orientalisation, even though in the context of her culinary fiction Lisa Lau's concept of "re-Orientalization" (that is, as Lau clarifies in the subtitle of her essay, the "perpetration and development of Orientalism by Orientals") seems more effective to describe the exoticising processes generated in *The Mistress of Spices*. In her examination of a new orientalism (re-orientalism), Lau focuses on what she discerns to be the disturbing effects of the ever-increasing role of diasporic Indian women writers in fabricating a reductive, fixed, and distorted idea of the subcontinent overseas. Such authors – Divakaruni is included in the group – are turning (indeed re-turning) the orientalist gaze back upon the "Oriental"/"Orient" in ways that are facilitated by their material agency and claims to cultural "authenticity."[20] As Lau compellingly argues, they have become re-orientalists on account of their positionality as "simultaneously that of the insider and outsider" (572). This vexed positionality has likewise been depicted by Rushdie in relation to diasporic Indian authors in Britain as being "at one and the same time insiders and outsiders," a condition that prevents them from using "whole sight," but grants them "stereoscopic vision" ("Imaginary" 19). These writers are endowed with a double perspective as insiders and outsiders, self and other. When they attempt to represent "India," Rushdie writes, they are "obliged to deal in broken mirrors, some of whose fragments have been irretrievably lost," a circumstance which "may actually be as valuable as the one which is supposedly unflawed" (10). The writer is aware of the necessarily problematic understanding of migrant writers as caught between – or, as he puts it, straddling – two cultures (10–15). Rather than falling *between* two "stools," for him it is more productive to see migrants' positioning as evincing a multiplicity of cultural points of identification. In an interview, he observes:

---

[20] For the sake of readability, I opt to elide the quotation marks when referring to the concepts of authenticity and inauthenticity hereinafter.

I think the way in which we experience the world is that we don't have all the pieces that explain it. We have some of them; our knowledge and our experience and the accidents of our lives give us, if we're lucky, enough pieces with which to make enough sense of the world. But I think that all of us are conscious of the fact that there're bits missing from the picture. There are pieces of the jigsaw that aren't there. There are bits of the broken mirror that got lost. And so I think I've tried to suggest in my books that that kind of fragmented vision is actually a truthful way of writing about the world—the world seen in fragments. (qtd. in Silverblatt 201–202)

If orientalism broadly refers to western discursive misconceptions of the East, it might be feasible to extend Lau's theorisation and read Divakaruni's novel as engaging in culinary re-orientalism. It might not be fair to state that the author had the calculated and conscious aim of profiting from the use of spices as the structuring motif of her novel. Perhaps the writer was not moved by what Vasco da Gama was pursuing, again according to Rushdie's narrator in *The Moor's Last Sigh*, i.e. "whatever was spicy and hot and made money" (59). Maybe it is too radical to assess *The Mistress of Spices* as the outcome of, as Leela Gandhi puts it, "an unwholesome partnership between neo-Orientalism and postcolonial opportunism" (128). Lau clarifies that "it is not [her] contention that the diasporic authors necessarily have any insidious intention, or consciously conceived aim, to re-orientalise" (574). Even granted that Divakaruni might not have chosen the theme of spices exclusively as a marketing manoeuvre to play the global market and increase the sales of her debut novel, it is still possible to detect a degree of authorial intent in the novel's re-orientalist codifications. In *The Mistress of Spices*, writes Amitava Kumar, "Indians are postcolonial chickens coming home to roost – as spicy, well-barbecued Tandoori," a fact that makes it obvious, in Kumar's words, "that the literary goods in question have been stamped, 'For Export Only'" being as they are nothing but "easy-to-swallow nonsense" ("Louder" 88).

In this respect, a connection can be established between Divakaruni's novel and Shoba Narayan's *Monsoon Diary: A Memoir With Recipes* (2003), a work that weaves South Indian vegetarian recipes with a personal narrative about the author's childhood and later "juggling of cultures, straddling lifestyles" in the US (102), and which might equally qualify as food pornography. This much is suggested by the book description included in the inside flap suggesting that Narayan's stories are "as varied as Indian spices – at times pungent, mellow, piquant, and sweet," and that "[t]antalizing recipes" spring from her "absorbing tales about food and the *solemn* and *quirky* customs that surround it" (emphasis added). In a review of Narayan's book reprinted in the hardcover edition, Sharon Boorstin describes it as "[a] taste of a life that is exotic yet familiar," and "as pungent and satisfying as a good curry." Reading *Monsoon Diary*, Boorstin concludes, made her "want to get on a plane to India—or at least eat in an Indian restaurant." The choice of the title word "monsoon," to a great extent inconsequential in narrative terms, functions as a hook for the global market. In fact, the use of the title of Mira Nair's hit film *Monsoon Wedding* (2001) for one of the chapter headings of Narayan's memoir seems to confirm this intention of capitalising on the exotic appeal of the term "monsoon."

Similarly to the comparison Divakaruni's narrator makes between India and the US, unfavourable to the latter, in the opening pages of her memoir Narayan draws a stark contrast between American fast food and Indian food while stressing the ritualistic nature of feeding Indian children (3–4). An emphasis on the idea of authentic – and hence dismissal of the hybrid – is resumed later in the memoir when, after a failed attempt to turn her husband Ram into a fusion cuisine lover, Narayan goes back to preparing "simple" South Indian food because he "was tired of entertaining the United Nations in [their] kitchen" (191). Likewise, *The Mistress of Spices* reinstates the stereotypical notion of Indians as consuming subjects of spicy food evocative of their "homeland," needing to continually feed a nostalgic longing. Indeed, Tilo associates the ingesting of particular Indian foods with being Indian, as if there were any clear cut correlations between ethnicity and food. She partakes of an understanding whereby immigrants ingest specific foods; in this way, the narrative is complexly situated within a racialising process which acts to confirm prevailing stereotypical notions about the South Asian community. To Divakaruni's essentialist narrator, what you eat is who you are. She attributes cultural determinism to food, understanding it as the ultimate cultural marker. This much is evident, albeit by contrast, in the depiction of the "rich Indians" who are clearly set apart from the rest of Tilo's customers. These wealthy Indians relate themselves almost wholly to white upper-class America to the degree of actually *passing* as white. Some of them "have forgotten to be Indian and eat caviar only" (76), she comments despondently. In this near-totalising remark, Tilo perceives those who have ceased to eat Indian food and started instead to favour western delicacies as Indians who have disregarded who they are. Divakaruni thus employs a pornographic culinary framework given that, ultimately, she participates in an ongoing pattern of re-orientalisation through which Indians are categorized and othered by what they eat.

*****

The fact that the marketing strategies used to promote both *The Mistress of Spices* and *Midnight's Children* to metropolitan readers have inescapably influenced their signifying processes points to the importance of examining the social biography of literary works. A relevant part of this biography is the winning of prestigious western literary prizes such as the Booker. The best example to illustrate the high profile attained by Booker prizewinning works is indeed *Midnight's Children*, which has been continually reprinted since awarded the prize in 1981, the Booker of Bookers in 1993, and The Best of the Booker in 2008. As Rushdie himself admits, prizes "[ha]ve become a marketing device, a way of selling books" (Thomson and Sylvester). Following this admittedly long introductory chapter, and after the brief, but necessary, digression that ensues on the book's structure, the chapter dedicated to the role of Rushdie as a gatekeeper begins by assessing the politics involved in playing the postcolonial, or the "Rushdie card," in the awarding of the Booker.

The Book's Skeleton

> My belief is that – in its eventual verdict – literary criticism will judge Rushdie as a novelist whose work, like that of Thomas Mann or D H Lawrence, is not easily divisible into "novels." What he is assembling, laboriously and inventively, is an oeuvre: a life-long structure.
>
> —John Sutherland

> The dubious critiques offered here are then compromised by my personal involvement in the to and fro of ... well, of a white boy writing about black music.
>
> —John Hutnyk 5–6

In an interview, Rushdie describes the form his novel *Midnight's Children* progressively acquired as "the shape of *the attempt to impose shape* on what seemed formless, which is why the book sort of has the meat on the inside and the skeleton on the outside, because the skeleton was gradually imposed on the book" (qtd. in U. Chaudhuri 23). I would like to borrow this image in an attempt to explain the construction of the present study, which is admittedly the result of a rather undisciplined and dispersed quest for new ways of thinking about, and researching, Rushdie's texts. In clear distance from abusing interdisciplinarity as "a fashionable academic catch-cry" (Huggan, *Interdisciplinary* 7), the approach to this oeuvre has been relational, both intertextual and interdiscursive. In effect, as Huggan perceptively observes about the field of postcolonial studies in general, "much of the work that goes on within it is inter*discursive* rather than inter*disciplinary*" (5). Because Rushdie's texts are shaped by other texts, engaging with a multiplicity of contentions and debates, and because other cultural producers also borrow from and hence transform the Rushdie canon, alluding to his texts and/or being influenced by them, this book moves from one cultural product to another to encourage implicit comparisons between them, while trying to escape the "anxiety of interdisciplinarity" that Huggan identifies in postcolonial studies (7). This is a literature-led work – having been trained primarily as a literary critic, I treaded with caution the border-zones between different disciplines and was especially wary of making claims to multidisciplinary expertise. Though suited to the tangled concerns of the present project, that relational methodology had its problems: the narrative seemed to take a life of its own sometimes, with its author (against informed advice) standing aside watching almost helpless as the project drew in, of its own accord, more texts ("the latest" book or "the most recent" film).

In the sense that narratives, ideas, arguments, and theories were picked up during the research that led to this work, it might well be the case that the result of the present research embodies and encapsulates a magpie tendency of its own, which I hope does not impede critical coherence. In particular, a project committed to examining not only Rushdie's writings, but also his subsumption into an image-making machinery as star literary author, global brand, and celebrity intellectual – a critical positioning which must be at the base of any reading of his work today – necessarily entails the use of interview material from multiple, and at times volatile and unreliable, sources in the media.[21] An additional challenge was offered almost on a weekly basis by Rushdie, the constant media presence and prolific author: during the writing of this book, he authored *Shalimar The Clown* (2005), *The Enchantress of Florence* (2008), *Luka and the Fire of Life* (2010), and *Joseph Anton: a Memoir* (2012). As its object of study is multisited, this work ultimately has a comparative dimension in the form of dialogic juxtapositions of cultural formations and textual practices.[22] However demanding, this process was felt to be inevitable. After all, one is attempting to map "a life-long structure," in John Sutherland's words quoted in one of the epigraphs above, which keeps on expanding, but nonetheless requires the positing of logics of association among these cultural texts and the creation of a critical space for the occurrence of new conversations, as well as the uncovering of connections between and across discourses and practices within larger cultural patterns. In effect, when it came to approaching Rushdie's works in tandem with the consideration of his roles as cultural broker, critical hybridity or "theoretical creolization," in Brah's phrase, emerged as a requirement. In ways that bear upon this project, Brah contends: "creolised envisioning is crucial ... if we are to address fully the contradictions of modalities of enunciation, identities, positionalities and standpoints that are simultaneously 'inside' and 'outside'" (210). The variety of registers mobilized in Rushdie's work, the multifariousness of sites of enunciation of his roles as cultural broker, and the multiplicity of spheres that his public life operates on were partly responsible for a creolized (hopefully not dispersive, nor atomized) theoretical framework.

Rushdie's work is, in all probably, one of the most discussed today in the area of postcolonial literary studies, to the point where Sabina and Simona Sawhney start off their essay "Reading Rushdie after September 11, 2001" (2001) by stating: "The appearance of yet another collection of essays on Rushdie's work will no doubt seem odd to many people." They rhetorically ask: "Isn't there too much already written about Rushdie, for Rushdie, against Rushdie? Can't postcolonial critics talk about someone else for a change?" (431). These two questions are clearly meant as a provocation, given that they introduce a special issue of the journal *Twentieth-Century Literature* entirely devoted to Rushdie's work. The reader who continues to be interested in engaging with this seemingly exhausted matter is thus forced to search within herself the source of her interest. As Hutnyk

---

[21] A note on reference style is due. Given my frequent use of interviews as source material in this study, I opted for considering them as indirect sources, signalled by the expression "qtd. in," in an attempt to distinguish the interviewer's statements from the interviewee's. For instance, the phrase "Salman Rushdie qtd. in Michael Silverblatt" in the first epigraph of this chapter follows words by Rushdie uttered in the context of an interview by Silverblatt.

[22] Thomas Cartelli defines "*dialogic* appropriation" as "the careful integration into a work of allusions, identifications, and quotations that complicate, 'thicken,' and qualify that work's primary narrative line to the extent that each partner to the transaction may be said to enter into the other's frame of reference" (18).

observes about the contingent critical terrain of his analysis of exotica, attention should also be drawn to the "desire [for exotica] that we all, to some degree, fall for" (5). As such, my own motivations have also been subject to scrutiny.

This book positions itself within the nexus of current debates concerning the co-option of South Asian cultural products by a "globalised *condition of postcoloniality*" that includes, as A. Ahmad argues, the process of description and discursive constitution by the postcolonial critic (9). One may also rhetorically ask whether it is at all possible for any practices in postcolonial studies to overcome these conundrums, or whether they must or should continue to haunt researchers. This work thus acknowledges the unattainability of a neutral way of seeing and recognizes the contingencies of the "locus of theoretical enunciation" from which one voices a critical narrative (Mignolo 112). This locus of enunciation is, in this case, epistemologically bound to a Portuguese cultural context, with an imperial back-story of its own, which demanded, to begin with, an internal examination of one's own intentionality in constructing the present work. This required a critical engagement not only with the texts under examination here, but also a recognition of the epistemes, in the Foucauldian sense, that have made those texts so appealing in the first place.

*****

Following the introduction, which set the conceptual ground for this study and provided a couple of illustrative case studies of cultural brokerism, the first chapter of this book is on Rushdie as a gatekeeper. It is intent on demonstrating to what extent the writer's cultural authority and impact on shaping current markets for IWE has been used by publishers to market potential IWE bestsellers and/ or prizewinners, thus maximising the profitability of cultural production. Such manoeuvre within the "economics of cultural prestige" (English, *Economy of Prestige* 4) is examined in the first section of the chapter with reference to the awarding of the Man Booker Prize for Fiction in 2006 and 2008 to Indian writers Kiran Desai and Aravind Adiga, respectively. The process of granting cultural legitimacy is exposed as a reciprocally constitutive act in which Rushdie, "the Booker heavyweight" (Muir), plays a pivotal role and influences the rules of the awarding game. This analysis is followed by a comparative reading of Rushdie's short story "The Free Radio" (1994) and Adiga's Booker-prize-winning novel *The White Tiger* (2008) that explores the ways an "Exotic Dark India" has been constructed and (un)authorized. Contributing to a critique of Rushdie's relation with the cultural industries, the chapter then pursues a consideration of the star principle, at the very core of the Adornian culture industry, in the making of Rushdie as a postcolonial literary star whose book sales and media attention are affected by his private life.

The chapter entitled "Exploding the Canon" focuses on the literary Rushdie and is inaugurated by a study of the short story "Yorick" (1994) from the perspective of revisiting the western canon. Using as contextual backdrop the Merchant-Ivory 1965 filmic production *Shakespeare Wallah*, which depicts the reception of Shakespeare's plays in India after the end of the British Raj, the first section deals with Rushdie's short story not only as a parodic rewriting of *Hamlet*, but also as a parody of postcolonial rewritings of Shakespeare. The notion of literary canons as sites of cultural conflict is taken up in the next section that examines the politics of anthologising in the volume co-edited by Rushdie and Elizabeth West, *The Vintage Book of Indian Writing*.

One of the many connecting threads of the above chapter is the quest for authenticity and its implications, though its focus is on the authenticity debate that has been raging around IWE for the past three decades. The ensuing chapter, "Film and television: showcasing pictures of India," further foregrounds the authenticity debate in connection to predominantly visual representations of India. It begins by probing various responses, including those by Rushdie and Arundhati Roy, to Danny Boyle's *Slumdog Millionaire* (2008). Despite (or because of) its mainstream success in the West, Boyle's film, like Adiga's novel *The White Tiger*, faced vehement accusations of complicity with a re-orientalist representation of a Dark India and thus illuminates paradoxes not just within the construction of pictures of India, but also within their contestation. Following this analysis of Rushdie's role as cultural broker in the controversy surrounding *Slumdog Millionaire*, and acknowledging the writer's magpie tendency, manifest through his active engagement with visual forms such as photography, painting, film, and TV, the chapter then focuses, in the subsequent section, on the writer's critique of the Raj revival in film and TV.

Building on the common ground between Adorno's and Horkheimer's critique of the political economy of the culture industry and Rushdie's undercutting of the high/low culture distinction in his creative practice, the succeeding chapter begins by adapting the concept of "culture industry" to the context of contemporary postcolonial cultural production of South Asian origin and rebrands it as "brown culture industry." It moves on to an examination of the ways in which rock-and-roll, a quintessential western discourse, acts as the prime structural underpinning of the novel *The Ground Beneath Her Feet*. In this novel, rock-and-roll is provocatively rendered as "not 'goods from foreign' but made in India" (96), with Rushdie placing the stress on the ambiguity residing between the resistance of the megastar protagonists to a global power structure and their capitulation to the seductiveness of Anglo-American popular culture.

The last chapter before the conclusion, on Rushdie as a public intellectual, endeavours to assess the author's apparently shifting political affiliations, emphasising self-reflexivity and self-irony in its critical effort to capture the complex positionality of Rushdie as cultural broker. The central concern of the first section is to tease out an interrelated set of elements that have contributed to shape the discursive predicament connected with the fatwa in which Rushdie has been trapped for decades. The chapter closes with an examination of the antagonism stirred up in the British press by Rushdie's knighthood in 2007 and an attempt to present an alternative approach to this polemic from the one outlined by commentators in the print media.

Chapter 1
Rushdie as Gatekeeper

Strategic re-orientalism in literature is, perhaps unavoidably so, complicit with what it seeks to refute, generating new discursive authorisations and mobilising new agents of legitimation, such as Rushdie himself. The scenarios of contestation over cultural legitimation postcolonial writers find themselves within, where the term "authenticity" is used and abused, as the critical debate on Adiga's *The White Tiger* aptly illustrates, require a reading attuned to the reconfiguration of (paraphrasing Brah) the diasporian in the native and the native in the diasporian (209). This chapter is attentive to the privileged positionality of postcolonial authors who benefit from the reach and distribution available to western publishing houses in the context of the global late-capitalist system. Agency is powerfully present within the complex networks of power that involve the social circulation of books, and the "Rushdie card" has even been played by Rushdie himself. Against this backdrop, the writer's self-critical articulation of opposition and complicity vis-à-vis his privileged market positioning and his "canonization as our Writer of the East" (Birkerts 233) are focal points of inquiry in this chapter. Rushdie functions as a power brand, capable of granting cultural capital to authors. Undoubtedly as part of a conscious brand management, he has blurbed various works, including Helen Fielding's *Bridget Jones's Diary* (1996), Don DeLillo's *Underworld* (1997) and Zadie Smith's *On Beauty* (2005). With a view to promoting a debate on the writer's literary stardom, this chapter concludes with an analysis that rests specifically on the interweaving of his authorial signature with the brand name "Rushdie." In other words, it examines how the author has been undergoing construction as a global literary celebrity, as a brand, ever since the fatwa.

The Postcolonial Card[1]

> ... [T]here's a kind of critical rhetoric in England about how nobody in England can write about contemporary England. And there are just all these Indian writers, winning all the prizes and so on while people are asking why can't anyone write about England any more, you know, what's wrong with us.
> —Rushdie, qtd. in Vijaya Nagarajan

---

[1] This section is an updated and substantially revised version of the chapter "Prizing Sameness? Kiran Desai and the Booker Prize" printed in Sunita Sinha and Brian Reynolds (eds), *Critical Responses to Kiran Desai*. New Delhi: Atlantic, 2009, 21–31, published with the permission of Atlantic.

Focusing on the Booker prize, the broad purpose of this section is twofold: first, to look at the star principle that has come to attach itself to Booker winners as well as to the cultural works themselves, and second, to examine the current hypervisibility of postcolonial literature from the Indian diaspora resulting from niche marketing strategies developed predominantly by Anglo-American publishing houses. In an interview with Jean W. Ross in 1982, when asked to consider what winning the 1981 Booker Prize for Fiction had done for him, Rushdie stated that a "huge aura has grown up around it" (1), especially in the preceding years, which contributed to the pressure exerted by the prize:

> It's had the most extraordinary effect, of a kind that the Booker Prize hasn't ever had before. ... [T]he immediate result was to turn my book into a great commercial success, which it certainly hadn't been up to that point. So it has obviously made a financial transformation in my life which I hadn't counted on. Apart from that, for about two months after winning the prize I found it almost impossible to do any work – not because of the prize itself, but because of the endless telephone calls and things that surrounded it. (1)

In tandem with increased opportunities for publishing contracts, winning or even being shortlisted for the Booker – the London-based literary award attributed annually to "the best novel written in English" by "citizens of the Commonwealth or the Republic of Ireland"[2] – represents extensive media coverage, bookshop displays, and worldwide readership, and consequently a significant impact on book sales. The Booker, Joe Moran argues, contributes "to create a kind of premier league of bankable literary names" (153). The critic draws attention to the inescapable fact that "publishing houses select which of their authors should be considered," which in reality "means that the real danger is that they give publishers' hype a veneer of cultural authority" (153). Bourdieu had already remarked that being granted access to the field of literature is similar to "getting into a select club" as "the publisher is one of those prestigious sponsors (together with preface-writers and critics) who effusively recommend their candidate" (77). Booker-prize books are hence instant bestsellers in the context of the celebrity-driven and market-oriented literary field. Another point of interest in the following section is that, as Huggan writes, the Booker "has tended to favour postcolonial writers – writers either based in countries of the former British Empire (Africa, the Caribbean, South Asia, Canada, Australia, New Zealand) or belonging to minority communities (Afro-Caribbean, South/east Asian) in Britain" (*Postcolonial Exotic* xii). This fact is certainly significant to the analysis that follows of Rushdie as "the Booker heavyweight" (Muir) and of his role as cultural broker, particularly as a gatekeeper, in the metropolitan literary industry.

*****

---

[2] It is worth pointing out here that "Commonwealth" includes the English-speaking world, second-language countries included, but that the Booker rubric excludes the US.

In the course of an interview given to the Booker website by Kiran Desai, the recipient of the award in 2006, the interviewer recalls that, briefly after winning, the writer had confessed that she would have liked to have been in India because there "they care for the Booker so much." Desai clarifies her earlier assertion regarding the high public profile of the prize in the subcontinent: "Indians have always followed the Booker – an old link, I suppose, and the fact that the prize is often given to books particularly pertinent to us" ("Kiran Desai"). It has without a doubt been quite distinctive of the Booker to promote fiction that concerns Britain's colonial history and its postcolonial present. Furthermore, the prize, with its eligibility prerequisites of Commonwealth (including British) or Irish nationality, raises issues connected with, as Claire Squires mentions, "the imperial history of Great Britain and the concomitant colonial structure of its publishing industry" ("Common Ground" 45).[3] Still, Kiran Desai might be referring also to the unprecedented visibility garnered by diasporic Indian authors writing in English in the last decades, and their favouring by the Booker and its shortlist.

Recent investigations of the politics of the book-prize industry have situated literary awards as a particular form of cultural capital within a contemporary "economy of cultural prestige." James F. English (2005) notes the remarkable rise of prizes in literature and the arts in general and identifies at the very heart of that industry the cultural capital of prestige. He argues that this immaterial economy displays a more sweeping globalisation than that which has taken place in the economy of material commodities. Moreover, according to John Street, "[t]he prize is a device for conveying market-relevant data," significant because "[c]onsumers need information in advance of their purchase of cultural goods" (820). In other words – those of Richard Todd, in what is to date the most comprehensive overview of the cultural politics of the Booker phenomenon, *Consuming Fictions* (1996) – the Booker acts as "a consumer guide to serious literary fiction" (61). If "contemporary literary canon-formation is subject to powerful, rapidly changing market forces affecting and influencing the consumer," one of these forces that has an impact on the Anglophone reader is indeed the Booker and its shortlist (9). This is what makes the British-based literary prize such an immense promotional venture and hence partly responsible for the hypervisibility of Indian fiction written in English in the global market, a role that led Huggan to describe the prize as "a popular retailer of the 'postcolonial exotic'" (*Postcolonial Exotic* 117).

---

[3] Huggan's discussion of the Booker's relation to the metropolitan literary industry also examines the ambivalent promotional role of the UK food wholesaler Booker Plc, established in 1834, commercial sponsor of the prize from 1968 to 2001, with a colonial history in the Caribbean sugar trade (*Postcolonial Exotic* 106–107). English characterises as "cultural money-laundering" the acceptance by the Booker-McConnell company to act as sponsors to this literary prize (*Economy of Prestige* 199). As English reports, in 1972, John Berger, winner of the prize for his novel *G.*, denounced the Booker sponsor as a colonialist enterprise and donated half of his prize money to the London branch of the Black Panthers (203). The investment company Man Group Plc began sponsoring the prize in 2002.

In an interview, Indra Sinha, an Indian writer whose novel *Animal's People* was shortlisted for the Booker in 2007, pondered the recurrent charges of exoticism attached to the prize and criticized the tendency of the British reading public to suspect a tokenistic inclusion of "people from faraway exotic places" on its shortlist: "And then they say things like, 'Three *desis* on the Booker List'? It shouldn't be like that, really, because it completely demeans and denigrates your book. And it's a bit sad if it's imputed that you are really there because of tokenism" (qtd. in Naravane). The spectre of tokenism haunting the prize, or the accusation of winning because of "brownie points,"[4] and the interrelated perceived co-optation of postcolonial literature by the cultural prestige of the prize, were remarkably satirized in a sketch broadcast in 1998 as part of the British TV comedy series *Goodness Gracious Me*.[5] This sketch depicts an interview conducted during a literary chat show – "The Book Programme" – which sets out to "discuss the phenomenal success of Asian writers in western literature." The show's host is joined by three authors on the Booker shortlist, including the fictional character Anita Devi, no doubt a reference to the eternal Booker bridesmaid Anita Desai: thrice Booker shortlisted, the first writer from the Indian subcontinent to have a novel shortlisted for the prize with *Clear Light of Day* in 1980, subsequently twice put on the shortlist with *In Custody* (1984) and *Fasting, Feasting* (1999), albeit in none of those three cases winning the prize, and mother to Kiran Desai, who did win the Booker in 2006. The host asks Anita Devi whether there is not "a certain amount of bandwagon-jumping going on, following the successes of such writers as Vikram Seth and Arundhati Roy," and whether she does not feel "the glut of novels by Asian authors" to be "just a fad." Devi rebuts these allegations, while celebrating and essentialising Asian writers as "natural authors" on account of "the rich depth of [their] cultural experience."

The ensuing discussion hosted by "The Book Programme" lampoons the fashionable critical discourse surrounding Indian literature in English, namely the celebration of the fertile creative ground made up of "the indelible scars" left by colonisation and by the fight for independence, as well as the disparagement of Eurocentric interpretations and imperialist preconceptions. The Booker-nominated books featured on the show are, according to their authors, inspired by "thousands of years of civilization," "the duality of the immigrant experience," and "the tradition of the pictorial in Indian literature." The shortlisted books turn out to be a children's book and a colouring book, nominated merely because of their authors' Asian-sounding names, as is the case with the outlandish Indira Pakistani character (who is, in fact, the white actor Jeffrey Archer), but whose book made the shortlist just the same. When the British-Punjabi novelist, playwright, and actress Meera Syal, performing the role of Anita Devi, confidently declares, tongue-in-cheek, that her work – titled *The Little Bear That Goes Shopping* because it deals in

---

[4] As Arundhati Roy punningly put it after receiving the Booker (Cowley 23), "brownie points" referring to the junior branch of the Girl Guides, but with "brown" meaning "Asian" connoted as well.

[5] Series 2, episode 3, 0:19:43–0:22:07.

reality with a little bear that goes shopping – did not make the Booker shortlist just because of her name, she seems to be echoing the recurrent debate surrounding the absence of English-sounding names on the list.

Cultural commentators, such as the creative team behind *Goodness Gracious Me*, have regarded with ambivalence the canonisation of postcolonial authors and their works by the Booker. The broadcast date of that comic sketch is significant: in 1998, there was a boom in IWE following Roy's *The God of Small Things* (1997) winning of the prize the preceding year. Writers such as Roy have been perceived as having commodified their literary works, benefiting from their postcolonial associations to sell the postcolonial exotic in the context of the Booker prize industry. However, approximately a decade after winning the Booker, Roy confessed in a 2008 interview with *Tehelka Magazine*: "Success devastated my life. It changed all the equations." According to Roy, the Booker "was simultaneously a release and a burden. ... [I]t became [her] middle name" ("Success Devastated"). In 2005 William Dalrymple described the frenzy that ensued in the publishing industry after *The God of Small Things* won the Booker:

> [I]nternational literary agents and publishers descended on India from London and New York, signing up a whole tranche of authors, many of whom received major advances for outlines of novels they had barely begun. Picador launched a list exclusively devoted to Indian writing in 1998; the office was soon buried under an avalanche of unsolicited manuscripts. Throughout the late 1990s, barely a month went by without the news of some fledgling scribbler being discovered lurking as a sub-editor on the Indian Express or pushing papers in the Ministry of External Affairs. ("The Lost Sub-continent")

Interestingly, a scene in Mira Nair's film *Monsoon Wedding* depicts the aura of profitability and prosperity surrounding the act of writing in English by Indians: when a member of the Verma family makes it known that she has applied for a creative writing course in the US, her entrepreneur uncle supports her immediately: "Lots of money in writing these days. Look at that girl who won the Booker: she became a millionaire overnight."

Not unrelatedly, Vikram Chandra detects a "censorious rhetoric about correct Indianness" ("Cult"), a point to be developed later in this chapter. He illustrates this rhetoric resulting from an "anxiety about the anxiety of Indianness" by quoting Namita Gokhale's words in *Sunday* magazine about the Indian-born Kiran Desai:

> The daughter of a famous Indo-Anglian novelist, she makes a cushioned landing into the world of people-like-us literati, with a fat advance from Faber and fleeting visits to the fatherland. ... Kiran Desai typifies a tendency of contemporary Indo-Anglian writing, of the author as a glib tourist guide of an alien sensibility rather than an introspective insider chronicling the life and times he or she lives in.

In *Consuming Fictions*, Todd explores the marketing strategies and interests that shape the Booker and notes how this prize influences media coverage and also publishing contracts through bidding wars between publishers and large advances for the subsequent books of the more visible authors. More than ever, the Booker has become a "household name" and a "nationally televised extravaganza" (English, *Economy of Prestige* 198–199), a fact that Todd, writing almost a decade before, had not fully apprehended.

The Booker has attracted considerable visibility, being as it is so highly promoted. Like arts prizes in general, it has "become a kind of spectator sport, attracting considerable media speculation and discussion, and [is] accompanied by organized betting" (J. Street 819). This is the result, among other factors, of a studied planning of media exposure, with a carefully staged controversy in the press and the organisation of a glamorized award ceremony, a media event in itself. J. Street writes that the media attention devoted to the Booker "not only includes fluctuations in the betting at the bookies, but also rumours about agents, editors and authors, or leaks about tensions between the judges" (839). One of the most notorious incidents has been, as English recounts, how when Rushdie did not win the Booker in 1995 with *The Moor's Last Sigh* he "pound[ed] his fists on the table, cursing at the prize's administrator, saying the judges knew 'fuck all' about literature" (206). In an effort to continuously cultivate the Booker mythology, the prize organizers announced in 2008 the one-off celebratory award The Best of the Booker to celebrate the fortieth anniversary of the prize. Unprecedentedly, the winning novel was selected by a public vote from among a shortlist of six novels previously chosen by a panel of judges. The winner of The Best of the Booker – *Midnight's Children* – was announced at the London Literature Festival in July 2008. This celebratory event was accompanied by an exhibition at the Victoria & Albert Museum and by a season at the Institute of Contemporary Arts entitled "The Booker at the Movies," featuring films based on Booker-winning novels.

Not only does the sketch from *Goodness Gracious Me* introduce issues of commodification and marketability connected with the commercial achievements of postcolonial literature, to which the Booker is certainly no stranger, but it also helps introduce the question whether or not a postcolonial card is being played – and if indeed it is, by whom – in the prize's acclaim of postcolonial writers, in this case, of South Asian descent.[6] To address this interrogation, the focus will now shift to the 2006 Booker round, considering how the winner Kiran Desai might be construed as a postcolonial commodity. Certainly, as Moran notes, literary celebrities, such as Rushdie and Kiran Desai, "cannot simply be reduced to their exchange value" given that "they are complex cultural signifiers who are repositories for all kinds of meanings" (9). Nonetheless, with Desai as a case study, this section attempts to map out the connotations that commodities – here, postcolonial authors circulating as commodities – come to acquire during their exchange. Accordingly, the writer Kiran Desai is here regarded as a product in the global literary marketplace, held to standards of financial viability.

---

[6] Chris Bongie's use of the expression "postcolonial card" is within the context of "university hiring practices" (para. 55).

It is commonly agreed that Indian fiction in English generated a considerable amount of interest at home and abroad after Rushdie's emergence in the 1980s as a leading literary father-figure. In effect, the enormous success of *Midnight's Children* paved the way for the appeal of Indian fiction written in English by "Rushdie's Children" in a large-scale literary marketplace. The label "Rushdie's Children" was without delay ridiculed by Amitava Kumar in a review: "We grew up in India under the stultifying shadow of the nationalist myth that we were all the children of Mahatma Gandhi. Now, if *The New Yorker* is to be believed, we are all the children of Salman Rushdie" ("God" 84). Kiran Desai, one of Rushdie's "daughters," was hailed by *The New Yorker* in 1997 as part of that emergent young group of Indian novelists writing in English when she was just working on her debut novel, *Hullabaloo in the Guava Orchard* (1998). Her only published work at that time was precisely the short piece included in that fiction issue of *The New Yorker* dedicated to India: "The Sermon in the Guava Tree," subtitled in the table of contents as "An author's debut." As Wachinger appropriately notes, "[i]t is not an overstatement ... to say that it was the *New Yorker* that turned Anita Desai's daughter into a member of the 'imagined community' of India's literary elite" (72). Still, *The New Yorker* was not the only stakeholder involved in turning this diasporic writer into a valuable cultural commodity: Rushdie himself offered her as "welcome proof that India's encounter with the English language, far from proving abortive,[7] continues to give birth to new children, endowed with lavish gifts" ("Damme" 1997: 61; "Introduction" xxii).[8] This "proof" consisted of the short story "The Sermon in the Guava Tree" – an extract from her first novel, at the time still an unpublished manuscript – which *The New Yorker* incorporated in its special fiction issue and Rushdie decided to include in his and West's *The Vintage Book* under the title "Strange Happenings in the Guava Orchard." The biographical note for Kiran Desai in this collection comprised only three lines and announced that Desai's first novel – at the time titled *Strange Happenings in the Guava Orchard* – was to be published by Faber and Faber ("Biographical Notes" 570–571).

---

[7] The use of the terms "encounter" and "abortive" echoes Naipaul's contention that "[t]he Indo-British encounter was abortive; it ended in a double fantasy. Their new self-awareness makes it impossible for Indians to go back; their cherishing of Indianness makes it difficult for them to go ahead. ... The penetration was not complete; the attempt at conversation was abandoned" (*Area* 233).

[8] Amit Chaudhuri, using similar terms but looking at this development from a different perspective, notes in an essay originally published in the *Times Literary Supplement* in 1999: "the two words, 'Indian' and 'English', which sat next to each other so uneasily [a few decades ago], their juxtaposition looked upon with as much suspicion from every side as if they were the progeny of warring families (which, in a sense, they were), are now wedded in a marriage that not only seems inevitable but health-giving; what might have been a tragedy has been turned, apparently, into a happy ending with numberless possibilities" ("Construction" xxiii).

Accounting for the growing status and rising notoriety of "'Indo-Anglian' literature" in the introduction to that co-edited anthology, Rushdie concluded: "[o]n the map of world literature ... India has been undersized for too long," and an "age of obscurity is coming to an end" (xxii). Interestingly for the purposes of interrogating the postcolonial associations of the Booker prize, Rushdie's selection features a number of Booker-shortlisted or Booker-winning authors: Anita Desai, Ruth Prawer Jhabvala (winner in 1979 with *Heat and Dust*), Rushdie himself (shortlisted with *The Moor's Last Sigh* in 1995, *The Satanic Verses* in 1988, and *Shame* in 1983; winner with *Midnight's Children* in 1981; longlisted with *Shalimar The Clown* in 2005), Rohinton Mistry (shortlisted with *Family Matters* in 2002, *A Fine Balance* in 1996, and *Such a Long Journey* in 1991), Arundhati Roy (winner with *The God of Small Things* in 1997), and Kiran Desai (winner with *The Inheritance of Loss* in 2006). Rushdie was longlisted again in 2008 for *The Enchantress of Florence*, and in the same year Amitav Ghosh (included in the anthology) made the shortlist for *Sea of Poppies*. Rushdie reiterates the idea that an "age of obscurity is coming to an end" regarding English fiction by Indian authors in a closing remark of the essay "Damme, This is the Oriental Scene for You," included in *The New Yorker* issue: "India's writers have torn up the old map and are busily redrawing their own" ("Damme" 61).[9] He describes Desai's début as "equally impressive" in relation to Roy's *The God of Small Things*, describing "Strange Happenings in the Guava Orchard" as "a Calvinoesque fable of a misfit boy who climbs a tree and becomes a sort of pretty guru," and ends by acclaiming it as "lush and intensely imagined"; he continues thus: "Kiran Desai is the daughter of Anita: her arrival establishes the first dynasty of modern Indian fiction. But she is very much her own writer, the newest of all these voices" (61). When Desai's novel was published the next year, Rushdie's previous promotional push was boosted. His blurb – "Lush and intensely imagined" – features on the front cover and right under the title of the book, while the authorising words originally written in the prologue to his and West's collection ("Introduction" xxii) are included in a three-page opening section under the heading "Further acclaim for *Hullabaloo in the Guava Orchard*."

Desai's second novel, *The Inheritance of Loss*, winner of the Booker in 2006, has been decried or praised, according to one's perspective, as a Rushdiesque novel. For instance, the writer Will Self, noting that the Booker has tended to celebrate books that represent "the creative collision of English-language fiction with an explosive, post-colonial world," stated that "Desai's victory seemed like a mainstream choice," and that the novel, "for all its individual sparkle and originality, is nothing if not a post-Rushdie novel." On another occasion, *The*

---

[9] The article entitled "Damme, This is the Oriental Scene For You" and subtitled "An Introduction to Indian Fiction" (*The New Yorker*, June 23–30, 1997) was subsequently published (or "enshrined," as Rajeswari Rajan pejoratively puts it) with slight adaptations in the introductory chapter of *The Vintage Book*. "Damme" was reprinted in Rushdie's collection of non-fiction *Step Across This Line* (159–173).

Inheritance of Loss was regarded by a representative of the British booksellers Waterstone's as maintaining "the fine tradition of Booker winners set in India" such as its predecessors *The God of Small Things* and *Midnight's Children* (Jury). Earlier, one of the blurbs to Desai's debut novel had read: "Desai spins a hilarious tale with a smattering of Rushdiesque flourish (*India Today*)." In fact, her work seemed to follow a step behind Rushdie, moving from a narrative with "lots of heat and dust, sweating men, lisping saris, and honking traffic, as well as plenty of yakking Indians" in *Hullabaloo in the Guava Orchard* (Kumar, "Louder" 83) to a more transnational setting in *The Inheritance of Loss*, a novel that spans the Asian and American continents and narrates the travails of illegal immigrants in New York.

Regarding Kiran Desai's standing as a diasporic Indian writer and winner of the Booker, if we adapt Huggan's general understanding of the award as an instance of "prizing otherness" and recast it as an example of prizing sameness, Desai is to be regarded as an author who is simultaneously marketed as the exotic other and as the recognisable exotic, made familiar through the comparisons with Rushdie. In "Culture Industry Reconsidered," Adorno writes: "What parades as progress in the culture industry, as the incessantly new which it offers up, remains the disguise for an eternal sameness" (100). Only after the connections to Rushdie and parallels with his work had been drawn, were Desai and her work made ready for metropolitan consumption. The prior history of her commodification as postcolonial author and the fact that her mother was shortlisted three times for the Booker but never won, also serve the commercial logic of the Booker prize. As J. Street remarks, "[a]rtists' previous success (and the reputation attached to it) are essential to the prize becoming a media event. If the shortlist consisted of unknowns, then it would not attract media attention" (838).

Without question, Rushdie granted a seal of approval to Desai with his generous praise. Both this acclamation and the comparisons drawn between her work and Rushdie's add cultural capital to her novels and inform the judgement of prospective readers. However, who gets the return from this investment when Desai's work is made to circulate in the global literary marketplace? If Desai is packaged, priced, and thrown out on the market with the help of exoticising marketing strategies, is not Rushdie, in this sense a postcolonial lobbyist, the one playing the postcolonial card? Is he not displaying a self-awareness of the field of meaning already constructed around the label "Rushdie"? In all probability, he is one of the best examples to demonstrate how postcolonial cultural artefacts are commodified and made to circulate in a context of "postcoloniality," i.e. "a global condition of cross-cultural symbolic exchange" (Huggan, *Postcolonial Exotic* ix), displaying an overt "contradiction between anti-colonial ideologies and neo-colonial market schemes" (413). Is he strategically playing with the perception, established in both the publishing industry and in academic circles, of "Rushdie" as brandname? Or is he an unavoidable part of the global cultural economy and its marketing tactic of commodifying a postcolonial writer, as much as his blurb to Desai's *Hullabaloo in the Guava Orchard* is an integral component of the novel's promotional logic? Rushdie may well be redistributing cultural capital, but does this in any way contribute to the restructuring of the metropolitan publishing industry? When an interviewer asked him how significant marketing is to literature, he answered that it was not relevant to literature, "but it's very important for the bank balance of the writer" (qtd. in A. Sawhney). Despite being inescapably part and parcel of the promotional circuit of postcolonial literature, there still subsist some difficulties in regarding Rushdie as fully co-opted by the metropolitan literary industry.

Rushdie, revered as the gatekeeper of IWE, to a certain extent because of his Booker profile, besides paving the way for the recognisability of diasporic South Asian authors, embraces the idea of acting as patron for upcoming writers. For example, the essay "The Best of Young British Novelists," where he describes the controversy surrounding Granta's second list of "Best of Young British Novelists," for which he acted as judge in 1993 (after having been himself selected as one of Granta's "Best of Young British Novelists" in 1983), is an unflinching defence of those "highly promising writers with some achievements and a great future ahead of them" (35).[10] Ardashir Vakil is yet another example of a young writer greatly extolled by Rushdie (Concilio 131). Rushdie's blurb – "Extraordinary ... amazing" – appears in block capital letters on the cover of the non-fiction work *Maximum City: Bombay Lost and Found* (2005) and heads the "Authors' praise" listing on the back of the front cover: "Suketu Mehta's *Maximum City* is quite extraordinary ... It's the best book yet written about that great, ruined metropolis." Later, he commended Ketaki Sheth for her book of photographs on Mumbai, *Bombay Mix: Street Photographs* (2007), extolling her work on the back cover with these words: "Ketaki Sheth's photographs, so formally interesting, so sharply seen, so deeply felt, give these street lives the greatest gift such work can offer: the dignity of art." Interestingly, a blurb by Rushdie – "Sheth's Bombay is subtle, considered and thoughtful, even when it is outwardly brutal. There is an incidental beauty in its people, in the midst of the grime ..." – also features on the dust jacket of Sheth's book, thus highlighting the circularity of the process of endorsement.

In the article "Is Salman Rushdie God?" Kumar denounces a partial view of Indian writers of English that should merit the attention of critics and is worth quoting at length:

---

[10] The list comprised: Iain Banks, Louis de Bernières, Anne Billson, Tibor Fischer, Esther Freud, Alan Hollinghurst, Kazuo Ishiguro, A. L. Kennedy, Philip Kerr, Hanif Kureishi, Adam Lively, Adam Mars-Jones, Candia McWilliam, Lawrence Norfolk, Ben Okri, Caryl Phillips, Will Self, Nicholas Shakespeare, Helen Simpson, and Jeanette Winterson. (34).

> I agree that "writers like Rushdie" or "not like Rushdie" continue to be categories under which most hacks prefer to slot Indian writers. But isn't this a shortcoming and shouldn't we be critical of this habit? ... And don't the writers who have emerged in India in the past two decades deserve more than what is given them when we treat them as clones? Yes, it is true that the writers who followed in the wake of Rushdie were inspired by his example, but it is important to take serious note of the different directions in which their work has gone. Their work, I believe, is a creative comment on Rushdie and his extraordinary output. Today, it is impossible to read any new work of Rushdie without also bringing into the discussion the new works by those who are patronizingly regarded as his literary offspring.

In fact, Indian writers of English are still categorized by being "like Rushdie" or "not like Rushdie." These labels are also used to enhance the cultural capital of the Booker shortlist. Indeed, the impact of the prize on the consumption of literary texts comes mostly from labelling: it distinguishes a cultural commodity through ascription of, among others, exotic qualities, with decisions resulting in canonisation. More than simply selling books, the Booker contributes to the canonisation of writers, and nowhere is this more evident than in Rushdie's case, an effect that also extends to his "children." This section has set out to inquire whether a "postcolonial card" has been played in the Booker prize given its favouring of authors from nations of the erstwhile British Empire or belonging to minority communities in Britain. It concludes by admitting to having somewhat dodged the question when it ended up replacing the "postcolonial card" by the "Rushdie card." In sum, the star principle that Adorno argues is prescient in the workings of the culture industry, and which is unquestionably attached to Rushdie, has extended to the Indian writer Kiran Desai. The focus of this section was based on Rushdie's strategic negotiation of the highly leveraged brand name "Rushdie" as a way of creating an artistic space or market niche for postcolonial diasporic work. Interrelatedly, this section briefly looked at the consecration of both Indian authors writing in English and of Empire-related themes by the Booker prize.

During the past three decades, an impressive inventory of Indian literary works written in English has been acquiring an unprecedented success in the cultural marketplace, mostly as an offshoot of being awarded (or longlisted for) literary prizes. In the case of the Booker prize, Aravind Adiga is the fourth Indian writer to win the award in 2008. The 2008 Booker longlist included the novels *The Enchantress of Florence* by Rushdie, *Sea of Poppies* by Ghosh, as well as *A Case of Exploding Mangoes* by Pakistani Mohammed Hanif. Out of the final six shortlisted authors in 2008, two (Adiga and Ghosh) were of South Asian origin. Most recently, Jeet Thayil was shortlisted in 2012 with the novel *Narcopolis*. The next section will maintain this focus on the promotional circuit surrounding Indian literature in English, though with reference to the Booker prize for 2008, awarded to Adiga for *The White Tiger*, and the ways the (anti-)Rushdie card was played in the process of branding Adiga's novel.

Exotic Dark India[11]

> Did *you* make me for the gap in the market
> Did *I* make me for the gap in the market
> ...
> Can I cream off awards from your melting-pot phase
> Do you medal yourselves when you meddle with my type [?]
>
> —Daljit Nagra 6–7

This section examines Adiga's *The White Tiger*'s staging of a Dark India as a newfangled object of exoticist discourses. It begins by considering the novel as an ironic uncovering of the subsumption of a Dark India into the global literary marketplace at a time of a perceived shift in re-orientalist representational practices and their western reception. Specifically, while taking the measure of the appraisal the novel has received, the premises that underpin the most vehement critiques directed at *The White Tiger* are questioned: on the one hand, that Adiga's work offers a purportedly long-awaited creative departure from Rushdie's; on the other hand, that the characterisation strategies followed by Adiga result in what critics have perceived as class ventriloquism and, correspondingly, in a re-orientalised title character equipped with an "inauthentic" voice.

*****

After decades of cashing in on the fascination with a mystical Eternal India, the idea of an ostensible Dark India has been acquiring of late a significant exotic cachet in the cultural industries. The representation of a Dark India is admittedly not new – it can be traced back to Mulk Raj Anand's groundbreaking novels *Untouchable* (1935) and *Coolie* (1936). More recent novels that could be read to a greater or lesser degree as depicting a Dark India are, for example, *A Suitable Boy* (1994) by Vikram Seth, *A Fine Balance* (1995) by Rohinton Mistry, *Sacred Games* (2006) by Vikram Chandra, and *The Glass Palace* (2000) and *Sea of Poppies* (2008) by Amitav Ghosh. Nonetheless, a revamped portrayal of a Dark India garnered an unparalleled visibility in 2008 with the awarding of the coveted Booker prize to Adiga's debut novel *The White Tiger*. The then chair of the Booker judging panel, former British Cabinet Minister and Conservative MP Michael Portillo, celebrated the novel as "an intensely original book about an India that is new to many of us." He further hailed it as "in many ways perfect" and added that the novel had "knocked [his] socks off" (E. Wagner). Looking at *The White Tiger* from a less favourable angle, Somak Ghoshal wrote that Adiga's narrative "turns out to be the ideal rough guide to Dark India: a series of extensive footnotes for the benefit of Western readers." "As Adiga shows," the Indian critic contended,

---

[11] This subchapter is a revised version of the article "Exciting Tales of Exotic Dark India: Aravind Adiga's *The White Tiger*," *The Journal of Commonwealth Literature*, 45. 2, June 2010, 275–293, published with the permission of Sage.

"the best bet for all those closeted novelists lurking in this country of a billion, is to write about the Darkness, the rural hinterland that lies stashed far away from the dazzling India of the big cities."

Ghoshal's conjecture that Adiga had "his eye probably set on a future screenplay for a Hollywood version of his book," might have some truth to it. In fact, a film adaptation of *The White Tiger* was to be made, with a script written by Oscar-nominated writer Todd Field, but production halted due to legal battles over rights in 2012. Adorno's and Horkheimer's thesis is that the culture industry "rejects anything untried as a risk. In film, any manuscript which is not reassuringly based on a best-seller is viewed with mistrust" (106); this process of capital formation is further echoed in the statement: "[t]his work process integrates all the elements of production, from the original concept of the novel, shaped by its sidelong glance at film, to the last sound effect. It is the triumph of invested capital" (98). As Blake observes, "it is probable that the criteria for publishability will become more closely tied to the notion of 'filmability'. Many publishers are already component parts of transnational corporations, which can maximize their investments in the few products which achieve global sales success by marketing them in different formats"; in fact, Blake sees this as "one of the [possible] reasons for Salman Rushdie's change of tactics towards producing more, shorter and sharper, novels [like *Fury*]" (71).

Judging from the title of Adiga's novel, the reader might reasonably expect to encounter a tale about a rare and exotic character.[12] Furthermore, given that the tiger is a symbol of power and might, the title *The White Tiger* also alludes to India's rise as a tiger economy, and thus conflates ideas of exoticism and unstoppable economic growth.[13] In ways that assist a more complex understanding of Rushdie as cultural broker, this subchapter joins in the ongoing critical debate as to whether Adiga's metaphorical construct of a Dark India undermines previous stereotypes associated with the representation of a magical Eternal India (and at the same time offers a corrective portrait of the "progress" resulting from the Indian IT and business outsourcing boom), or whether his novel is yet another covert means – through the use of extremely effective self-reflexive representational strategies – of selling a refurbished exotic idea of the subcontinent to western readers. In this

---

[12] The uncommon coloration of white tigers has made them popular attractions in zoos and shows that showcase wild animals. For example, the German-American illusionists Siegfried & Roy were famous for having bred and trained white tigers for their much-publicised shows in Las Vegas.

[13] The term "tiger economy" refers to the accelerated growth undergone by the economy of a country. While this expression was initially applied to the "East Asian Tigers" (Hong Kong, Taiwan, Singapore, and South Korea), India is currently described too as a tiger economy, in the sense that it is propelled by the vertiginous development of its globally-oriented economy and the burgeoning of an affluent urban middle-class. Furthermore, India is part of the BRICs, an acronym that refers to Brazil, Russia, India and China, countries sharing a booming economic development.

respect, a critical approach to the impact of *The White Tiger* in the western literary marketplace might well be induced by a question that the Indian writer K.R. Usha poses in her review of the novel: "To whom is Adiga addressing this unleavened story, in his faultless prose?" The answer is seemingly quite obvious for Usha, considering that "[a]ny Indian who reads the newspaper knows that India isn't shining."

One of the main points Huggan makes in *The Postcolonial Exotic* is that India as exotic spectacle has progressively become available for global consumption. Through his formulation of the "postcolonial exotic," Huggan critiques "the global commodification of cultural difference" as a "general mechanics of exoticist representation/consumption within an increasingly globalized culture industry" (vii). Within this "alterity industry" (x), one of the agents involved in the mediation of the "aesthetic value of cultural difference" (13) is the literary marketplace. As stated in the introduction, the arguments presented here are not based on an overriding pleasure principle guiding the western publishing industry. Still, what is suggested here is that Adiga's novel contributes (even if unintentionally) to sustaining such an alterity industry. The marketing potential of *The White Tiger* lies in two distinct but nevertheless related ideas – that of "the exotic" and that of "dark" – which are in turn associated with cultural difference. In this sense, the novel's revamped spectacle of India is achieved through representational strategies that conflate an Exotic India with a Dark India.

The act of reading Adiga's Dark (Exotic) India as a staged phenomenon is inspired by the (self-ironic) confession on the part of the narrator of *The White Tiger* that his knowledge of the history of India's booming neighbour, China, came from a book – significantly entitled *Exciting Tales of the Exotic East* – which he found when browsing at a secondhand book market in Delhi (5). This account of how the image of China in the protagonist's mind was built around a book with that clichéd title might be interpreted both as a satire of exoticising western notions about the East and as an exposure of the metropolitan consumer-reader's complicitous desire for such alluring tales. Specifically, while taking the measure of the appraisals *The White Tiger* has received, this subchapter questions one of the premises that underpin the most vehement critiques directed at the novel: that Adiga's work purportedly offers a long-awaited creative departure from Rushdie's, hence the awarding of the Booker in 2008.

In a nutshell, *The White Tiger* is about an India that is "two countries in one: an India of Light, and an India of Darkness" (14). The India of Light is that of wealth, technology, and knowledge, while the India of Darkness (where the majority of Indians live) is that of misery, destitution, and illiteracy. The novel describes how its protagonist/narrator Balram Halwai managed to claw his way into the Light of Delhi and Bangalore, out of the Darkness of Laxmangarh, a small remote village in the poor state of Bihar, in eastern India, on the banks of what he calls the "the black river" (14), a reference to the river Ganges. Balram refers here to the revered icon of Spiritual India in the western imaginary ever since the Beatles, in their legendary sojourn in the subcontinent in 1968, arrived at Rishikesh, a city bathed by the sacred river, to visit Maharishi Mahesh Yogi's ashram.[14] Whereas the Darkness, where Balram is born and bred, flows from the Ganges into rural India, the Light, on the opposite side of the spectrum, surges inward from the coast. Balram holds the river responsible for "bring[ing] darkness" to the country (14) and describes it in its materiality as "full of faeces, straw, soggy parts of human bodies, buffalo carrion, and seven different kinds of industrial acids" (15). This representation of the Ganges undermines the feeling that, as Shivani cuttingly remarks in relation to a recent strand of IWE, "you [the western reader] can safely dip your toes into the exotic mystical waters of the East" (9). After deconstructing the touristy image of the Ganges (and also the argument that all IWE represents India in ways likely to please western tourist urges), the narrator states that he is definitely "leaving that river for the American tourists" (18) who come in their hundreds "each year to take photographs of naked sadhus" (15). The narrator also undermines the spiritual reputation of his home village Laxmangarh, which is just a few miles from the Bodhi Tree under which the Buddha obtained enlightenment ("Bodhi"). While it is reported that the Buddha walked through Laxmangarh, in the protagonist's version "he ran through it – as fast as he could – and got to the other side – and never looked back!" (18).

The White Tiger is a first-person *Bildungsroman*, recounting the ascent of its protagonist from servant to "self-taught entrepreneur" (6). The plot centres on Balram's character formation, or rather on his long and arduous fight for survival in a way which attests, in Rushdie's words, to "the Indian talent for non-stop self-regeneration" ("Imaginary" 16). Against all odds, he sheds the venomous mud of the Ganges, "the rich, dark, sticky mud whose grip traps everything that is planted in it, suffocating and choking and stunting it" (15). Defying the expectations of his caste of sweetmakers (56, 63) and the destiny into which he was born as the child of a cycle-rickshaw wallah in the Darkness, he is hired as a driver by a rich local landlord for his son Mr Ashok and his spoiled daughter-in-law Pinky Madam, who have returned from the US. Balram moves with the couple to Gurgaon, an affluent Delhi suburb where new shopping centres selling luxury brands conceal in their interior run-down segregated markets for the staff, and where luxurious high-rise apartment complexes, such as the kitsch Buckingham Towers[15] where Mr Ashok and Pinky Madam live, coexist with the cockroaches and mosquitoes in the servants' cramped quarters. In the India of Light, he witnesses the rampant consumerism of one of India's booming cities and faces the downside of a consumer-oriented elite among whom brown envelopes circulate freely.

Somewhat unaccountably, Balram conspires to murder his corrupt master. He cuts Mr Ashok's throat with a broken bottle of Johnny Walker Black Label,

---

[14] See Saltzman's album of photos *The Beatles at Rishikesh* (2001), which documents the Beatles' stay at Yogi's ashram.

[15] In *Midnight's Children*, baby Saleem grew up in Buckingham Villa. Methwold's Estate consists of four houses named after European palaces: Versailles, Buckingham, Escorial, and Sans Souci.

escapes with his dirty money, the product of landlordism and corruption, and then finds a place in Bangalore's entrepreneurial class. As would the protagonist of an archetypal *Bildungsroman*, he re-integrates into society as Ashok Sharma, the apparently upper-caste owner of a prosperous taxi service in the India of Light. So, from one point of view, the criminal anti-hero murders his boss and uses his money to finance his way into the India of Light and does not seem too perplexed by his nefarious actions. From another point of view, the entrepreneurial hero breaks with his past in the India of Darkness and to that extent triumphs despite his unpromising initial station in life. Again, as in a *Bildungsroman*, Balram is paradoxically an anti-hero and, in keeping with India's newfangled economic strength, "a modern Indian hero" who features in "a parable of the new India" (Kapur). In the narrator's own phrasing, his life's story should be entitled "The Autobiography of a Half-Baked Indian."[16] When Balram was still at school, an inspector pointed his cane straight at him and said: "You, young man, are an intelligent, honest, vivacious fellow in this crowd of thugs and idiots. In any jungle, what is the rarest of animals – the creature that comes along only once in a generation?" In reply to this, he answered "[t]he white tiger," and the school inspector retorted "That's what you are, in *this* jungle" (35). Balram, the White Tiger, struggles to survive in the post-independence Indian wilderness because, as he notes, "on the fifteenth of August, 1947 – the day the British left – the cages had been let open; and the animals had attacked and ripped each other apart and jungle law replaced zoo law" (64). To Balram, pre-independence India, "in its days of greatness, when it was the richest nation on earth, was like a zoo. Everyone in its place, everyone happy" (63). Along similar lines, Rushdie draws a satirical portrayal of the end of the "roseate age of England's precedence":

> how fine was the manner of [the imperial sun's] setting; in what good order the British withdrew. Union Jacks fluttered down their poles all round the world, to be replaced by other flags, in all manner of outlandish colours. The pink conquerors crept home, the boxwallahs and memsahibs and bwanas, leaving behind them parliaments, schools, Grand Trunk Roads and the rules of cricket. ("New Empire" 129–130)

The British imperial project incorporated the exotic space of India into colonized territory partly by classifying its inhabitants as exotic animals living in the wild, conveniently setting them apart and exhibiting them in a state of near cultural captivity. In the aftermath of the British Empire, according to Balram, formerly colonized subjects had to adjust to "the law of the jungle"; when the British departed, the orderly zoo became a landscape of destitution and inequality, a corrupt jungle where local elections were customarily bought and sold, and where villagers from the Darkness prattle about them "like eunuchs discussing the Kama Sutra" (98). "[T]hanks to all those politicians in Delhi," independence

---

[16] This is a parody of the title of *The Autobiography of an Unknown Indian* (1951) by Nirad C. Chaudhuri.

has resulted in repeated clashes between Balram's desires to escape casteism and classism and the constraints of a culturally-embedded corruption (64). In India's current state, the cunning and resourceful protagonist posits that there are only two ways that an uneducated and underprivileged individual can rise above the restrictions imposed by caste and class: crime and politics. In effect, there are only two destinies in India: either "eat – or get eaten up" (64).

Presenting himself as "A Thinking Man / And an entrepreneur / Living in the world's centre of technology and outsourcing" (3), Balram pens an uninvited series of letters to the Premier of China, Wen Jiabao, to prepare him for his upcoming official visit to India. In the course of seven nights, from "Electronics City Phase 1 (just off Hosur Main Road), / Bangalore, India" (3), he sets out to introduce the Chinese leader to the "realities" of his country's recent economic boom. It is from the clichéd location of the bustling city Bangalore, along with Hyderabad one of India's fastest-growing high-tech centres, that Balram intends to correct the misconceptions about the country fostered by Indian entrepreneurs and corrupt politicians for their own self-aggrandizement. "One fact about India," he remarks, "is that you can take almost anything you hear about the country from the prime minister and turn it upside down and then you will have the truth about that thing" (15). The White Tiger, the Indian entrepreneur, wants Wen Jiabao, the Prime Minister of China, to return to his country with the "truth" he is revealing because "[i]f anyone knows the truth about Bangalore, it's [*him*]" (4). Indeed, the trajectory of his life purportedly reflects the actuality of Rising India where the IT boom masks poverty, corruption, and inefficiency.

Artists, Rushdie suggests, are in the business of cultural mapping. In an interview, he argues that *Midnight's Children* attempted to answer a cartographical imperative – to chart a new aesthetic map of his birth country – because "India may be an ancient civilization but it's also a new country." He reasserts that "[o]ne of the things you have to do with new countries is to draw maps of them"; after providing the reader with these imaginative maps, writers can then "put [themselves] on the map" (qtd. in U. Chaudhuri 28). *The White Tiger*, published 27 years after *Midnight's Children*, sets out to chart the underside of India's newfound economic prowess by the hand of a protagonist who stands for "tomorrow" (6). Even though Adiga's mapping of a Dark India might be seen as an opportunistic depiction of Indian destitution, it represents to some critics the future of a nation coming to terms with images of endemic poverty and underdevelopment, and of a literature in search of a new creative path away from what they perceive as worn-out Rushdiesque motifs.

In a rave review of *The White Tiger*, *The Economist* lionizes Adiga as "the Charles Dickens of the call-centre generation" ("His Master's"). Following a familiar practice of comparing Indian novelists to Dickens (a critical tradition that seems to descend from Mulk Raj Anand, a writer said to be "India's Charles Dickens"[17]), Charlotte Higgins describes Adiga's portrayal of India's glaring

---

[17] See e.g. Behera 90 and Burke 170.

social contrasts as "almost Dickensian," basing her comparison on the fact that, in the novel, "the unpleasant reality of contemporary Indian society is revealed via mordant sketches of characters, from millionaires in their air-conditioned tower blocks to the unfortunates who are trapped in poverty and who live literally below them, catering to their every whim." Indeed, Adiga considers that "the criticism by writers like Flaubert, Balzac and Dickens of the 19th century helped England and France become better societies" (qtd. in "I Highlighted"). Perhaps unwittingly, these reviewers hint at a further connection between Dickens and Adiga besides an allegedly Dickensian ability to convey experience that they perceive in the latter: the fact that Dickens was seen by his contemporaries as a nineteenth-century Adiga. Indeed, anxiety over the commodification of literature dates back at least to Dickens's age. While these reporters liken Dickens to Adiga, Rushdie regards the Victorian novelist as "quintessentially Indian," in terms which could include the Delhi depicted in Adiga's novel:

> Dickensian London, that stenchy, rotting city full of sly, conniving shysters, that city in which goodness was under constant assault by duplicity, malice and greed, seemed to me to hold up the mirror to the pullulating cities of India, with their preening élites living the high life in gleaming skyscrapers while the great majority of their compatriots battled to survive in the hurly-burly of the streets below. ("Influence" 71)

In *The Independent*, David Mattin hails *The White Tiger* as "an Indian novel that explodes the clichés – ornamental prose, the scent of saffron – associated with that phrase" because it introduces readers instead to "an India where Microsoft call-centre workers tread the same pavement as beggars who burn street rubbish for warmth." In this context it comes as no surprise that Adiga's narrative is greeted by David Sexton, writing for the *Evening Standard*, as a "scathing, abusively satirical antidote to the romance of Rushdie" and that, in *The Independent*, the reviewer Boyd Tonkin writes that "Adiga could be classified as the anti-Rushdie, cleansing florid exotica from the fiction of India" ("General Fiction"). Might these responses signal a shift taking place in the western reception of Indian novelists in English? While this remains as yet an open question, the fact is that, in the control of cultural authenticity effected by these agents of legitimation, the positive valuation of *The White Tiger* (and, significantly, the shortlisting of Thayil's *Narcopolis* for the Booker) depends on an apparent opposition to a perceived tendency of IWE towards formal experimentation and exotic spice-related metaphors that readers generally tend to connect in their minds with Rushdie's novels, and that some authors themselves repudiate, as manifested by Thayil during an interview: "I try to avoid sentimentality and I try to avoid the easy cliché. I try to avoid any mention of mangoes, of spices and monsoons. The problem with those books about India which paint Indian society in soft focuses [is that] I find it very difficult to recognize the country I know in those books" (qtd. in "'Narcopolis': Inside India's Dark Underbelly").

The epigraph introducing this subchapter presented the British poet Daljit Nagra's self-reflexive remarks on the cultural commodification and consumption of otherness. His allusion to the possibility of "cream[ing] off awards" encapsulates a problematic this chapter attempts to unpack: how literary works and authors function as tradable commodities within re-orientalist patterns. Given that the marketing strategies used to promote *The White Tiger* to metropolitan readers clearly influenced its signifying processes, it is relevant to examine the social biography of the novel. As Appadurai contends, "we have to follow the things themselves, for their meanings are inscribed in their forms, their uses, their trajectories" ("Introduction" 5). As consumer items and marketable goods, Indian writers in English and their works are consistently classified into one of two categories, following niche marketing strategies: they are either "like Rushdie" or "not like Rushdie," as Kumar observed. Such labels were used to boost the cultural capital of the Booker shortlist in the 2007 competition when the Indian-born author Indra Sinha, shortlisted for his novel *Animal's People*, was recurrently related to Rushdie in the print media. "Everyone pigeonholed as an 'Indian writer' is inevitably compared to Salman Rushdie," remarks Sinha ("Q&A"). Indeed, Rushdie's career, which began in advertising, served as a sanctioned precedent for Sinha's literary celebrity debut. The interviewer Anil Thakraney even went to the lengths of asking the author if it would be "correct to say that [his] life has turned out rather like Rushdie's" given that he had "followed his career in almost every single way, except for the fatwa and Padma Lakshmi." To this provocation, Sinha sarcastically retorts:

> "Why do you say that? Is it because we both grew up in Bombay, both went to Cathedral school, both were at public schools in England, both read English Literature at Cambridge, both went into advertising as copywriters, both worked at Ogilvy & Mather, both worked with the same art director, Garry Horner, on the same Fresh Cream Cakes account? We differ in that Mr Rushdie claims to have written the slogan 'Naughty but Nice' and I do not. Also, I have not won a Booker Prize, did not suffer a fatwa, have no friends among the jet-set and society hostesses don't seem to have my number."

In the 2008 Booker competition, critics in the media seemed to be pitting Rushdie against Adiga, who was welcomed as the voice of the new generation of IWE. Much of the media attention at the time focused on the fact that Rushdie's *The Enchantress of Florence* made it to the Booker longlist but did not make the cut to the shortlist. According to Julie Bosman in *The Times*, this decision "both startl[ed] and delight[ed] British critics and subsequently prompt[ed] the Booker judges to explain why Mr. Rushdie was snubbed." Portillo, chair of the judges, apparently felt he needed to justify this decision: "In the opinion of these five people taken together, Salman Rushdie's was not one of the top six books for us" (Bosman). In lieu of referring to Rushdie as "an authoritative literary father worthy of affiliation" (Wachinger 83), as was in all probability the case with the 2006 Booker awarded to Kiran Desai, Adiga allegedly functions as foil to both the

Booker heavyweight himself and to Indian writers of "florid exotica" in general. In this sense, at work was not so much the playing of the Rushdie card, as analysed in the previous subchapter with reference to Kiran Desai, as an anti-Rushdie one. Instead of prizing sameness, in 2008 the strategy was seemingly to prize difference in relation to Rushdie. Viewed in the context of a multidimensional model of the literary field (English and Frow 45), Adiga's appraisal relies – albeit in reverse – on Rushdie's status as marketable commodity in the literary marketplace. As Erica Wagner comments in *The Times*, "it is perhaps fitting" that in the year when *Midnight's Children* was elected The Best of the Booker to celebrate the fortieth anniversary of the prize, the winner should be "a compelling portrait of modern India, *The White Tiger*, that takes his country – and the reader – into the present day, a follow-up to the moment of a country's conception that Rushdie portrayed." Likewise, praising Adiga's novel as charting a new imaginative territory, Sudipta Datta asked Adiga in a post-Booker interview whether he thought IWE "has finally shed the Rushdie hangover." Adiga answers that he does not believe "it had a hangover"; he adds that authors such as Kiran Desai, Amitav Ghosh, and Rohinton Mistry are not "remotely like Rushdie" and yet "each is a very great writer," this demonstrating the vibrancy and diversity of current South Asian writing.

According to Todd's analysis of literary texts as market commodities, the particular process of literary canon-formation facilitated by the Booker prize is "commercial as well as literary (what's 'in'? what's everybody reading this season?)" (101). It is necessary then to regard the above critical exchanges as artificial and strategic. Besides, the opposition between Rushdie's and Adiga's narrative thematics is ill-founded. Both writers are social commentators attuned to the inequalities in Indian society. Rushdie's vision of India in the short story "The Free Radio," for instance, is possibly as dark as Adiga's unremitting satire and gore-and-grime realism in *The White Tiger*. In Rushdie's collection of short stories *East, West*, the "East" section starts out in the subcontinent, and could not be further removed from the idea of a magical Eternal India. "The Free Radio" is the tragicomic story of another "half-baked" Indian: Ramani, a naïve rickshaw driver who voluntarily submits to a vasectomy for the sake of his new wife, a widow with five children, but especially because he believes he will win a transistor radio. The historical setting of the short story is the dark political climate of Indira Gandhi's emergency suspension of civil law in 1975 – "the beginning of a continuous midnight," as Rushdie's narrator Saleem puts it in *Midnight's Children* (419). In defiance of a court order calling for her resignation following a conviction for election malpractices (and which ultimately resulted in the collapse of her administration in 1977), Indira's "modernisation" included the imprisonment of political opponents, vote-buying, press censorship, and sterilisation by vasectomy targeted at the lower castes, either for payment or under coercion.[18] Referring to this intensive programme, Indira was reported as stating: "Some personal rights

---

[18] ReVelle and ReVelle note that "[a]lthough the government did not mount a national campaign of compulsory sterilization, individual states were encouraged to do so," and that

have to be kept in abeyance for the human rights of the nation: the right to live, the right to progress" (ReVelle and ReVelle 137).[19] "The Free Radio" particularly exposes the major "nasbandi" (sterilisation) campaign carried out under the direction of Indira and her son Sanjay. Efforts to control population growth in India have been under way since the early 1950s.[20] Medical personnel had sterilisation quotas to fill, and money or a "brand-new first-class battery-operated transistor radio" ("Free Radio" 25) were the incentives offered to those willing to submit to the procedure (ReVelle and ReVelle 137). It is in this context that Ramani, a representative of the uneducated and economically deprived Indian underclass, enters the "big white caravan" of the Indian National Health Service in exchange for a free radio ("Free Radio" 24).

This short story is but one of the many incursions on Rushdie's part into the criticism of Indira's inadequate policies. *Midnight's Children* also portrays the unpalatable atrocities of the Emergency resulting from the overall suspension of civil liberties in the name of social and political reforms. In effect, Indira is recast in Saleem's nightmares as the Wicked Witch of the East from *The Wizard of Oz* (207–208). In the essay on Fleming's film Rushdie wrote for the BFI, he compares Indira with Margaret Hamilton, the actress who played the witch in *The Wizard of Oz*: "the nightmare of Indira Gandhi is fused with the equally nightmarish figure of Margaret Hamilton: a coming-together of the Wicked Witches of the East and West" ("Short Tale" 33). The writer also comments on Indira's tendency towards absolutism in the essay "Dynasty": "Unlike her father, Mrs Gandhi was clearly suffering badly from the grandiloquent, *l'état c'est moi* delusions of a Louis XIV. Her use of the cult of the mother – of Hindu mother-goddess symbols and allusions – was calculated and shrewd" (50). In *Midnight's Children*, the protagonist Saleem has to be sterilized because of the potential threat he poses as one of the "midnight's children" to the "Only True Succession." As Kavita Daiya argues, the physical mutilation of Saleem's body acts as an allegory for the Indian nation in the sense that it incarnates the spatial and social partitions of the postcolonial national body (44–45).

The government programme of mandatory family planning equally figures in Rohinton Mistry's *A Fine Balance* (1995), a novel set against the backdrop of the Emergency. Similarly to Adiga's novel, *A Fine Balance* portrays the widespread

---

"[i]ncentive payments to those who submitted to vasectomies were a part of the law, as were payments to informers" (137).

[19] The full quote reads: "We must act decisively and bring down the birth rate ... We should not hesitate to take steps which might be described as drastic. Some personal rights have to be kept in abeyance for the human rights of the nation: the right to live, the right to progress" (ReVelle and ReVelle 137).

[20] As late as 2008, government officials in the Indian state of Madhya Pradesh were still using incentives to convince men to undergo sterilisation given their failure to meet the targets set by the family planning program. Instead of a free radio, vasectomy camps offered fast-track gun licenses, so that the men who had agreed to the invasive procedure would "not feel less manly" ("India Uses").

corruption, bigotry, and poverty afflicting India, although its setting is the 1960s and 1970s. Mistry's novel hints that Indira's "voluntary" sterilisation programme was in fact so only for the upper classes. Two of the main characters of Mistry's narrative, the tailors Om and Ishvar, coming from the untouchable castes, are forcibly sterilized as a result of imposed quotas (372). *A Fine Balance* also makes clear reference to the distribution of free transistor radios – for example, in a passage in this novel a character reports that men are subjecting themselves twice to the same operation because of the "benefits" entailed: the chance to own two radios (165). When Rushdie's character in "The Free Radio" belatedly finds out that this compensation scheme had already been abandoned, he nonetheless pretends to have received a radio (27–28). After realising there is no reward, he moves to Bombay in search of Bollywood stardom. Ramani is described by the narrator, a retired teacher, as "an innocent, a real donkey's child" (19), and this innocence is also political (Iftekharuddin 368). Through this self-delusional character of a rickshaw-wallah, Rushdie uncovers birth control as a nationally contentious issue in India and also exposes the naïvety of those who think that politicians provide "free radios to people who are so keen on popular music" (25). In this sense, Balram's life story and *The White Tiger*'s dissection of India's economic success might well be construed as a follow-up to Rushdie's story's depiction of the Emergency period.

Even though the reaction of Indian readers both in the subcontinent and in the diaspora to *The White Tiger* was multifarious, neither wholly hostile nor adverse, Adiga still faced the recurrent accusation of complicity with inauthentic representations of India. In this respect, Kanchan Gupta claims that

> [the writer] crafted his novel in a manner that it could not but impress the Man Booker judges who see India as a seething mass of unwashed hordes which worship pagan gods, are trapped in caste-based prejudices, indulge in abominable practices like untouchability, and are not worthy of being considered as an emerging power, never mind economic growth and knowledge excellence.

Rushdie celebrates the idea of "hybridized, mongrel truth" and contends that "we should avoid at all cost any pedigreed version of the truth" (qtd. in Cronenberg 176). Against those such as Gupta who posit that authentic representations depend upon finding a space exterior to western market forces, this subchapter maintains that a "hybridized, mongrel truth" is enabled in *The White Tiger* by playing the rules of the global literary marketplace, rather than by escaping from it. Ultimately, both the protagonist of Adiga's novel and the "truth" he tells about Rising India play out a "hybridized, mongrel truth." Furthermore, Balram and his "reality" are strategically inauthentic: through intentional self-contradiction and ironic character development, Adiga's failure to achieve an in itself untenable authenticity is deliberate. In Huggan's formulation, authenticity stands as the "currency at play in the market place of cultural difference" (*The Postcolonial Exotic* 158). By describing cultural authenticity thus, the critic underscores the crucial importance of having access to specific means and modes of cultural representation. *The White Tiger* takes Huggan's terms one step further by blatantly choosing to stage inauthenticity while simultaneously holding up for critical scrutiny the novel's own complicity with the marketing of an Exotic India, along terms similar to Rushdie's *Midnight's Children*. Departing from the view of those critics who find a re-orientalist construction of India in *The White Tiger*, this subchapter situates the debates over the perceived authenticity/inauthenticity of Adiga's portrait within the broader problematic of so-called "real" Indianness. As has been argued in countless studies, the quest for authenticity in IWE is inescapably doomed to failure because that would imply the existence of a tangible origin (undermined from the outset by the use of a non-autochthonous language introduced via British colonisation) against which to gauge it. Rushdie had already exposed in the early 1980s the "bogy of Authenticity" haunting the then fashionable critical label "Commonwealth literature" which he defines as

> that body of writing created, I think, in the English language, by persons who are not themselves white Britons, or Irish, or citizens of the United States of America. I don't know whether black Americans are citizens of this bizarre Commonwealth or not. Probably not. It is also uncertain whether citizens of Commonwealth countries writing in languages other than English – Hindi, for example – or who switch out of English, like Ngugi [wa Thiong'o], are permitted into the club or asked to keep out. ("Commonwealth" 63)

The writer was one of the leading voices to question the antithesis between English and "Commonwealth" literature. He jettisons the latter label, seeing it as part of a "ghettoization" tactic aimed at excluding a "bunch of upstarts" from the realm of "English literature, the great sacred thing itself," to be reserved for native English-speakers only (62). To substantiate his argument against this critical label, Rushdie describes an episode featuring a patronising "lady from the British Council":

> When I was invited to speak at the 1983 English Studies Seminar in Cambridge, the lady from the British Council offered me a few words of reassurance. "It's all right," I was told, "for the purposes of our seminar, English studies are taken to include Commonwealth literature." At all other times, one was forced to conclude, these two would be kept strictly apart, like squabbling children, or sexually incompatible pandas, or, perhaps, like unstable, fissile materials whose union might cause explosions. ("Commonwealth" 61)

Sharing an understanding of the untenability of a Commonwealth literature, Amitav Ghosh withdrew his novel *The Glass Palace*, named the Eurasia regional winner for the 2001 Commonwealth Writers Prize, from that prize's final stage. The Commonwealth Writers Prize is a leading award for fiction established in 1987,[21] but Ghosh protested against his work being categorized as Commonwealth

---

[21] The Commonwealth Writers Prize is administered by the Commonwealth Foundation, an intergovernmental organisation. Its mission statement is "[t]o encourage and reward the upsurge of new Commonwealth fiction and ensure that works of merit reach

literature, when only works written exclusively in the English language are, as Rushdie words it, "permitted into the club." According to Ghosh, the phrase "Commonwealth literature" describes an outmoded reality – it "anchors an area of contemporary writing not within the realities of the present day, nor within the possibilities of the future, but rather within a disputed aspect of the past"; accordingly, the rubric of "the Commonwealth" implies a "particular memorialization of Empire" and, as such, competing for the Commonwealth Writers Prize would mean "betraying the spirit" of Ghosh's anti-imperialist *The Glass Palace* ("Commonwealth").[22]

Although the concept of authenticity has been discredited by many in contemporary critical discourse, it continues to play a prominent role in the debates over IWE and remains a crucial element in enhancing the appeal of non-western cultural products in a global market. Because it continues to provide, in the context of certain critical agendas, a fertile ground for the discussion of IWE, the explanatory potential of the concept of authenticity should not be dismissed. As previously alluded to, the "anxiety of Indianness" – or rather "anxiety about the anxiety of Indianness," as Chandra characterizes it in a direct reference to the title of an influential essay by the critic Meenakshi Mukherjee – ultimately structures the reception of IWE novels and most of the fiercest responses to them. In this "anxiety about the anxiety of Indianness," diasporic authors are accused of domesticating difference and of developing work that is by and large driven by the need to represent India to a largely western readership.

For the remainder of this subchapter, the workings of the rhetoric of "real" Indianness, as Chandra describes it and as it is used repeatedly by reviewers, will be outlined and then a reframing of this issue in relation to *The White Tiger* will be advanced. Such change of perspective will allow for a reading of Adiga's novel unconstrained by the unavailing longing for authenticity under the guise of "real" Indianness. The issue of the Indianness of Indian English writing has elicited a considerable amount of critical attention in recent years, as well as motivated numerous quarrels between critics and writers. This discussion tends to retread the same issues periodically. In the essay "The Anxiety of Indianness" (1993),[23] Mukherjee addresses the (conceivably self-conscious) anxiety besetting Indian English fiction, which she suggests results in a tendency to rely on an overabundance of markers of "real" Indianness. Whereas the cause of this anxiety in earlier Indian English authors such as Raja Rao, Mulk Raj Anand, and R.K. Narayan "came out of their own desire to be rooted," in the case of the new generation of writers, in Mukherjee's words, it "may be attributed to the pressures of the global marketplace" (181).

---

a wider audience outside their country of origin" (in http://www.commonwealthfoundation.com/culturediversity/writersprize/).

[22] See Ghosh's letter to the administrators of the Commonwealth Writers Prize, reproduced at: http://www.thedailystar.net/2003/06/07/d30607210169.htm. Conversely, the writer at no stage withdrew his shortlisted *Sea of Poppies* from consideration for the 2008 Booker.

[23] Reprinted in Mukherjee's *The Perishable Empire* (2000): 166–186.

In reaction to Mukherjee's critique, Chandra, in a perceptive and polemical examination of what he dubs "The Cult of Authenticity," strikes back at what he calls the "anxiety about the anxiety of Indianness," that is, the accusation that "a real reality that was being distorted by 'Third World cosmopolitans.'" In what has become a classic reference text in this debate, the novelist argues that Indian "cultural commissars" (for the most part critics such as Mukherjee) traffic in authenticity; in doing so, they act as gatekeepers of Indianness, arrogating to themselves the ability to "identify a 'Real India'" and monitoring which aesthetic practices are "properly Indian" and which are not. He quite straightforwardly resists the idea of an authentic Indian literature springing from "a deep, essential connection to a 'real' Indianness." The publication of *The White Tiger* once again resurrected the debate over authentic literary representations of India by Indian English writers, and markedly so after the novel was awarded the Booker. In the midst of competing claims made of the authentic, critiques focusing on the inauthenticity of Adiga's novel particularly questioned the capability of a highly educated author (who studied English literature at Columbia and Oxford universities and who is a former correspondent in India for *Time* magazine) to grasp the experience of the Indian underclass. Specifically, some reviewers accused the novelist of devising an inauthentic lead character. For instance, Akash Kapur pointed out that Balram's "credulousness and naïveté often ring false"; the critic illustrated this by referring to particular scenes in the novel and proceeded to conclude that, "[i]n their surfeit of emblematic detail," these sequences "reduce the characters to symbols."[24]

Adiga had the stated intention of writing a novel about, in his own phrase, the "invisible men within India,"[25] that is, about individuals coming from a cultural and social background very different from his own. Nonetheless, he would inevitably have to face the customary critical accusation of fabricating narratives about the poor of India chiefly for an affluent and/or western readership. Whereas for the chauffeur-turned-entrepreneur the murder of his employer might function as an emancipatory tool in resisting class constraints, critics posit that Adiga's apparently subversive narrative does not empower the poor and uneducated. The novelist's endeavour to grant visibility to the rage of the Indian underclass is seen as inadequate to a number of commentators who fault the writer for aping the voice

---

[24] Interestingly, this discussion centred on the lack of verisimilitude of a writer coming from a privileged background mimicking the voice of the poor classes echoes E.M. Forster's arguments in the preface to Anand's *Untouchable*. According to Forster, *Untouchable*, a novel depicting the daily routine of an untouchable, Bakha, a sweeper and toilet-cleaner, "could only have been written by an Indian who observed from the outside. No European, however sympathetic, could have created the character of Bakha, because he would not have known enough about his troubles. And no Untouchable could have written the book, because he would have been involved in indignation and self-pity. Mr. Anand stands in the ideal position" ("Preface" vi–vii). It is worth noting that Anand was a close friend of Forster, who was instrumental in helping him secure a contract to publish *Untouchable* after nineteen publishers rejected the manuscript (Ranasinha 18).

[25] See Adiga, interviewed at: http://www.youtube.com/watch?v=s4tAPvWVorY.

of an imaginary subaltern. For example, Somak Ghoshal, in a rather literal critique of the "readability" of *The White Tiger*, notes that "Adiga tries to do a clever first-person voice, spoken by Balram, in a choppy, Indianized English; but his effort, alas, is a huge flop." Somewhat overlooking Adiga's ironic character development, Subrahmanyam foregrounds what he reads as the disconcerting "dissonance" and the "falsity" of the narrator/subaltern's voice: "What does [Balram] sound like? ... whose vocabulary and whose expressions are these? On page after page, one is brought up short by the jangling dissonance of the language and the falsity of the expressions. This is a posh English-educated voice trying to talk dirty, without being able to pull it off" ("Diary"). "It may have won the Booker, but it rings false and flat," writes Salil Tripathi in a review of the novel.

Even though Adiga might be prey to the "anxiety of Indianness" and, furthermore, the lead character of *The White Tiger* does promise to "tell the truth about Bangalore," this subchapter argues that the novel does not attempt to comply with the strictures of authenticity. Rather, as K.R. Usha discloses, Adiga's narrative bypasses the expectation that it was construed as a real-life portrait of the Indian underclass. "I'm no philosopher or poet, how would I know the truth?" (8), Balram asks rhetorically at the beginning. According to Usha, the protagonist "is very obviously ventriloquising for the author who is refracting Balram's sensibility through his own lens"; despite finding this representational strategy tenable, the critic considers that it results in extreme essentialisation to the point that "every nuance is beaten out." However, Adiga seems to be quite explicitly mocking the longing for the ideal of authenticity through the construction of an overtly essentalised lead character. Besides, like Rushdie in *Midnight's Children*, Adiga disavows any attempt to legitimize his depiction of India as "real" by setting *The White Tiger* against a deliberately inauthentic historical background. Indeed, the writer warps the purpose of Wen Jiabao's actual Delhi visit in April 2005, whose stated aim was not to discover the "truth" about Indian entrepreneurship but rather to contribute to resolve the longstanding border dispute between India and China. Adiga thus destabilizes historical facts in his retelling of a real event of recent Indian history. Likewise, Rushdie's Saleem is an unreliable first-person narrator who, by his own admission, is untrustworthy. If the protagonist of *Midnight's Children* is an unreliable narrator in the sense that he subverts the official version of modern Indian history, Adiga's Balram is an unreliable, because "unreal," Indian subaltern subject. While the critical rhetoric of Real India seems to imply a discarding of impurity and hybridity, *The White Tiger* strategically stages its inauthentic Dark India.

Attesting to the pervasiveness of the "anxiety of Indianness," Adiga himself seems to have – maybe unwittingly – succumbed to such angst. In an interview published on the Man Booker Prize website shortly after *The White Tiger* was included on the 2008 longlist, the writer's claiming, or rather reclaiming, of a "real" Indianness echoes Chandra's parodic description quoted earlier: "It's a great thrill to be longlisted for the Booker. Especially alongside Amitav Ghosh and Salman Rushdie. *But* I live in Mumbai, where not many people know of the

Man Booker Prize; *I'm still standing* in long queues and *standing* in over-packed local trains in the morning and *worrying* about falling ill from unsafe drinking water. Life goes on as before" (qtd. in "Aravind Adiga"; emphasis added). Echoing Chandra's ironic reading of the criticisms directed at Indo-Anglian literature, Adiga's assertions of authenticity are based on his groundedness in a "Real India" where, among other features, speakers of English only amount to a meagre percentage of its inhabitants. "[N]ot many people know of the Man Booker Prize" in a country populated by individuals such as Balram, who, though represented through the medium of English, does not speak it, as he clarifies from the outset (3). Not unrelatedly, Rajeswari Rajan questions the authenticity of Indian writing penned in a language that will only be accessible "to an elite audience that constitutes less than two per cent of the population," although Rajan's figure may be an underestimate. The "realities" of Adiga's India, that is, the specific material circumstances under which *The White Tiger* was produced, are made obvious by the adversative conjunction "But" that clearly distances his artistic predicament from Ghosh's and Rushdie's. Those diasporic writers, besides being part of the Indian English-speaking élites, share an additional commonality with Adiga in that they also authored novels that were longlisted for the Booker in 2008. Nevertheless, unlike him who currently *lives* in Mumbai (after spending many years abroad), Ghosh and Rushdie are both mainly domiciled in New York[26] and are hence removed, at least physically, from the actuality of the country.

Adiga here seems to partake of the recurrent criticism according to which commercial success for Indian English writers depends on their voluntary expatriation to countries in the West or, as Chandra ironically puts it, to "faraway air-conditioned regions of *vilayat*."[27] In opposition to the (at the time of speaking) western-located NRIs Ghosh and Rushdie, Adiga suggests in this interview his intimate knowledge of India provided by an unfiltered, first-hand access to its "reality." By foregrounding the material and cultural differences between him and westernized diasporic writers, Adiga is privileging a notion of authenticity based on a stark divide between the national and the diasporic subjects. However, Adiga's claims of a sort of unprivileged positionality as a writer based in India are deeply problematic: the distinction between authors either inside India or outside is not productive because of the complexity of being "inside" or "outside"; besides, and despite claims of rootedness, Adiga himself is positioned both "inside" and "outside" India in fundamental ways. "For some," Rushdie argues, "English language Indian writing will never be more than a post-colonial anomaly, the bastard child of Empire, sired on India by the departing British; its continuing use of the old colonial tongue is seen as a fatal flaw that renders it forever inauthentic" ("Introduction" xii). In an ironic take on this, Chandra remarks, "if you write in English, and are improperly contaminated by the West, if you've travelled across the Black Waters and lost your caste, then the 'Real India' is by definition beyond

---

[26] Ghosh has returned to India to work on the Ibis trilogy.
[27] See Rushdie, "Introduction" xiii.

your grasp." Adiga's use of the present continuous verb tense in "I'm still standing" and "[I'm still] worrying" again stresses his rootedness in present-day Mumbai, while his reference to the queues, the over-crowded trains, and the contaminated drinking water seems to sustain Chandra's argument that Real India, seen as a site of everyday concrete struggle, is "approachable only through great and prolonged suffering."

For Rushdie, authenticity is "the respectable child of old-fashioned exoticism" in the sense that "[i]t demands that sources, forms, style, language and symbol all derive from a supposedly homogeneous and unbroken tradition. Or else" ("Commonwealth" 67). The author cuts his last phrase short in all probability to draw attention to the fact that cultural expressions falling outside the "fantasy of purity" are regarded by the self-appointed gatekeepers of authenticity as non-existent and are therefore left unacknowledged. Rushdie's intertextual narratives suggest that cultural purity is nothing but a fictional construct. The accusations faced by Adiga of inauthenticity in the representation of a Dark India and of complicity with a pernicious re-orientalism, originating for the most part from Indian critics, are far from original. The inauthenticity backlash has been dealt with at some length in this section to show how difficult it has been to overcome what is probably one of the most contentious critical issues in IWE. The hand-wringing over authenticity will no doubt continue to divide commentators, and will almost certainly continue to frame further discussions of *The White Tiger*. Indeed, it seems that the spectre of authenticity in IWE refuses to be exorcized. Following the pervasive rhetoric that Chandra deconstructs in "The Cult of Authenticity," authors such as Adiga (and to some extent Rushdie) seem to be inescapably constrained by the need to "explain" India to western readers and hence fall back on easily decoded rhetorical tropes of "real" Indianness. In the end, Adiga's "anxiety of Indianness," as expressed in the Man Booker Prize website interview, illustrates the multiple ways in which India is enmeshed in an unending process of cultural commodification. Indeed, the appeal of a Dark India in the literary marketplace – or, more accurately, the favouring by the Booker judges' of representational strategies that purportedly offer a revamped orientalised India to the twenty-first-century (western) reader – relies heavily on a previous contestation of discourses, facilitated by authors such as Rushdie, surrounding India and its allure as exotic other.

Salman Rushdie Superstar[28]

> I seem to have fallen into a Rip van Winkle sleep at some point. Now, in the new century, I wake up and blink at the bright lights that glare down at a stage on which stands that frightened creature – the writer – pulled out of the burrow and

---

[28] This section is a revised and shortened version of the chapter "Salman Rushdie Superstar: The Making of Postcolonial Literary Stardom," printed in Rainer Emig and Oliver Lindner (eds), *Commodifying (Post-)Colonialism: Othering, Reification, Commodification*

revealed in the full glare of publicity, trying desperately to retain a few rags of decency in this harsh spotlight.

—Anita Desai, "Rip Van Winkle"

As an attempt to study Rushdie's work in its relation to cultural brokerism must include a reflection on the workings of the cultural industries today, this section is motivated by the following questions: What is the relationship between the writer's life, works, and critical reception and these industries? In what ways has his fiction, and the author himself, provided a resource for them? In addition, this section attempts to offers tentative answers to an additional question: How is the writer made to *perform* – in other words, present, re-present, as well as exaggerate or underplay – the role of the postcolonial writer? In Rushdie's case, this section argues that the construct of a postcolonial celebrity space articulates on several nodes. Attention is drawn to the strategic negotiation of his celebrity status, particularly to the ways he strives, not only through constant media appearances (motivated, for instance, by the fatwa, the knighthood for his services to literature, or the celebrity wedding to Padma Lakshmi, soon followed by divorce), but also in his practice as writer in exposing, intervening, and manipulating the machinery of celebrity to meet his own ends (for example, to open up a space in the global literary market for diasporic South Asian artists).

*****

The distinction between the renowned writer and the media star cannot stand in Rushdie's case. As in numerous occasions, in May 2008 the spotlight was directed yet again on the writer. The reason behind the hubbub in the media was that he made a cameo appearance – "a crazy fluke" in his own words (qtd. in Banay) – in the video of actress Scarlett Johansson's début single "Falling Down."[29] Rushdie is seen nuzzling the actress-turned-singer's neck, making her giggle, and then grinning at the camera. A news story in *The Sunday Times* reporting the event begins by warning its "[r]eaders of a more sensitive nature" to "look away," and proceeds thus:

> Scarlett Johansson's latest conquest is not a Hollywood hunk with a six-pack and a surf habit, but none other than our very own paunchy, hood-eyed, middle-aged genius Salman Rushdie. ... Well, well. Hasn't he done well? The busty star is just the latest in a long line of stunning gals to be seen swimming upstream with Salman. ... So, *what's the pull?* It can't be his looks — the man has the face of an outraged woodpecker. ("Middle Youth"; emphasis added)

---

and the New Literatures and Cultures in English. Amsterdam and New York: Rodopi, 2010, 219–238, published with the permission of Rodopi.

[29] This single is included on her album *Anywhere I Lay My Head*, Atco/Rhino Records, 2008.

In early 2009 *The Daily Mail* ran an article on Rushdie's allegedly "radical image makeover" and "come-and-get-me-girls" appeal after his divorce from the model, actress, chef, and reality-show hostess Padma Lakshmi in 2007:

> Since the break-up Rushdie has rarely been seen without a glamorous woman on his arm and has been overseeing his own radical image makeover. He has treated himself to an oversized "bling" watch that might be more at home on the wrist of David Beckham or the rapper Jay-Z. The wordsmith has taken to wearing sunglasses indoors and even toyed with getting fit. He also issued a "come-and-get-me-girls" invitation in the *New York Times*, when he announced: "I'm totally eligible, single and available." ...
>
> He is significantly lacking in the hair department and suffers from a rare inherited condition called ptosis, which gives him the droopy-eyed look of a man fighting a losing battle with sleep. In short, when it comes to looks, Rushdie is no catch. (Bates)

A more recent article on glamorous women who favour "nerds," published in *The Times of India* by Nona Walia, discusses Rushdie's "secret formula" thus:

> The poster boy of intellectualism, Rushdie has successfully flaunted his pretty poster girls. Be it the sensual Padma Lakshmi or Pia Glenn, he always gets the best women. Recently, the *Globe and Mail* reported how the podgy intellectual's sex appeal was his power and status, which made him a babe magnet. The *Daily Mail* debated on Rushdie's secret formula, as he flaunted his new squeeze! Says London-based film producer, Jagmohan Mundra, "Salman always gets the best girls. Intellect is still rated high in the dating world. Women find his attention hard to resist. There's an 'awe factor' being seen with Rushdie, and women love his attention and gaze, with the cameras clicking away." ("Women")

In 2006 a headline in the online edition of *The New York Post* had already depicted in its gossip section Rushdie and his son Zafar as "babe magnets." In similar vein to the above pieces from *The Sunday Times* and *The Daily Mail* – the latter a newspaper that does not always consistently display an interest in literature matters – the anonymous reporter adopts an admonitory tone when describing the Casanova-like conduct of both father and son:

> Lock up your daughters when Salman Rushdie and his son hit the party circuit. The acclaimed author and his offspring are talking each other up as powerful chick magnets no woman can resist — with Zafar Rushdie, 27, even confessing he's used his 59-year-old father's prowess to score. "Most people who go to a party with their parents try to run away from them. Not me. If I want to meet girls, I just stand near him. ("Rushdies")

"Known across the world for his flamboyance and ... err ... luck with the ladies, as much for his writing skills," as Purnima Sharma puts it in *The Times of India*, Rushdie's complex positioning as literary star is well illustrated by his cameo appearance in Johansson's music video and by the "chick magnet" label that has come to attach itself to the writer, most visibly after his fourth divorce. Suffice to recall here the title of an article published in *The Independent* on 25 October 2009 by Katy Guest: "Beauty and the Brain: So, What Attracted You to a Short, Balding Egomaniac?" Reiterating the question posed by the reporter in *The Sunday Times* article, what indeed is "the pull"? What social meanings are behind such pulling power? What makes Rushdie the object of such frequent media attention and headline-grabbing? At the same time, why would this acclaimed author be so willing to allow his image to be used to advertise the launching of Johansson's at the time new artistic pursuit, when he gladly abandoned a career in the advertising industry in the 1980s? A possible answer to this question is provided by A.N. Wilson: "The lessons Rushdie learnt in the world of advertising – about keeping a product everlastingly in the public eye, about promoting merchandise however unsaleable, in short, the art of manipulation and persuasion – were useful ones which have never left him." Following this reasoning, promotional actions such as these help us further understand the creation of postcolonial celebrity as a commodity.

There has been a surge of celebrity studies since the 1960s which includes the pioneering works *The Image* by Daniel Boorstin (1962) and *The Society of the Spectacle* by Guy Debord (1967), as well as *Stars* by Richard Dyer (1979), *The Frenzy of Renown* by Leo Braudy (1986), and *Celebrity and Power* by P. David Marshall (1997). Although these works remain central to star studies today, they have somehow failed to address the specific issue of literary fame in a comprehensive way. Filling that gap in the reserarch, Joe Moran argues in the study *Star Authors* (2000), an examination of literary celebrity in the US, that celebrity writers tend to be figures who "straddle the divide" between literary elitism and popular readership. As Moran notes, literary celebrity "raises significant questions about the relationship between literature and the marketplace, and between 'high', 'low' and 'middlebrow' culture" (4).

On account of the development of star studies, current criticism of Rushdie's work has been increasingly attentive to his location as literary star in the field of postcolonial cultural production. At least since the late 1980s, Rushdie has been the object of rumour and speculation in the British press. At that time, as Sanjay Subrahmanyam recounts in his examination of the two decades of the fatwa, "[w]eekend newspaper supplements retailed gossipy accounts of how *The Satanic Verses* had failed to win the Booker prize, with malicious claims regarding Rushdie's tantrums when this happened" ("Angel"). Mondal frames Rushdie's current work as springing from "within the celebrity glasshouse"; to Mondal, this is dilemmatic in the sense that the writer's texts are "as much a reinforcement of his own celebrity as an indictment of the culture that sustains it" (174). Even though the non-literary avatar connected to the fatwa nearly engulfed Rushdie's career as a writer, the death sentence is one of the central factors of his fame in academia because, as Subrahmanyam caustically remarks, "[n]o postcolonial literary critic can seemingly make a career without a comment on the matter" ("Angel"). It might be too simple to state that the writer was either an innocent victim or a manipulator of his circumstances at the time of the fatwa. Departing from Huggan's arguments, and considering that Rushdie is seen at times by commentators as actively pursuing self-promotion and recognition in international literary circles, an examination of his status as the most visible face of the postcolonial glitterati can only be achieved through a critical understanding of the interplay between three inextricable domains of the brand name "Rushdie."

These domains are: first, and perhaps foremost, the celebrity status acquired in the aftermath of the fatwa; second, the academic canonisation resulting from Rushdie's critical acclaim as a postcolonial writer and the inclusion of his works in university syllabi;[30] and third, the fame built up through strategies of self-publicity. These promotional strategies demonstrate that the author's role in the celebritisation of authorship has increased in the last decades. Promotional events included participating in Johansson's video and in U2's video "The Ground Beneath Her Feet" (in what may be called a joint collaboration from 2000, the lyrics being taken from Rushdie's novel of the same name), as well as granting several promotional interviews to high-profile talk-show hosts, appearing in public as intellectual and political advocate, presenting lectures at universities and taking part in literary festivals as writer and critic, accepting an invitation to be Distinguished Writer-in-Residence at Emory University's Department of English (even if "Sir Salman CANNOT be contacted through the English Department," as spelled out in the web page[31]), actively involving himself in organisations such as International PEN (as honorary Vice-President, Member Trustee-at-Large, and President of PEN American Center) and the International Parliament of Writers (as its founder and first President), and also being a regular presence in society columns. The author's celebrity status owes much to the skilful participation in the promotional circuit and to the careful negotiation, management, and self-creation of these multiple associations, to some extent buttressed by a "minority" appeal, which are all included in the promotional circuit of publishing. Furthermore, Brouillette notes how authors "act as consumers of their own images as they react to their own personae in their literary works, often through attempts at theorizing the process itself" (3). Novels such as *The Ground Beneath Her Feet* and *Fury* are self-reflexive of the literary celebrity constructed by and imposed on Rushdie. For example, *Fury*'s character Little Brain is a "monster of tawdry celebrity" and "a creature of the entertainment microverse," both "a video game" and "a cover girl" (98).

The writer became internationally renowned in the 1980s for having "redr[awn] the literary map of India," as the *New York Times* put it, with the critical acclaim granted to his *Midnight's Children* (Kadzis, "Salman Speaks" 216–217). This novel was the recipient of the James Tait Black Prize and of the high-profile Booker Prize for Fiction; subsequently, it was first voted The Booker

---

[30] This aspect will be addressed in detail in the next chapter, "Exploding the Canon."
[31] See http://www.english.emory.edu/people/faculty/Rushdie.htm.

of Bookers in 1993, being regarded the best novel to have won the prize in the 25 years since its inception, and later awarded the one-off The Best of the Booker to celebrate the fortieth anniversary of the award in 2008. Besides his proven track record as a bestselling author, Rushdie's works have won him major international prizes, such as the Whitebread Prize for Best Novel, the European Aristeion Prize for Literature, and the French "Prix du Meilleur Livre Etranger." The writer's celebritisation results in part from the burgeoning "literary-value industry" made up of individuals and institutions committed to "producing the reputations and status positions of contemporary works and authors, situating them on various scales of worth" (English and Frow 45). Still, Rushdie is probably best known globally for the 1988 novel *The Satanic Verses* and on account of the fatwa decreed by Ayatollah Khomeini, Iran's then spiritual leader and head of state. The decree pronouncing the death sentence against Rushdie was received by the author on 14 February 1989, a date he looked back on a decade later as a rather "unfunny valentine" ("My Unfunny" 28). More startlingly, the fatwa was also construed as "an extreme form of literary criticism," as V.S. Naipaul notoriously declared, though, as he later clarified, such a comparison between literary criticism and the silencing by death of creative expression was intended to be read "as a joke" (Gussow). The worldwide recognisability of Rushdie as the epitome of the conflict between freedom of speech and the defence of religious beliefs prompted Kadzis, a decade later, to write in the foreword to an interview he conducted with the author that, as a result of the "distinction" conferred upon Rushdie by the Iranian government, and "although he may have wished otherwise," he had been turned into "perhaps the most famous writer in the world" ("Salman Speaks" 216). Such a view held true as late as 2007, with Teverson starting his monograph on Rushdie with the statement that the writer's fame "is not hard to establish" (3) and devoting the opening paragraphs of his introduction to an itemisation of the various areas comprising the writer's celebrity status.

Jay McInerney's 9/11 novel *The Good Life* (2006) evinces the connection Teverson draws between the Rushdie affair and the "exclusive" news reports dealing with the writer's "complicated love life" (4) by fictionalising and using as creative material the hullabaloo, duly played out in the media, of Rushdie's involvement with Lakshmi, and subsequent divorce from Elizabeth West, his third wife. *The Good Life* opens with a dinner party where Rushdie was expected to appear and a last-minute cancellation. One of the references to the writer in McInerney's novel stresses precisely Rushdie's and, somewhat by extension, Lakshmi's standing as troublesome celebrities: "It wasn't just Salman and his heady aura of celebrity; his new girlfriend was absurdly beautiful, to the point of being a socially disruptive force" (10). Supposedly, Rushdie is scheduled to embark the next day on his book tour for the novel *Fury*, but the dinner party host Corrine Calloway, instead of being upset, actually feels relieved by the absence of the "illustrious guest" (9–10): "they'd been friends with Salman's wife, the mother of his youngest child," and even though she "didn't believe everything she read in the tabloids and she refused to take sides in marital disputes ... this one hit a little closer to home."³² Furthermore, Corrine "was still worried that a bomb might go off in his vicinity, although supposedly the fatwa had been lifted;" after all, "[t]he people who wanted him dead weren't the forgive-and-forget type" (10).

As a result of the non-literary polemic which catapulted Rushdie to fame and turned him into a target of religious hounding due to alleged insults to Islam, the writer spent nearly a decade in hiding under British governmental protection. Even though it is still uncertain whether the fatwa has been withdrawn or is in fact continuously renewed, some commentators say that "now he's only hunted by cameras" (P. Cohen), as the title of an article printed in the *New York Times* in 2008 put it. The label "Rushdie" has been undergoing a process of self-fashioning at least since the publishing of *The Satanic Verses*, to the extent that the text itself suggests the author was cognisant that his words would spark controversy. "It's true that some passages in *The Satanic Verses* have now acquired a prophetic quality that alarms *even me*," the writer declares in his essay "In Good Faith" (407; emphasis added). He might well be referring to sentences such as "[y]our blasphemy, Salman, can't be forgiven. Did you think I would not work it out? To set your words against the Words of God" (*Satanic* 374), and, most likely, the almost divinatory passage printed in the closing section of the novel – more accurately, on its penultimate page: "Salahuddin was thinking … about how he was going to die for his verses, but could not find it in himself to call the death-sentence unjust" (545–546).

As John Updike trenchantly argues, the period corresponding to Rushdie's self-described "dark decade" ("Dream" 196) increased the writer's mastery of celebrity-related topics. Updike remarks that the writer's "fascination with fame and theatricality, movies and rock music predated the fatwa" and still continues to imprint on his fictional work "a distracting glitter, like shaken tinsel" ("Paradises Lost"). This view of the writer's fascination by celebrity is reiterated (albeit more forthrightly) by A.N. Wilson in *The Daily Mail*: referring to Rushdie's post-fatwa work as devoid of "literary merit," Wilson argues that the writer "had become one of those people who are famous for being famous, and the books were sold on the back of this fact. … The more unreadable he becomes, the more the publishers promote him as a celebrity." Despite his literary achievements, the post-fatwa Rushdie might seem to have vanished into the gossip page. Here, I am rewriting Martin Amis's notable phrase according to which Rushdie "had vanished into the front page" as a result of *The Satanic Verses* affair (Brennan 69).³³ Alluding to Amis's expression during an interview to Nagarajan in 1999, the writer confirmed

---

³² For instance, Geetha Ganapathy-Doré reads *Fury* as "the almost public statement" of Rushdie's "marital troubles" ("Orphic Journey" 17).

³³ Amis's words were originally published in "Rendezvous with Rushdie," *Vanity Fair* Dec. 1990: 161. Brennan writes alternatively that "Rushdie, as a whole, has been foreshortened by the [Rushdie] affair" (69). Likewise, the novel *The Satanic Verses* disappeared into *The Satanic Verses* affair.

that that was "more or less exactly how it felt" and that what he was trying to accomplish at that moment was "to reappear in the cultural section."[34]

Regardless of Rushdie's professed intent in the late 1990s, two of the newspaper extracts quoted at the beginning of this section are from "Page Six," a gossip column included in *The New York Post*,[35] and from the "life and style" section of *The Sunday Times*. While these are not representative of the entire media output pertaining to the author over the post-fatwa decades, they nevertheless illustrate a fundamental contention of Adorno who argues, in relation to music and the culture industry in the essay "On the Fetish Character of Music and the Regression of Listening," that "[t]he reactions of the listeners appear to have no relation to the playing of the music" (a comparison with literature and readership is being drawn here). Adorno continues thus: "They have reference, rather, to the cumulative effects which, for its part, cannot be thought of unalienated by the past spontaneities of listeners, but instead dates back to the command of publishers, sound film magazines and rulers of radio" (35–36). The critic claims that "[t]he star principle has become totalitarian" (35) and, by the same token, the media responses to Rushdie have tended to record his fondness for partying and attraction for stunning women, bearing at times little relation to his literary achievements. It has been in this media environment that Rushdie's star image has been made to circulate; in this sense, the following comment voiced by the first-person narrator in the novel *The Ground Beneath Her Feet* might be seen as echoing the author's own musing on the workings of celebrity:

> We always did prefer our iconic figures injured, stuck full of arrows or crucified upside down; we need them flayed and naked, we want to watch their beauty crumble slowly and to observe their narcissistic grief. Not in spite of their faults but *for* their faults we adore them, worshipping their weaknesses, their pettinesses, their bad marriages, their substance abuse, their spite. (20)

This passage is significant both for disclosing the centrality of the subject of fame permeating Rushdie's work, as well as for signalling the writer's own anxieties resulting from an undesired, overwhelming celebrity. Huggan contends that Rushdie's prominence in the 1980s as a star of the postcolonial literary field was at least partly the result of commercial strategies devised by publishers and literary prize sponsors such as the company Booker-McConnell, the sponsor of the Booker from 1968 to 2002, to "market the margins" and "prize otherness." By many accounts – and Huggan's is no exception here – Rushdie stands as one of the most canonical and critically lauded Indian postcolonial writers, but notwithstanding this critical praise, he is often depicted, and accordingly attacked, as a writer who is entangled in the superficial world of celebrities and glamour. For instance, the critic Harish Trivedi regards the writer's fame as incommensurate with his literary

---

[34] He had already declared on the *Charlie Rose Show* on January 18, 1996: "I have been trying to emerge from that front page ever since, to become visible again" (Rose 210).

[35] Since 2006 *Page Six* has been an associated magazine of the newspaper.

achievements, declaring to *The Times of India* that "Rushdie's fan following is more for his worldly success than his writing" (Walia, "Our Sheikhspeare?").[36] Nonetheless, it is precisely his "wordily success" that needs to be thought through and even embraced as essential to an understanding of the author today.

Instead of celebrity simply being imposed on writers, it is now commonly agreed that they, as creative individuals, retain a degree of agency in the negotiation of their own celebrity (Moran 10). Given this circular nature of celebritisation, even if Rushdie's private life is ransacked, the strategic administration of the author's multi-mediated image on the public stage is in all probability more impressive than his portrayal of celebrity culture in the novel *The Ground Beneath Her Feet*. An incomplete list of Rushdie's incursions into film and TV is impressive. In fact, the writer has been the theme of a *Seinfeld* episode[37] and appeared as "himself" in the film *Bridget Jones's Diary* (dir. Sharon Maguire, 2001) and in the near-slanderous political quiz show *Have I Got News for You*, while archive footage of a book signing of *The Satanic Verses* was used in Kenneth Branagh's film *Peter's Friends* (1992). Rushdie starred as the obstetrician-gynaecologist Dr Masani in Helen Hunt's film *Then She Found Me* (2007), side by side with seasoned actors Bette Midler, Colin Firth, and Matthew Broderick.[38] In addition, the openly hostile Pakistani film *International Guerrillas* depicts him as a villain involved in an international criminal gang and as such deserving of a righteous killing. A film version of *Midnight's Children* was released in 2012, and rumour had it that he was planning on taking up a role in the adaptation (which turned out not to be the case). "If Gore Vidal can do it, I thought, so can I," Rushdie confides during an interview (qtd. in P. Cohen), alluding to Vidal's part as the villain Director Josef in *Gattaca* (dir. Andrew Niccol, 1997). In fact, the writer spent much of his time at Cambridge involved in his second passion after writing (H. Ahmad 1319) and, due to what remains an "unscratched itch about acting," he considers that a "late career" like Vidal's is more suitable to his more mature talents (qtd. in Kadzis, "Rushdie Rocks").

While in hiding, Rushdie also made frequent, highly publicized appearances in a variety of media as a spokesperson for free speech. During his "plague years," he took dramatically to the stage at a U2 concert at Wembley Stadium in 1993 and carried out a dialogue routine the band and he had rehearsed backstage beforehand. Later, Rushdie sent U2 a copy of *The Ground Beneath Her Feet*, "really expecting nothing" (qtd. in Nagarajan), and the band set the writer's words to music as their song also entitled "The Ground Beneath Her Feet" – specifically using the lyrics of the sad love hymn the character Ormus dedicates to Vina, his deceased lover – whilst afterwards Rushdie made a cameo appearance in the video that was

---

[36] To this criticism, Rushdie might retort that "in some Indian literary quarters, it has become fashionable to denigrate [his] work" ("Dream" 196).

[37] Episode "The Implant," number 59, season 4 (1992–1993), broadcast on 25 February 1993.

[38] Episode 7.8 (1994).

released to promote the song. He appears very early in this video, contemplatively staring out the window of a room full of candles and writing into a book. The video is a promo clip for Wim Wenders's film *The Million Dollar Hotel* (2000), which includes U2's song "The Ground Beneath Her Feet" on its soundtrack. Feeding the writer's celebrity image, there are online newspaper articles on him, or making reference to his name (mostly in relation to the fatwa), appearing on a daily basis (at least at this time of writing). After the public wedding to Lakshmi in 2004, a celebrity event in itself, and the divorce in 2007 – with rumours about the impending break-up of the marriage leaking into the press well before it was made official – the press announced, almost weekly, a new girlfriend for Rushdie. In an interview, the writer belittles the media frenzy following his fourth divorce as a mere "occupational hazard"; nevertheless, as he himself recognizes, it lends a gloss to his public image: "Nobody thinks less of Arthur Miller because he was married to Marilyn ... . They probably think more of him" (qtd. in Banay).

The "practices, meanings and manipulations acted out in public culture" that Ommundsen refers to as being (self-)enforced upon star authors seem to be in Rushdie's case for the most part self-constructed through repeated performance in the media. This grants the writer, as literary superstar, an aura through mass reproduction, echoing Benjamin's considerations on film celebrity in "The Work of Art in the Age of Its Technological Reproducibility" (1939). Instead of a shattering of the aura, a process that Benjamin associates with the production of commodities through mass reproduction as opposed to the reception of rare artworks, present here is a sense almost of awe and veneration in Rushdie's proximity. That aura inheres not in the writer himself, but rather in external attributes of elusiveness and proximity associated to the buzzword "Rushdie." These attributes have been built by actions presumably tailored for a mass audience, such as the restriction on his appearances on account of the fatwa, his overtly publicized opinions as a public intellectual, and his lectures as an invited speaker at universities, among others. Moreover, in a way that might also be construed as a strategy of product placement of "Rushdie" as commodity, the writer has become a habitué of the international dinner-party circuit and as such a coveted item by the paparazzi. This celebrity phenomenon relates to Benjamin's assessment of film stardom in the late 1930s: "Film responds to the shrivelling of the aura by artificially building up the 'personality' outside the studio. The cult of the movie star, fostered by the money of the film industry, preserves that magic of the personality which has long been no more than the putrid magic of its own commodity character" ("Work of Art" 261). Adorno rejects Benjamin's reasoning that the advent of mechanical reproduction and the democratisation of art had brought about a complete eradication of the aura. According to Adorno, Benjamin neglects to take into consideration the autocratic "star principle" at the very core of the culture industry ("Fetish Character" 35), that is, the consumer attraction to glamour and celebrity. Rushdie as literary star, and the individual processes of cultic worship on the part of cultural consumers of the commodity "Rushdie" expand and complicate both the concept of "aura," one of Benjamin's most influential critical contributions, and Adorno's theory of the culture industry. In fact, Rushdie's literary celebrity status is more than sheer commodification of culture, but relies instead on a complex transaction between high and popular cultures.

This subchapter is posited on the assumption that the construct of Rushdie as a postcolonial celebrity author articulates on several nodes. The author is by all standards as much a literary as a popular culture phenomenon, as much a postcolonial icon as a media star. Undoubtedly, the separation between these areas is artificial given that Rushdie's stardom, as is the case with the celebritisation of authorship in general, stands astride two discourses which might be regarded as distinct – the popular and the literary. Literary celebrity undermines and complexifies a reading of fame as more commonly a by-product of the cultural industries. Not only Rushdie's strictly literary career, but also his private life as represented in the media illustrate the notion of "journalistic capital," a concept comprising "visibility, celebrity, scandal," which English proposes as the transformative and mediating power between economic and cultural capital ("Winning" 123). Rushdie as star conflates the field of literary production with tabloid culture. His stardom reflects the economy of literary celebrity culture because, more than suggestive of a pervasive celebrity-driven and market-oriented cultural production and "[r]ather than being a straightforward effect of the commodification of culture" (Moran 4), it concurrently mobilizes a set of convergences and clashes between high cultural capital and the marketplace which, as Moran argues, are at the heart of the construction of literature as a cultural category.

Rushdie stands as a key nodal point for a discussion about the workings of postcolonial celebrity culture in the way that he provides a mix of aura, literary capital, academic canonisation of the postcolonial, and media buzz. In other words, the writer's celebrity status is the result of a convergence (at times perceived as a clash) of diverse discourses of fame: popular, literary, and postcolonial. He carries the aura, as much as – or even more than – his work. Indeed, it seems at times that the cultural commodity being fashioned, circulated, and consumed is not so much the writer's texts, but the brand "Rushdie." Expanding on a "broader historical shift over the last century" from authorial signature to brand name, English and Frow argue that the specificity of contemporary literary celebrity is that it conflates "a notion of authenticity and of personal presence that characterized the Romantic regimes of authoriality, of signature, and of copyright; and a model of seriality that is characteristic of the contemporary culture industries" (51). Rushdie is conscious of this since celebrity "seems to enforce self-reflexiveness: for those authors who experience it, it often becomes a constant preoccupation – they talk and write about it constantly, in both fictional and non-fictional forms, usually describing fame as a negative influence pervading their whole life and work" (Moran 10). As he confesses to Kadzis, he is "interested in the way in which we as a culture use celebrities. In that respect they are quite like the old pantheons of gods, who, you know, behaved very badly" (qtd. in "Salman Speaks" 225).

Finally, how does the writer position himself in relation to his own stardom? "It is a terrible thing to be famous for the wrong thing," he is reported as saying apropos the fame foisted onto him by the fatwa (H. Ahmad 1330). Rushdie's disenchantment and uneasiness about celebrity are replayed in Mike Collett-White's article "For Salman Rushdie, Celebrity Is a Curse" (2005), where the writer is described as being overburdened by the persona constructed by the machinery of fame. Feeling the weight of his own literary stardom, he compares instant fame to Islamic radicalism: "The problem is that when you are well known there is a desire in some bits of the media to write about you at times when you don't have a book to talk about .... In the same way Islamic radicalism is one of the curses of our times, so is celebrity culture." The author is exceedingly conscious of his writing *and* of himself as a commodity; he is aware, as well, of his status in the image-making industry that has informed his writing from very early on. This is probably why Rushdie has always felt uneasy about having a film made about his life: around the time of the fatwa controversy, director Miloš Forman approached him with a film project, but he declined the offer. On this proposal, he asserts: "if there's going to be anything on my life, I'd rather write it myself, rather than have somebody else portray my life, leaving me with no control of how it turns out" (A. Sawhney). Not unrelatedly, he observes in "In Good Faith": "When I am described as an apostate Muslim, I feel as I have been concealed behind a *false self*, as if a shadow has become substance while I have been relegated to the shadows" (405). The writer similarly laments when interviewed by Boyd Tonkin: "I think that when people become famous, there's a public perception that they are not human beings any more. They don't have feelings; they don't get hurt; you can act and say as you like about them" (qtd. in "Salman Rushdie"). The uneasiness disclosed by these statements is similar in tone to a confession he makes in the travelogue in which he narrates his first visit to India in twelve years: "My metamorphosis from observer to observed, from the Salman I know to the 'Rushdie' I often barely recognize, continues apace" ("Dream" 221). Additionally, in an interview to Kadzis, he remarks that his main reaction to being "perhaps the most famous writer in the world" is one of disappointment.

Rushdie has dealt at length with the phenomenon of stardom in his work. The characters in his latest novels (*The Enchantress of Florence* (2008) excluded) – Max Ophuls,[39] Malik Solanka, Vina Apsara, and Ormus Cama – are all stars, in one way or another. The latter two characters are even depicted as displaying an "almost frighteningly totemic celebrity" (304). Vina herself reports to having seen a light on Ormus, "[a] radiance, an aura .... Not excessive?, but definitely emanating. About equivalent to a hundred-watt bulb, that is to say, enough to illuminate an average-size room. Which was plenty" (129). Metadiscursively, in its focus on celebrity culture, *The Ground Beneath Her Feet* is the novel that displays the most visible concern with the postmodern political conundrum of living in a world dominated by media exposure and constructed media-images.

---

[39] Rushdie's character, "a man of movie-star good looks and polymathic accomplishment" (*Shalimar* 161), takes his name from the influential German film director Max Ophüls (1902–1957).

For instance, the narrator attributes the diverse versions in circulation of the first encounter between the romantic couple in the novel, the mega-celebrities Vina and Ormus, to

> the clouds of mythologisation, regurgitation, falsification and denigration that have surrounded their story for years: depending which journal you read, you might have heard that he transformed himself into a white bull and carried her away on his back while she, warbling gaily, clutched with erotic delight at his two long, curved and gleaming horns; or that she was indeed an alien from a galaxy far, far away who, having identified Ormus as the most perfectly desirable male specimen on the planet, beamed down smack in front of him at the Gateway of India, holding a space flower in her hand. (90–91)

In the face of this awareness of how stifling stardom can be, one is only left to wonder what strategies the writer will devise to leave the "Rushdie" he time and again hardly recognizes out of "that zone of celebrity" that the novel narrator's evocatively describes as a place "in which everything except celebrity ceases to signify" (425).

Chapter 2
Exploding the Canon

This chapter attempts to contribute to a broader understanding of the changing nature of contemporary literary publishing, and of the position of the postcolonial writer in the face of market pressures and readership expectations nurtured, to a significant extent, in the criticism itself. Postcolonial studies have been pursuing a sustained examination of the inclusions and exclusions of canonical formations, drawing attention to the provisional and relational nature of "the canon," but processes of canonisation are readily discernible in the field of postcolonial literature. In a chapter devoted to practices of canon-formation, it should be noted from the outset that these have for the most part been legitimized, regulated, and mediated by western academia. The idea of a postcolonial canon (or canons, as in the thriving IWE canon of which Rushdie is unquestionably one of the strongest representatives) complicates the notion that postcolonial narratives of otherness are – as if *by definition* – excluded from the canon. Tracing the "social life of things" in the production, marketing, and reception of South Asia-related or South Asia-originating postcolonial literature involves an examination of its relationship to the canon given that, as David Damrosch notes, studies devoted to postcolonial literature might be "reproducing the hypercanonical bias of the older Europe-based fields" ("World Literature" 49).

The two sections of the present chapter share an explicit oedipal link. The short story "Yorick," at the centre of the first section, has been read as Rushdie's oedipal attempt at murdering his literary predecessors: Shakespeare and the western canon in general (Nogueira; Meyer). The second section builds on the popular understanding of contemporary Indian writers such as Vikram Seth, Amitav Ghosh, Shashi Tharoor, and Rohinton Mistry as "Rushdie's children," along with others included in Rushdie's and West's anthology *The Vintage Book of Indian Writing*. Against this context, Amit Chaudhuri, one of "Rushdie's Children" – or "Midnight's grandchild," as Pankaj Mishra calls him (Schürer 84) – edited a few years later the competing *The Picador Book of Modern Indian Literature*. Even though Chaudhuri straightforwardly asserts that *The Picador Book* "is not a riposte to any other anthology" ("Note" xxxii), it might be construed as an oedipal attempt at murdering the primal father and leading contemporary Indian literary star. In Freud's shadow, the second section of the chapter stages opposing arguments, as fleshed out by Rushdie and Chaudhuri, on what constitutes Indian literature.

In the Canon's Mouth: "Truly, a Velluminous history!"

> The distributed copies of the Bible, which even in translation remains the "English" book, are not read but willingly received to be sold or bartered, and to be used as waste or wrapping paper.
> —Homi Bhabha, *Location of Culture* 122

"Yorick's" narrator assumes the role of the Bard who is constantly trying to persuade the reader that his (and not Shakespeare's) is the "real" version. This section focuses on the ways the intertextual re-construction of *Hamlet* in Rushdie's short story reverses metropolitan readers' expectations of a straightforward "postcolonial retelling" of Shakespeare's play. Such expectations are nurtured, to a great extent, by postcolonial analysis of writing-back processes to the hegemonic centre, of the sort Said eulogizes: "Many of the most interesting postcolonial writers bear their past within them – as scars of humiliating wounds, as instigation for different practices ... as urgently reinterpretable and redeployable experiences, in which the formerly silent native speaks and acts on territory taken back from the empire" (*Culture and Imperialism* 34–35).

*****

The Siege of Krishnapur, a pastiche Victorian novel written by J.G. Farrell in 1973, depicts the siege of an imaginary Indian town during the Uprising of 1857 from the point of view of the British community occupying a secluded Victorian outpost. As the Uprising spreads across the subcontinent, in fictional Krishnapur, British officials disregard the rumours of civil unrest unfolding elsewhere. Until they inevitably find themselves under siege, the officials remain undaunted, counting on their military (and above all cultural) supremacy against an army of sepoys. As the novel reaches its epilogue, the narrator details how, when ammunition becomes too scarce to defend the besieged garrison, the British decide to turn into makeshift weapons the heads of electroplated statuettes of "great men of literature, of Dr Johnson, of Molière, Keats, Voltaire, and, of course, Shakespeare" (16). The circumstances of the siege thus force the Collector, the owner of these statuettes and also the character who commands the British occupancy in town and presides over the Krishnapur Poetry Society, to extend his belief in the civilising power of the European cultural heritage, epitomized by these "great men of literature," to a confidence in the statuettes' heads efficiency as cannonballs:

> ... of the heads, perhaps not surprisingly, the most effective of all had been Shakespeare's; it had scythed its way through a whole astonished platoon of sepoys advancing in single file through the jungle. The Collector suspected that the Bard's success in this respect might have a great deal to do with the ballistic advantages stemming from his baldness. The head of Keats, for example, wildly festooned with metal locks ... had flown very erratically indeed, killing only a fat moneylender and a camel standing at some distance from the action. (304)

Following Bhabha's theorisation of the "English book" as "an insignia of colonial authority and a signifier of colonial desire and discipline" (*Location* 102), the Shakespearean text was as much a "sign taken for wonders" as the Bible in the sense that both were emblematic of "those ideological correlatives of the Western sign – empiricism, idealism, mimeticism, monoculturalism ... that sustain a tradition of English 'cultural authority'" (105). With Shakespeare's head at its head, the above passage from Farrell's postmodern and postcolonial encounter with Victorian fiction satirically dramatizes the assumption that English literature, again with Shakespeare at its head, was instrumental to the exercise of imperial power.

Recent decades have witnessed an amplified interest in the colonial and postcolonial variations of the Bard's texts. Studies by Ania Loomba (*Gender, Race, Renaissance Drama* 1989), Jyotsna Singh ("Different Shakespeares: The Bard in Colonial/Postcolonial India," 1989), and Nandi Bhatia (*Acts of Authority/Acts of Resistance* 2004) on the intricacies of Shakespearean production in the subcontinent and on the indigenisation of the Bard's plays in vernacular theatres highlight that, even if the English book endures as a "hallowed entity" in postcolonial India (J. Singh 457), authority is never without ambiguity or double-edgedness. In Benita Parry's words, "a textual insurrection against the discourse of colonial authority is located in the natives' interrogation of the English book within the terms of their own system of cultural meanings" (25); or, in Bhabha's phrasing, "[t]o the extent to which discourse is a form of defensive warfare, then mimicry marks those moments of civil disobedience within the discipline of civility: signs of spectacular resistance" (*Location* 172). Of particular interest here is the notion of "mimicry," according to which the colonized's imitative performance of the colonizer's culture undermines the authority of that culture. Bhabha argues for more subtle, discursive modes of resistance practised by colonized people: rather than mimesis providing proof of the realisation of the civilising intent of colonisation, it establishes a partial and distorted representation which menaces the colonizer more than it comforts. In Bhabha's understanding, the mimetic performance of the colonized subject – in which that subject takes up the guise of the colonizer – subverts the project of colonialism not because it might be a conscious act of misappropriation, but because it has a menacing effect which is produced by colonialism's own paranoia. The colonizer recognized his/her ambivalent situation, "tethered to, *not* confronted by, his dark reflection, the shadow of the colonized man, that splits his presence, distorts his outline, breaches his boundaries, repeats his actions at a distance, disturbs and divides the very time of his being" (44). Colonial ambivalence thus produces hybridity, which is not just a mixing together – it is a dialogic dynamic where certain elements of dominant cultures are appropriated by the colonized and rearticulated in dissident ways. Bhabha's pivotal – and exhaustively rehearsed – argument is that the English book, read as a fetishized sign that magnifies western hegemony, is paradoxically a marker of the colonial ambivalence that lends colonial discourse vulnerable to mimetic subversion.

Critics have demonstrated the influence of Shakespeare, whose name is seen as one and the same with high art and elite culture, on Bollywood cinema, the epitome of Indian popular culture, and the Merchant-Ivory production *Shakespeare Wallah* displays this productive tension. The film depicts the reception of the Bard's texts in India after the end of the British Raj, and plays precisely on the idea of the fracturing of the English text as it is rearticulated in the cultural context of both post-imperial Britain and post-independence India. The representation of theatrical performances by a group of Shakespearean actors in India and the unexpected (because manifestly unappreciative) audience responses to them allow for a refashioning of a monolithic colonial cultural heritage into a *multi*lithic construct in a postcolonial setting. Relatedly, Luke Strongman (2002) contends that Booker-winning novels such as Farrell's *The Siege of Krishnapur* have reinvented, both individually and collectively, the colonial hangover in the aftermath of the British Empire by dealing with the emergence of hybrid cultural formations at a time of transition to a post-imperial stage. Even if "[n]ot all the winning novels are actively engaged in 'de-scribing' or dismantling of empire," Strongman argues that "all are part of the after-text of empire" (xii) and, in this sense, contribute to the constant reinterpretation of imperial legacies. Grouping Booker-prize-winning novels into categories such as "Novels of the Raj" and "Postcolonial Pessimisms," Strongman charts an even if somewhat ambivalent orientalism and nostalgia for the Raj in novels such as Farrell's *The Siege of Krishnapur*, Ruth Prawer Jhabvala's *Heat and Dust* (1975), and Paul Scott's *Staying On* (1977); disaffection and malaise in V.S. Naipaul's *In A Free State* (1971), Nadine Gordimer's *The Conservationist* (1974), J.M. Coetzee's *Life and Times of Michael K* (1983), Keri Hulme's *The Bone People* (1985), and Peter Carey's *Oscar and Lucinda* (1988); as well as post-imperial insularities or narratives of the "Empire's twilight" in Kazuo Ishiguro's *The Remains of the Day* (1989).

To put *Shakespeare Wallah* into a nutshell, the film portrays the erosion of British cultural power at a particular point in time when the old order, the British Raj, overlaps with a new order, that of the aftermath of Indian independence. The film is nostalgic for an empire in which Shakespeare performed a crucial role, given that the playwright was enlisted as an edifying agent in the educational system of the British Empire. In this respect, Lubna Chaudhry and Saba Khattak contend that *Shakespeare Wallah* betrays an "underlying nostalgia for the colonial period" that "makes the political stance represented in the film problematic" (21). This subchapter is concerned with the re-articulation, not without the internal contradictions and ambiguities noted by Chaudhry and Khattak, of the relationship between colonial cultural hierarchies, epitomized by Shakespeare, and postcolonial subjects who perform back or subvert expectations of writing back. This section attempts a nuanced approach to *Shakespeare Wallah*, beyond binary oppositions, an approach which relies on the idea of transcultural negotiations and contestations. Because this approach is attentive to the ways in which the film appropriates the western canon and, particularly, the Bard's plays as productive sites of cultural conflict in a postcolonial milieu, it frames the ensuing analysis of Rushdie's short story "Yorick."

Released in 1965 by the Ismail Merchant-James Ivory production team, with a screenplay by Ruth P. Jhabvala, *Shakespeare Wallah* is usually lauded for its attention to visual detail, a characteristic we have come to readily associate with Merchant-Ivory heritage films. The film is loosely based on actor-manager Geoffrey Kendal's diary of the tour across India in 1947 of "Shakespeareana," his troupe. Actually, the film's casting relies heavily on performers from the Shakespeareana theatrical company – Kendal and Laura Liddell, his wife, play the Buckinghams, the fictionalized version of themselves, while their daughter, Felicity, plays the character of Lizzie. Even though the Kendals triumphantly toured Shakespeare productions in the country for nearly two decades, *Shakespeare Wallah*'s mostly British troupe, the Buckingham Players,[1] are now facing difficulties prompted by political transition. Independence, accompanied by the burgeoning popularity of India's film industry, has led to a change in taste among audiences who had before received Shakespearean theatre (apparently) with excitement. Tony, Mr Buckingham, confides to Carla, his wife: "We should have gone home in '47 when the others did." Another character grumbles about how the Indians are insensitive to Shakespeare's plays and react to his texts with indifference: "It's not like the old days. What do these people know about our theatre? Shakespeare and all that?" According to director James Ivory, the film was meant to be seen as "a metaphor for the end of the British Raj" (87). It should come as no surprise then that the adaptation of the Kendals' experience was politicized: actual events were remade and the audience reception of plays performed by the Buckingham Players was deliberately represented as resistive and disruptive. The Indian response to Shakespeare's plays after independence is thus reshaped in the filmic text by having the performances often interrupted. If in Kendal's autobiography/diary, Indians are depicted as "the most rewarding audiences in the world" (Kendal and Clovin 107), in the film, Buckingham rethinks his favourable opinion of them. A feeling of nostalgia prompts him to lament the loss of the audiences that "laughed at all the jokes, cried in all the right places."

As Thomas Cartelli observes, this Merchant-Ivory film "is symptomatic of a transitional stage ... when an enforced identification with the colonizing power becomes displaced by the espousal of indigenous cultural icons that underwrite emerging nationalist aspirations"; as he goes on to add, in *Shakespeare Wallah* the Bard's plays "no longer serve as a dependable, or commercially viable, item of cross-cultural exchange. The Shakespeare wallah can no longer market plays whose ideological supports have been pulled out from under him" (105). In the film, the cultural struggle between the former British colonizers and the newly independent subjects is framed as a clash between high culture, exemplified by Shakespeare's plays, and indigenous popular culture, typified by Bollywood films.

---

[1] Rushdie in *The Satanic Verses* refers to a theatrical company, named Prospero Players after the magician character in Shakespeare's *The Tempest*, which goes on tour in India to present plays such as *The Millionairess* by George Bernard Shaw. Saladin, one of the novel's protagonists, accompanies the troupe playing the role of an Indian doctor (49).

In this context, the Bengali director Satyajit Ray's involvement in the musical score of Merchant-Ivory's work is consistent with the Indian filmmaker's recurrent sharp critiques of Bollywood's reliance on nonrealist and melodramatic codes of representation. Even though theatre and popular cinema are, to some extent, put into dialectical conflict in *Shakespeare Wallah*, the film is ambivalence-ridden in its questioning of the place of the privileged Shakespearean text in postcolonial Indian culture. The film does go beyond a clean contrast between cultural matrixes, or even between high and low cultures. Ambiguity is embodied by the character of the young playboy Sanju. During the film, Sanju is expected to choose between two women who act as representatives of antithetical media and cultures. He has long been romantically involved with the Bollywood film star Manjula, but now he also feels drawn to Lizzie, the Buckinghams' daughter. Clearly, Sanju's interest in Lizzie is related to both his reverence for the world of Shakespeare and his contempt for popular Bombay cinema. *Shakespeare Wallah* draws a line between the talented English actress and the Indian femme fatale. The latter, the calculating and seductive Manjula, is the personification, so the film seems to convey, of the crassness and debauchery of Indian mass culture. Her cultural upper hand and the indisputable star power she possesses in India as a Bollywood actress are overtly contrasted with the now démodé Shakespearean troupe. Indeed, what the Buckingham Players struggle against is their ousting by Indian popular cinema, a displacement which *Shakespeare Wallah* satirizes and exposes as a depressing but inevitable outcome of independence (Lanier 46).

The film exacerbates the division between the Indian audiences and the British performers. Merchant-Ivory's cinematic text uses the device of textual juxtaposing, de-contextualising scenes from various Shakespearean plays to achieve an effect of narrative fracturing that amplifies the cultural demise of the British Empire (Kapaau, "Shakespeare Transposed" 45). A particularly telling scene in this respect is the performance by the "Shakespeareana" of Desdemona's murder in *Othello*: Manjula, the Bollywood celebrity, in her efforts to deflect Sanju's attention away from Lizzie (who plays the role of Desdemona), arrives late, poses for pictures, and gladly signs autographs, thus disrupting the English text. As Valerie Wayne puts it, *Shakespeare Wallah* "dramatizes hybridity both on stage and in the box at the theatre, for black Othello is murdering white Desdemona while the Indian film star is challenging her lover's desire for the British actress by, quite literally, killing the scene" (98). At this point, Buckingham loses control over the text by attempting to recoup the gaze of the audience: he steps out of his role as Othello and reproaches the audience for their distraction, trying somewhat pathetically to re-assert Shakespeare's authority in the early days of post-independence India (Wayne 98–100). Nonetheless, the lines of us and them, Shakespeare and Bollywood are not as strictly drawn as this scene would seem to suggest. The oppositions on which the film rests, anticipated by its title, between Shakespearean theatre and Indian cinema, high and low cultures, British and Indian, are historically not as sharply differentiated as might at first appear. *Shakespeare Wallah* does not offer any easy resolution to Sanju's split loyalties. Even if he is asked to choose between Lizzie and Manjula, he is ultimately unable to do so given that he is constructed as an uneasy hybrid of eastern and western cultural identifications. While he is attracted to a foreign actress and her cultural heritage, he also inhabits the conflicting subject position of an Indian aware of the alien and enforced presence of the British Raj.

Shakespeare Wallah appropriates and reimagines Shakespeare through an indigenous, or local frame. This echoes Bhabha's formulation of the Janus-faced boundary of national culture which is "always a process of hybridity, incorporating new 'people' in relation to the body politic, generating new sites of meaning, and, inevitably, in the political process, producing unmanned sites of political antagonism and unpredictable forces for political representation" ("Introduction" 4). Cultural practices such as cinema provide a significant entry point into the complex issues that the discourse of hybridity invokes, hybridity being one of the favoured images around which cultural and postcolonial studies have theorized the question of identity. According to Bhabha, the aim of cultural hybridity is not to define or to delimit; its usefulness is in opening up a discursive space – a "third space" – where transformations are made possible and newfangled identities are articulated (qtd. in Rutherford, "Third Space" 211). The Merchant-Ivory film under scrutiny here is easily viewed within an either/or paradigm: either as recuperating a nostalgic longing for colonial times when Shakespeare's authority was seemingly unquestioned, or as a subversive transgression, or even disruption, of the iconic play *Othello*. In this latter respect, the Indian audience's response was construed as overtly confrontational, contesting the ascribed "civilising" function of the Shakespearean text and appropriating it counterdiscursively to celebrate Hindi popular cinema.

These readings ultimately underwrite binary oppositions that Rushdie's "Yorick" neutralizes altogether. This subchapter will now proceed to examine that short story as a counterpoint to *Shakespeare Wallah*, as not only a revisiting of the western canon, but most importantly as a parodic appropriation of postcolonial appropriations of western canonical works, with specific focus on Shakespeare's *Hamlet*. Rushdie's self-reflexive move relies on readers' familiarity with this authoritative literary text – the writer invokes knowledge of the play, using it as a frame story, to then suspend a feeling of familiarity, telling the story anew. An alternative plot to that of the Elizabethan play is offered, in which the narrator assumes an authorial persona who is constantly trying to persuade the reader that his (one assumes) version can rightfully coexist with the Bard's. In this version, for instance, Hamlet's remark, following the appearance of his father's ghost, that something "is rotten in the state of Denmark" refers to Ophelia's foul breath (66). The narrator defends his alternative story thus: as "these matters are shrouded in antiquity, ... there's no certainty in them; so let the versions coexist, for there is no need to choose" (81).

Rushdie's relation to literary canons is worth elaborating on at this point. Richard Todd argues that since the early 1980s we have been living in a "general atmosphere of canon formation" (9). Because the concept of canon entails exclusion, selection, and privilege, postcolonial critics have been particularly attentive to the implications of processes of canon-formation for the generally perceived anti-canonical field of postcolonial literature. John Marx identifies three fundamental and overlapping assumptions about the interaction between postcolonial literature and the western canon: first, "postcolonial writing is held to *repudiate* the canon"; second, "postcolonial literature has been shown to *revise* canonical texts and concepts" (83); and last, "postcolonial literature increasingly *defines* a new canon from an established position inside its boundaries" (85). What Damrosch calls the "persisting divisions between the hypercanon and the counter-canon of world literature" ("World Literature" 53) should be regarded, Marx concludes from these dominant conceptualisations of the interaction between postcolonial literature and the western canon, as a "competition within a shared field of operation" (95). Hyper- and counter-canonical literary works are thus interdependent. In this respect, the canonisation of postcolonial writers such as Rushdie, Wole Soyinka, Derek Walcott, Nadine Gordimer, and J.M. Coetzee, to name a few (all but Rushdie Nobel laureates), is at least partly the result of the institutional status of postcolonial studies today. More than seeing postcolonial writing and the western canon as "embattled allies" (Marx 95), we should be attentive to the fact that western academia guides practices of postcolonial canon-formation, in the same way as there is a postcolonial studies industry that commodifies and markets the postcolonial intellectual.

Rushdie's work cannot be adequately considered an appendage of the western literary canon. His privileged status within the so-called postcolonial canon and his writing himself, however critically, into the British canon are unquestionable. Attesting to this double positioning is the fact that his short story "Chekov and Zulu" is included in *The Longman Anthology of World Literature* (edited by Damrosch et al.[2]) under the heading "Post-Colonial Conditions," and his short story "Christopher Columbus and Queen Isabella of Spain Consummate Their Relationship" (1994) is equally collected in *The Longman Anthology of British Literature* (edited by Damrosch et al.[3]) in the section "World War II and the End of Empire." In addition, the fact that the Cambridge University Press series "Cambridge Companions to Literature" has devoted one of its volumes to Rushdie, edited by Abdulrazak Gurnah in 2007, is one of many indicators of the writer's canonical status, a status which had already been further established by Emory University's purchase of his personal archive in 2006, followed by an exhibition. On a related level, the writer publicly acknowledges the influence western canonical authors such as Shakespeare have had on his work:

> [O]ne of the great gifts of Shakespeare to writers in the English language was to show that a work of literature can be many things at once – it doesn't have to be just one thing.
>
> An example I sometimes use: look at the sequence of opening scenes of *Hamlet*. The first scene is a ghost story. The second scene is intrigue at court.

---

[2] Volume F: The Twentieth Century.
[3] Volume 2C: The Twentieth Century.

> The third scene is a love story. The fourth scene is knockabout comedy. And the fifth scene is a ghost story again. What Shakespeare showed is that you could do all that. ... Shakespeare said, *Mix it all up. You can have comedy, history, and tragedy all wrapped into one. And all you have to do to pull it off is be Shakespeare.* (qtd. in Weich)

At stake here is a double influence, in the sense that Shakespeare's global canonicity continues to develop through appropriations of and allusions to his plays (Kapadia, "Transnational Shakespeare" 1–2). Themes, topoi, events, characters, and scenes from Shakespeare punctuate Rushdie's work.[4] For example, in *The Satanic Verses* there are allusions or direct references to the Bard himself (109), to the plays *Othello* (248) and *Hamlet* (228), and to Shakespearean characters such as Brutus (316), Shylock (398), Othello (466), and Iago (466). In that novel one also encounters a *Romeo and Juliet*-inspired balcony scene (371) and a theatrical troupe called "Prospero Players" (49). An instance of the multilayered intertextual use of Shakespeare's work and its translation into post-imperial London occurs when the protagonist Saladin declares, when courting the English character Pamela Lovelace, that *Othello*, "'just that one play', was worth the total output of any other dramatist in any other language"; in the face of this statement, Pamela "professed herself horrified, bracketing Othello with Shylock and beating the racist Shakespeare over the head with the brace of them" (398). In *Fury*, Eleanor Masters, the former wife of the protagonist Malik, presents the proposition of her doctoral thesis as being based on the fact that "at the heart of each of the great tragedies were unanswerable questions about love" such as:

> Why did Hamlet, loving his dead father, interminably delay his revenge while, loved by Ophelia, he destroyed her instead? Why did Lear, loving Cordelia best of his daughters, fail to hear the love in her opening-scene honesty and so fall prey to her sisters' unlovingness; and why was Macbeth, a man's man who loved his king and country, so easily led by the erotic but loveless Lady M. towards the evil throne of blood? (10)

Nowhere is the Shakespearean intertext more evident than in Rushdie's "Yorick," the first short story in the "West" group in the collection *East, West* (1994), narrated by a descendent of Yorick, where the Bard himself is referred to as "Master Chackpaw" (81). The story's intrusive narrator, with the help of a vellum in his possession, presents his own alternative version of *Hamlet*. He focuses on the jester Yorick, who marries Ophelia and later kills the King of Denmark, whose name is Horwendillus according to the Danish historian Saxo Grammaticus. This is "[t]ruly, a velluminous history" and the intention of the narrator is "not merely to abbreviate, but, in addition, to explicate, annotate, hyphenate, palatinate & permanganate – for it's a narrative that richly rewards the scholar who is

---

[4] Shakespearean intertextuality in Rushdie's fiction has been comprehensively addressed in Geetha Ganapathy-Doré's essay "Shakespeare in Rushdie/Shakespearean Rushdie" (2009).

competent to apply such sensitive technologies" (64). Rushdie's story is about "both the tale of the vellum itself and the tale inscribed thereupon" (64). Besides, the self-referential, intrusive narrator "appeals to the reader as a co-performer in the text as a script" (Meyer 126), inviting her to creative collaboration. He asks for her opinion about characters' motivations and invites her to imagine hypothetical scenarios: "Your fancy, from which all these dark suppositions have issued (for I began this passage by swearing myself to silence), is proved by them more fertile & convincing than my own" ("Yorick" 78). He even scolds her for supposedly reacting to discrepancies between Shakespeare's *Hamlet* and his own version: "What's this? Interruptions already?" (65). At the end of the story, the narrator reveals that Yorick's son by Ophelia "survives, and leaves the scene of his family's tragedy; wanders the world, sowing his seed in far-off lands, from west to east and back again; and multicoloured generations follow, ending ... in this present, humble AUTHOR" (83).

Critics such as Adelaine Nogueira, Michael Meyer, and Geetha Ganapathy-Doré propose a psychoanalytical reading of "Yorick" as Rushdie's oedipal attempt at murdering his literary fathers, cutting off a branch of the family tree of his predecessors, namely Shakespeare and the western canon in general. Ganapathy-Doré even suggests that the writer's use of Shakespeare as a point of reference "may simply have been a creative outlet to resolve the tension in his relationship with his father" ("Shakespeare in Rushdie" 21). There is a Freudian shadow hanging over the story and the first-person narrator even jokes about a psychoanalytic reading of *Hamlet*: "I'm just surprised that nobody's pointed out that Ophelia is *O phallus*" ("Yorick" 20). Are we then to read "Yorick" as a counter-text to Hamlet? What this subchapter argues is that texts such as this story, an example of mixture and interpenetrating cultural influences, cannot be adequately analysed by deploying a binary logic. As Said states, "cultures are too intermingled, their contents and histories too interdependent and hybrid, for surgical separation into large and mostly ideological oppositions" (*Representations* xi).

Parmita Kapadia contends that the presence of Shakespeare's play in "Yorick" may be viewed not so much as an attempt to deconstruct and subvert the canon, but rather as prompting a critique that undermines the constraining binary logic that confronts canonical texts with counterdiscursive ones ("Transnational Shakespeare" 5). As she argues, the use of Hamlet in "Yorick" resists the counterdiscursivity model of postcolonial appropriation by challenging the binary structuring that "haunts most contemporary appropriations of Shakespeare" (2). Bhabha's concept of "translation" is apt here to analyse the Shakespearean intertext in Rushdie's "Yorick." Following Bhabha's theorisation, this story might represent a "way of imitating ... in such a way that the priority of the original is not reinforced"; through this process, a hybrid product "sets up new structures of authority" and "new political initiatives," making up a "third space" that "displaces the histories that constitute it" (qtd. in Rutherford "Third Space" 211). Were Rushdie to use *Hamlet* as its source text, "Yorick" would be easily pigeonholed as an appropriation of Shakespeare. In Kapadia's words, Rushdie constructs a narrative "that promotes historical alterity and hybridity within an Occidental, not a postcolonial, context" ("Transnational Shakespeare" 6). According to Bhabha, hybridity is not as a simple process of accumulation that fuses different cultural forms into a homogenous whole. On the contrary, "hybrid hyphenations emphasize the incommensurable elements – the stubborn chunks – as the basis of cultural identifications" (*Location* 219). These "chunks" are irreducible to fixed categorisations and thus create an "interstitial space in-between" which allows for new world views (38).

The "manifest" intertextual[5] re-construction of *Hamlet* in "Yorick" reverses metropolitan readers' expectations of a straightforward "postcolonial retelling" of Shakespeare's play. As Chris Bongie puts it, "[t]he revisionist move, such an attractive option for postcolonial writers in the past, has become so familiar, so obvious, so calculated, it might be argued, that little or no case can be made for its 'innovative' or 'resistant' possibilities" (para. 41). Rushdie's "innovative" and "resistant" narrative articulates on three levels. Translation, rather than writing back to the western canon, is at issue in "Yorick." On one level, considering that parody and pastiche imply the active encoding of mimicry, or imitation with critical difference, within a text, this revisiting of *Hamlet* – "which ruins at least one great soliloquy" ("Yorick" 81) – is a pastiche of the postcolonial revisionist text. On a second interrelated level, the refusal of a counterdiscursive gesture on Rushdie's part can be seen as a denial to satisfy metropolitan readers' expectations of revisionist narratives by postcolonial writers of works belonging to the western canon . To a great extent, such expectations are fostered by the story's title, which seems to introduce a narrative told not from the perspective of the main characters in Shakespeare's play, but by the subaltern character of the court jester. In Rushdie's re-construction of *Hamlet*, an anticipated writing-back-with-a-vengeance story (the eastern-author-responds-to-the-western-canon narrative) is enacted as parody. Against expectations, the writer does not give voice to the subaltern Yorick. He takes the master narrative of postcolonial revisionism and plays with the anticipated readings of its short story, also targeting academic readings of Shakespeare through a postcolonial lens. Whereas the narrator of this tale is self-ironically construed as a fool, the scholar is someone who applies "sensitive technologies" (64). The story thus questions Shakespearean textual critics' authoritative hold over the text by interrogating the supposed totality, reliability, and authority of the Shakespearean canon. On a third level, "Yorick" sets up new structures of discursive authority, not by denying Shakespeare's continuing authoritative presence and iconicity, but by not reinforcing the priority of the "original" Shakespearean text. In conclusion, "Yorick" eludes the politics of polarity. It self-reflexively transcends the discursive dichotomies in which postcolonial appropriation is often mired. The story draws upon both Shakespeare's global cultural capital and readers' expectations of a

---

[5] Norman Fairclough distinguishes between "manifest" intertextuality, that is, "the explicit presence of other texts in a text," and "interdiscursivity," i.e., "the constitution of a text from a configuration of text types or discourse conventions" (10).

counterdiscursive and revisionist move on Rushdie's part to challenge catch-all claims about the all but innate oppositionality of postcolonial appropriations of canonical western texts.

*****

Referring to Rushdie's canonical status, Sandra Ponzanesi writes that "[b]y carving out for himself the role of the migrant author hovering between two cultures, Rushdie managed to become the leading spokesperson in literary and personal terms of a whole new generation of diasporic writers from former European colonies, especially India" (107). Likewise, English and Frow observe that "[b]y virtue of this apparently seamless legitimacy on the literary field, coupled with his outsized ego and knack for attracting the media, Rushdie had become the most visible representative and spokesman for 'Black British' culture" (53). The next section will focus on the ways Rushdie's canonical power is played out in his role as cultural broker of post-independence Indian literature, with specific reference to his role as anthologist.

Canon Wars

> ... it is perhaps one of the more pleasant freedoms of the literary migrant to be able to choose his parents.
> —Rushdie, "Imaginary Homelands" 20–21

By deliberately equating "Indian writing" with "Indian writing in English" – and in the process partaking in what might be construed as a reductive, unilingual understanding of post-independence literature – Rushdie's and West's 1997 anthology *The Vintage Book of Indian Writing* stands as a conflict-ridden selection from the outset. The broad purpose of this section is to investigate the ways in which *The Vintage Book of Indian Writing* and *The Picador Book of Modern Indian Literature*, a succeeding anthology edited by Amit Chaudhuri in 2001 including texts originally written in both English and the vernaculars,[6] are constituent parts of a symbolic economy wherein diverse "agents of legitimation" (Huggan, *Postcolonial Exotic* 5) grant cultural authority and even canonical status to writers and works, regulate the constitution of a literary star system, and facilitate success in a global market. Interrelatedly, this section examines the ways in which *The Vintage Book* and *The Picador Book* present competing canons of Indian writing and, on a more general level, addresses the problematics of canon-formation of IWE and its vexed relationship with the vernacular languages, providing an

---

[6] The term "vernaculars" is here used to refer to all languages used in India other than English, therefore including Hindi.

overview of extant critical opinions.[7] In examining the contending processes of canon-formation involving IWE and Indian writing in the vernaculars as mirrored by the scope and aims of *The Vintage Book* and *The Picador Book*, this section introduces the component of *failure*, proposed by Chaudhuri, as a referential model to the anthologist. The idea of failure results from the acknowledgement of the unfeasibility of representing totality (Chaudhuri, "Travels" 144) – in this case, the entirety of modern Indian literature, or even the work of Indian writers over a 50-year period. Ultimately, out of failure, it is possible to establish a new interpretational basis for reading anthologies of Indian literatures and, in particular, for moving beyond the conundrum of the "Indianness" of Indian fiction in English and in the vernacular tongues.

*****

Selecting a title for a book necessarily entails exclusion and elision. To an even greater extent, the same proves true when editors compile anthologies of literary texts. Referring to Rushdie's and West's *The Vintage Book of Indian Writing*, Huggan perceptively inserts "in English" into square brackets and places this phrase at the end of the anthology's title (*Postcolonial Exotic* 274). He thus draws attention to the heavy ideological baggage that the selection of the title carries, as this English-language anthology of post-independence Indian fiction consists almost entirely of texts written in *one* of the many languages spoken in the subcontinent. In fact, the volume includes 32 texts – in some cases extracts from longer works – by 30 Indian and two Pakistani writers, and, except from a short story translated from Urdu, all the texts were originally written in English. Controversially enough, this anthology purports to be a gathering of, in Rushdie's own phrasing, "the best Indian writing of the half-century since the country's independence" ("Introduction" ix). The polemic surrounding the anthology was compounded by the fact that Nobel laureate Naipaul is "regrettably absent from this book," not by editorial decision, but of his own volition (xix). This might be explained by Naipaul's belief that English in India "remains a foreign language", and that, as he proceeds to add, "the psychological damage caused by the continued official use of English, which can never be more than a second language, is immense" (*Area* 222).

On the surface, the process of anthologising is a response to a pre-existent body of creative works. There is, of course, more to this than meets the eye, as

---

[7] It is beyond the scope of this subchapter to exhaustively address existing critical work on anthologies of Indian literature as well as current debates on the anthology genre. For an authoritative discussion of competing models of Indian literary canons which includes "bhasa" literary production, see Francesca Orsini's essay "India in the Mirror of World Fiction" (2004) and, with reference to the emerging field of anthology studies, Leah Price's *The Anthology and the Rise of the Novel* (2000) and Jeffrey Di Leo's *On Anthologies: Politics and Pedagogy* (2004).

demonstrated by the publication of *The Vintage Book of Indian Writing*[8] and its successor *The Picador Book of Modern Indian Literature*. By contrast to Rushdie's and West's editorial decisions, Chaudhuri includes texts by 38 writers, 18 English originals, and 20 translations from a diversity of vernaculars. Chaudhuri later clarified in his collection of essays *Clearing a Space* (2008) that there lies at the heart of *The Picador Book* a conscious attempt to question the very existence of an Indian literature, instead of taking it as a "fait accompli." This, in the anthologist's mind, "is not necessarily to be insulting, but to invite one to conceptualize the matter in a new way"; *The Picador Book* is hence to be received as a question, rather than as a statement ("Travels" 142). In sum, Chaudhuri's anthology should not be read as an anthology of the "best" modern Indian writing, but as a critique of the taken-for-grantedness of Indian literature. If we extend this critique to Rushdie's and West's selection, *The Vintage Book* is purportedly informed by a notion of the pre-eminence of Indian prose literature *in English* when it sets out the goal of including within its covers "the best Indian writing of the half-century since the country's independence" (Rushdie and West ix).

This subchapter focuses on the above fault lines as spaces where, in the past three decades, canon wars have been fought over what constitutes Indian literature. The stated intentions of the editors is to present "the best Indian writing" since independence (Rushdie and West ix), or to provide a sense of "the quite amazing shape of modern Indian literature and narrative, and its provocative and engaging heterogeneity" (Chaudhuri, "Note" xxxii). Nonetheless, to mirror in an anthology such "endlessly rich, complex and problematic entity" (Chaudhuri, "Modernity" xvii) is necessarily a flawed ambition, as the editors themselves duly recognize. In this respect, Rushdie clarifies about his and West's selection: "It is of course true that any anthology worth its salt will reflect the judgements and tastes of its editors. I can only say that our tastes are pretty catholic and our minds, I hope, have been open. We have made our choices, and stand by them" ("Introduction" xi). Both anthologies are acts of editorial inclusion and omission that work, inevitably, to endorse exclusionary readings of Indian literature.

Despite Rushdie's disclaimer – "there is not, need not be, should not be, an adversarial relationship between English-language literature and the other literatures of India" (xvi) – the views expressed by Chaudhuri and him in their respective anthologies have often been flattened and essentialized, turning them into opponents in a literary canon war. Chaudhuri's understanding of an anthology as "an extended essay with very large quotations" and, in connection to this idea, of anthologies as "an accumulation of fragments" ("Travels" 144) might be an endeavour to outplay the canon war raging on the "Indianness" of Indian writing in "bhasa" languages and in English, a sterile debate that has beyond any doubt influenced the critical reception of *The Vintage Book* and *The Picador Book* alike.

---

[8] In the US the anthology was retitled. It was published by Henry Holt as *Mirrorwork: 50 Years of Indian Writing: 1947–1997* (1997) and later by Vintage as *The Vintage Book of Modern Indian Literature* (2004).

"The anthology, like most anthologies, is an odd book," asserts Chaudhuri, pointing out as the "particular oddity" of *The Picador Book* the inevitable fragmentary and incomplete nature of the project ("Travels" 142). As he anticipates:

> A representative anthology of Indian literature would have to be an ongoing project, and would probably run into several volumes; an attempt to present everything at once would risk either engulfing and overwhelming the reader, or missing him or her altogether, like one of those meteorites that hurtle past earth without making any noticeable difference to its atmosphere. ("Note" xxxii)

Correspondingly, Rushdie recognizes: "Fifty years of work, by four generations of writers, is impossible to summarize, especially when it hails from the huge crowd of a country ... that vast, metamorphic, continent-sized culture that feels, to Indians and visitors alike, like a non-stop assault on the senses, the emotions, the imagination and the spirit" ("Introduction" ix). Chaudhuri's anthology spans over 600 pages and showcases major Indian literary works from the mid-nineteenth to the late twentieth century. Nonetheless, its "more disgruntled reviewers" vociferously found it wanting and question, "Why was there so much Bengali and English; and so little Tamil, and no Punjabi?" ("Travels" 142). James Procter's comment on The British Council website – "the Picador anthology is certainly not without some glaring absences: Arundhati Roy, Rohinton Mistry, not to mention the complete absence of Gujarati and Marathi writers"[9] – exemplifies this reaction. Tarun Tejpal likewise draws attention to the omission of authors Kiran Nagarkar and Bharati Mukherjee in Rushdie's and West's anthology ("Rushdie"). According to this perspective, Chaudhuri concludes, "'Indian literature' was the sum of its significant parts; you would arrive at it if you added them all up" (142). Running counter to this, when putting together *The Picador Book*, the editor-writer opted for a critical departure from the strategy followed in the exhaustive and inclusive anthologies of modern Indian writing produced by the Sahitya Akademi (India's National Academy of Letters),[10] which for him illustrate the "bureaucratic cast of mind indispensable to the high moral tone of post-Independence India" (143). These anthologies amount to, in Chaudhuri's words, "a Borgesian attempt to map infinitude" and thus paradoxically mimic "the colonial explorer's striving towards control of alien terrain through classification and sampling" (143). By refuting the Sahitya Akademi's conception of anthologies, Chaudhuri undermines the taken-for-grantedness of an Indian literary canon. The editor chose the following alternative route in *The Picador Book*:

---

[9] This comment is under the heading "Critical perspective" on the page dedicated to Chaudhuri (http://www.contemporarywriters.com/authors/?p=auth21).

[10] The Sahitya Akademi's *Modern Indian Literature: An Anthology* (chief editor K.M. George) is made up of three volumes: volume one is *Surveys & Poems* (1992, xxix + 1148 pp.), volume two is *Fiction* (1993, xvii + 1192 pp.), and volume three is *Plays & Prose* (1994, xvi + 728 pp.).

> I began by abandoning the assumption that 'modern Indian literature' was 'out there' in the world, available for judicious representation and transposing to within the covers of a book. A literature, like an anthology, is not a collection of extraordinary achievements but a field of interrelationships; and it is part of the anthologist's job – his or her critical function – to contribute to interpreting and even creating one possible version of that field. (143)

In his manifesto-like introduction to *The Vintage Book*, Rushdie does not seem to share Chaudhuri's critique of a literature, or an anthology, as "a collection of extraordinary achievements" when, celebrating the booming interest in "Indo-Anglian" letters in the late 1990s, he (in)famously claims that "Indo-Anglian" literature "is proving to be a stronger and more important body of work than most of what has been produced in the [then] 16 'official languages' of India,[11] the so-called 'vernacular languages'" (x).[12] Works by "Indian writers working *in English*" stand for Rushdie as "perhaps the most valuable contribution India has yet made to the world of books" (x). Such optimistic (and deliberately provocative) rendering of the, at the time, "new, and still burgeoning" IWE (x) is based on the tenet that "parochialism is perhaps the main vice of the vernacular literatures" (xv). From this tenet – one that has been criticized for fuelling the opposition between "elitist" and "parochial" (Rajan) – follows that post-independence Indian writers of English have been garnering an impressive hypervisibility since the 1980s because, in Rushdie's words, they have been "too good to fall into the trap of writing *nationalistically*" and are thus capable of "holding a conversation with the world" (xv). Bearing out India's conflictual relationship with English as the idiom of the ex-colonizer, Rushdie contends that "India's best writing since independence may have been done in the language of the departed imperialists is simply too much for some folks to bear" (xiv).

According to the author, there are not one, but many English literatures. As he puts it during an interview with Rani Dube, "the most interesting things" in literature in English "are happening through people who have nothing that could remotely be called an Anglo-Saxon attitude: the Caribbean writers, African writers, Indian writers, others who are writing in English" (12). For him, English literature in India is Indian literature. As he argues in the 1983 essay "'Commonwealth Literature' Does Not Exist," "English is an Indian literary language"; furthermore, as he goes on to add, authors such as Mulk Raj Anand, Raja Rao, Nirad C. Chaudhuri,[13] and others gave it "quite a pedigree" in the early 1980s (65). The English language, the writer posits, has long "ceased to be the sole possession of the English" (70). Indeed, as early in his writing career as 1982, when he had just

---

[11] There are now 23 (including English).

[12] While the two editors undertook the selection jointly, the introduction is signed by Rushdie alone.

[13] Elsewhere, he includes these writers in "the generation of independence, 'midnight's parents'", and credits them, among others, as "the true architects" of IWE ("Introduction" xvii).

published *Midnight's Children*, he celebrates linguistic cross-breeding and extols the "reverse takeover" of the British colonizers' language by Indian authors that was in full swing at the time:

> the English language got exported as part of the great gift the British gave the world, and it probably is their most valuable gift, beyond parliaments and Taj Mahals[14] and schools and trunk roads and all that. ... It's like a reverse takeover of the Empire. It's as though the people who were colonized are now doing the colonizing. (qtd. in Dube 12)

He further celebrates the "reverse takeover" of the English language as follows: "those people who were once colonized by the language are now rapidly remaking it, domesticating it, becoming more and more relaxed about the way they use it – assisted by the English language's enormous flexibility and size, they are carving out large territories for themselves within its frontiers" ("Commonwealth" 70). Ultimately, according to Rushdie, "to conquer English is to complete the process of making ourselves free" ("Imaginary" 17).

Rushdie nonetheless admits that it is "not appropriate for India" to write about the subcontinent "in classical English, a very cool, precise, dainty, beautifully made English, which is the English of the Great Tradition" (qtd. in Dube 13). In *Midnight's Children*, the author strove to transpose "the rhythms of Indian speech and thought" into a narrative written in English, because "only if you can do that to English can you legitimately claim to be writing authentically about India in English," he claims (14). These words significantly echo Raja Rao's oft-quoted earlier arguments, expressed in the introduction to his Indo-Anglian novel *Kanthapura* (1938), Rao's first novel, concerning the need for Indian authors to bypass the alien sensibility of a language linked to colonialism and to build an Indian English for themselves. Rao exhorted his fellow writers to decolonize the English language, infusing it with Indian cadences, rhythms, and allusions so as to capture the deep structures of Indian cultures and accommodate diverse experiences. In other words, he wanted to expand the flexibility of English and urged Indian writers to participate in a process of nativisation of the "alien language" as "[t]he tempo of Indian life must be infused into our English expression" (vii). Likewise for Rushdie, who, as a language magpie, has consciously and consistently been involved in linguistic experimentation at several levels, it is an incorrect proposition "that English, having arrived from outside India, is and must necessarily remain an alien there" ("Introduction" xii). Without question, he has routinely defended English as a full-fledged Indian language in interviews and essays.[15] Still, Amit Chaudhuri in part refutes Rushdie's frequently rehearsed arguments by stressing

---

[14] Rushdie notes in a later essay that "the Taj, which in the mid-nineteenth century had been all but abandoned, and had fallen into a severe state of disrepair, would probably not be standing today were it not for the diligent conservationist efforts of the colonial British" ("Taj Mahal" 186).

[15] See e.g. Dube 14.

both the inescapability and ambiguity of the position of English as a subcontinental language in the post-independence period: "to say that English is now an Indian language – while that may be true – requires all kinds of qualifications and a careful re-examination of that claim; for English is not an Indian language in the way it is an American language; nor is it an Indian language in the way that Bengali or Urdu, for instance, is one" ("Modernity" xxii). The above words, initially published in the *Times Literary Supplement* at about the same time as *The Vintage Book*, seem a direct rebuttal of a passage in Rushdie's introductory chapter where he, considering the global pre-eminence of the English language, observes that English is a transnational language not only because of the influence of the British Empire, but also because of the current political and cultural hegemony of the US:

> Indian English, sometimes unattractively called 'Hinglish', is not 'English' English, to be sure, any more than Irish or American or Caribbean English is. And it is a part of the achievement of the writers in this volume to have found literary voices so distinctively Indian, and also as suitable for any and all of the purposes of art, as those other Englishes forged in Ireland, Africa, the West Indies and the United States. (xiii)

As Rushdie argued on a different occasion, while the initial pre-eminence of English was "the result of the physical colonization of the globe by the British," English as a transnational language is "a kind of linguistic neo-colonialism, or just plain pragmatism" ("Commonwealth" 64). Despite acknowledging that the English language is inextricably woven into the Indian cultural fabric, Chaudhuri contends that to investigate its "most profound impact and extraordinary outcome" in India, "one has to turn, paradoxically, from English and the issue of colonialism to the vernacular languages and indigenous history" ("Modernity" xxii). In this respect, Rushdie certainly recognizes the quality of "bhasa" writing: in 1983 he stated that "major work [was] being done in many languages other than English" ("Commonwealth" 69), and later observed that "the century before independence contains many vernacular-language writers who would merit a place in any anthology" ("Introduction" xvi). However, when putting together *The Vintage Book*, to his and West's "considerable astonishment," only a translation from the Urdu of S.H. Manto's short story "Toba Tek Singh" "made the final cut" (x). Similarly, Chaudhuri introduces the following cautionary note to *The Picador Book*:

> This is not a representative anthology; there is nothing, for instance, from Assamese, Gujarati, Marathi, and Punjabi, to take four languages at random. This is so partly because I couldn't find enough translations of quality in these languages from which to make a selection, and partly because there wasn't enough space to accommodate all the important writers in any one language in this anthology, let alone include something from every language. ("Note" xxxii)

The rubrics for *The Vintage Book* and *The Picador Book* are not entirely identical, and this should be borne in mind when comparing them. Whereas the first includes nothing from before 1947, the latter, by contrast, goes as far back as Michael Madhusudhan Dutt (1824–1873). Because *The Picador Book* covers a larger time-span, Chaudhuri includes a number of nineteenth- and early twentieth-century vernacular writers, among them Rabindranath Tagore, from a tradition which Rushdie praises in his introduction. Although unconvincingly in the opinion of some reviewers, Rushdie accounts for the absence in *The Vintage Book* of works in vernacular tongues, with the exception of Manto's short story, due to the "genuine problem of translation in India"; in an attempt at pre-empting criticism, he concedes that "it is possible that good writers have been excluded by reason of their translators' inadequacies rather than their own" (x). Another plausible reason for the near-exclusion of writings in the vernacular tongues might be that, as he had diagnosed more than a decade earlier, "outside India there is just about no interest in any of this work" because the "Indo-Anglians seize all the limelight" ("Commonwealth" 69).

Rushdie's polemical tone certainly aided sales of *The Vintage Book*. Still, Chaudhuri condemns the "sanctimoniously outraged and self-congratulatory response" that Rushdie's statements received in "liberal, middle-class India" ("Note" xxxiii–xxxiv); to overcome these "fatuous quarrels," he argues that such statements should be understood in the context of the "multiple, occasionally competing, traditions embedded within traditions" that comprise modern Indian literature (xxxiii). Without doubt, the scope and underlying aims of both *The Vintage Book* and *The Picador Book* mirror the debate on the processes of canon-formation involving IWE and Indian writing in vernacular languages and, in particular, on the "Indianness" of these contending, but nonetheless interconnected, traditions.

The present section introduces the issue of "Indianness" – "whatever that infinitely complex thing is" (Chaudhuri, "Construction" xxx) – as it is drawn into this debate, before considering its interrelationship with practices of canon-formation in Indian writing. In the context of the critical exchanges that tend to set English against vernacular languages, it is worth revisiting Vikram Chandra's oft-quoted essay "The Cult of Authenticity," where the writer reflects on certain Indian reactions to the much debated achievements of IWE in the western literary marketplace. Chandra comments on the "indigenous" reaction to Rushdie's assertions in the introduction to *The Vintage Book*, and summarizes the quasi-moral debate that opposes "Indo-Anglian writers" to "regional writers." He recounts being scolded at a reading at the British Council in New Delhi by the renowned critic Meenakshi Mukherjee, who all but charged him with blatantly selling out to "an all-devouring and all-distorting West" because he used the Sanskrit terms "Dharma" ("duty"), "Artha" ("material prosperity"), and "Kama" ("enjoyment"), the first three goals of human existence ("purusharthas") according to Hinduism, as titles for three of his short stories in *Love and Longing in Bombay* (1997). If Mukherjee accuses Indian English writers of essentialising India, critics such as herself, "[d]espite all their demurrals about not essentializing Indianness, and their ritual genuflections in the direction of Bhabha and Spivak," might also be held responsible for essentialising Indian artists, argues Chandra. The artistic achievements of "regional" writers are hailed by critics such as Mukherjee as possessing an "untouched and original Indianness"; in this way, the aesthetic and political validity of "regional" writing – ultimately, its authenticity – seems to be predetermined. Relatedly, at the time of the publishing of *The Satanic Verses*, Rushdie worried about the reception of that novel in India because he felt it was bound to be read in a reductionist manner. In the author's own description, *The Satanic Verses* "isn't specifically 'Indian'", a fact that would not "please many purveyors of the 'authentic'"; furthermore, he got "the 'un-Indian' tag all the time" (qtd. in Mitchinson 96). Following Rushdie's reasoning in a coetaneous essay, critics who endow "regional" or vernacular writing with cultural authority under the guise of authenticity should reflect upon the implausibility of the "fantasy of purity" (Rushdie, "Commonwealth" 68) and their own assimilation of the inauthentic cultural practices from which they strive to distance themselves. In fact, as Chandra ironizes, "when judged by their own rather bizarre standards, these gatekeepers are about as 'authentically Indian' as Pamela Anderson" ("Cult").

According to Mukherjee (2000), Indian novels in English fall into the trap of artificially attempting to certify their authenticity to counteract their use of a non-autochthonous language. As such, this anxiety of authenticity manifests itself in contemporary Indian English fiction through overly descriptive and ornate writing, the selection of ostensibly "Indian" settings, and the mobilisation of a plethora of exotic images. As opposed to Indian writers in English, regional or "bhasa" authors, because they write in "legitimate" Indian languages, she argues, do not have to display any badges of authenticity or protest their "Indianness," nor do their readers ever question it. As "bhasa" literally means "language," Chandra notes that Indian English writing is hence "non-language writing"; if regional writers are construed as national subjects, those who use English seek to be pan-Indian – they are ghettoized as "writers from nowhere who write in a non-language." The English language, which has unquestionably complicated and problematized the position of the "bhasas," is seen in post-British India as an agent of hybridisation and thus contamination of the "pure" indigenous cultures (Ashcroft et al. 21). The celebration and iconising of regional writers might be interpreted as betraying nostalgia for a "Real India," that is, for an autochthonous "original" cultural matrix untainted by the English language and hence untamed by former colonial rule.

Chandra champions the artistic autonomy that runs the risk of being dangerously hampered by what he calls a "censorious rhetoric about correct Indianness," while making an argument for the cultural hybridity at the heart of Indian literature. In an analogous way, Rushdie rebels against the absurd notion of a pre-existent "pure, unalloyed tradition" from which Indian writing springs, preferring instead to evoke images of intermingling. Indian culture is a mixture of many different influences:

> [W]e possess a mixed tradition, a *mélange* of elements as disparate as ancient Mughal and contemporary Coca-Cola American. To say nothing of Muslim, Buddhist, Jain, Christian, Jewish, British, French, Portuguese, Marxist, Maoist,

Trotskyist, Vietnamese, capitalist, and of course Hindu elements. Eclecticism, the ability to take from the world what seems fitting and to leave the rest, has always been a hallmark of the Indian tradition .... ("Commonwealth" 67)

Rushdie returns to this argument during an interview conducted by Una Chaudhuri when he contrasts his own understanding of "Indian tradition" with E.M. Forster's vision of irreconcilable cultural territories in the novel *A Passage to India* (1924). Forster's novel construed the subcontinent, in Rushdie's phrasing, as "containing lots of different, separate cultures which collide," set against the backdrop of the British Raj; furthermore, Rushdie vehemently objects to what he regards as the artificial creation of "a kind of pure Indian tradition," positing instead that "the tradition of India is a mixed tradition" (qtd. in U. Chaudhuri 23–24). The fallacy of a "pure" Indianness is again articulated in *The Satanic Verses* through the character of the Bombay socialite and art critic Zeeny Vakil. Opposed to myths of authenticity, Zeeny contends that the palimpsestic and syncretic characteristics of "original" Indian tradition are the inevitable outcome of hybridity. The presupposition that Indian culture is inescapably the result of cultural imbrications and eclecticism leads Zeeny to formulate the simple but relevant question: "Why should there be a good, right way of being a wog?" (52). In her critical work *The Only Good Indian* – a provocative title which contributed to the negative reaction it received – Zeeny seeks to replace "the confining myth of authenticity, that folkloristic straitjacket" by "an ethic of historically validated eclecticism," for, as the narrator posits, "the entire national culture [was] based on the principle of borrowing whatever clothes seemed to fit, Aryan, Mughal, British, take-the-best-and-leave-the-rest" (52).

One cannot disregard the extent to which the publishing of *The Vintage Book*, which coincided with the fiftieth anniversary of Indian political independence, was driven by the dictates of corporate profit. As Tarun Tejpal perceptively observes in a review of *The Vintage Book* entitled "Rushdie and the Sea of Prejudice" (a fairly obvious pun on the title of Rushdie's novel *Haroun and the Sea of Stories*):

> Since celebrity and commerce are inextricably linked in the modern world, publishers need big names as anthologists. It's doubly helpful if the big name also writes some kind of introductory essay, tying up his material and its themes – the essay then becoming a kind of template for whatever the arbitrary grouping yoked together. In this scenario, Vintage Books, UK, have managed to put together the ultimate masala: a huge occasion, 50 years of Indian independence; the most happening camp in world literature, Indians writing in English; and stirring it together as anthologist and essayist, the most famous Indian writer in the world, Salman Rushdie.

In this respect, Huggan regards the overabundance of highly publicized celebratory products and events surrounding India's fiftieth-year anniversary festivities as part of a "spectacularising" phenomenon. It is interesting to note against this backdrop that Rushdie was barred from the Indian Consulate's celebrations of the fiftieth anniversary of independence in New York ("Dream" 196). Besides *The Vintage Book*, Huggan includes the "50 Years of Independence" issue of the magazine *Granta* and the special fiction edition of *The New Yorker* devoted to Indian writing in a strand of products marketed to coincide with the Golden Jubilee year, to which one can add Divakaruni's novel *The Mistress of Spices*.

Besides authors and editors, other major players involved in a western-led process of the canonisation of Indian writing must now take centre stage: publishers, booksellers, marketers, sponsors (such as Booker Plc), reviewers, and the critical industry in general located in the West. As hinted by Chaudhuri in an article originally published in the *Times Literary Supplement* in 1999 and later reprinted in *The Picador Book* as one of the introductory essays, canon-formation is guided by "the assumptions that inform the expectations of publishers, writers and critics, even when they haven't been consciously articulated by them" ("Construction" xxiv). Elsewhere, in an essay published two years earlier, Chaudhuri cautions: "How much of the resurgence [in Indian writing (in English)] has to be with what publishers in England consider the marketability of Indian fiction, and how much of it is genuine achievement, will take at least twenty or thirty years, or more, to decide" ("Modernity" xvii). As Rushdie observes, the fact that in 1997 "Western publishers and critics [had] been growing gradually more and more excited by the voices emerging from India" ("Introduction" xiv) verifies the critical relevance of examining the role of these agents in shaping audiences' expectations and tastes. It is observed by Rushdie that "some 'home' commentators" might even feel "a canon is being foisted on them from outside" on account of "the power of the English language, and of the Western publishing and critical fraternities" (xiv). The author takes note of the Indian critiques of IWE which disparaged it as: "being less popular in India than outside India; for possessing inflated reputations on account of the international power of the English language, and of the ability of Western critics and publishers to impose their cultural standards on the East; for living, in many cases, outside India; ... for being the literary equivalent of MTV culture, of globalising Coca-Colonisation" (xiii). An example of this is Chaudhuri's reproach of the metonymical representation of Indian literature by a select body of work created by "a handful of writers who write in English, who live in England or America and whom one might have met at a party, most of whom have published no more than two novels, some of them only one" ("Modernity" xvii).

Rushdie's and West's anthology might well be construed as a device for reinforcing the presence of IWE in the global literary marketplace, at the same time as it actually shaped an idea of India and its literature. Paradoxically, the marketing of *The Vintage Book* as a national anthology further contributed to limiting western awareness of Indian writing to an elite group of writers recognized worldwide with Rushdie prominently at their head. Consecrated as *the* Indian postcolonial literary icon, the author is endowed with the cultural authority to select Indian literary texts that might appeal to a designated target readership explicitly located "outside India." A veneer of cultural authority (or authenticity) is highly desirable in the marketing of a product such as *The Vintage Book*. It is relevant to recall here that Rushdie's Booker prize in 1981 and Booker of Bookers in 1993 with *Midnight's Children* not only promoted the writer's ascent to the status of postcolonial literary icon, but also reinforced the hypervisibility of Indian fiction written in English in the context of a global literary marketplace. *The New York Times* sings the novel's praise thus: "The literary map of India is about to be redrawn. ... *Midnight's Children* sounds like a continent finding its voice" (Blaise) – a voice, one might add, that expresses itself in English. The London Review of Books characterizes it as "[a] brilliant and endearing novel, the latest of India's many contributions to English fiction, and the most remarkable of them all."[16] Harold Bloom, in a self-defined act of cultural prophecy (548), includes *Midnight's Children* in the appendixes to *The Western Canon* (1994), accompanied by R.K. Narayan's *The Guide* (1958) and Ruth Prawer Jhabvala's *Heat and Dust* (1975), further building and consolidating the novel's canonical status. Moreover, Rushdie's and Jhabvala's novels were recipients of the Booker Prize, whose relevance in the canonisation of postcolonial writing tradition has already been addressed.

In a review of Amitav Ghosh's novel *Sea of Poppies*, Shashi Tharoor uses an overtly celebratory tone when describing the influence of *Midnight's Children* on the development of IWE:

> Since the publication of Salman Rushdie's *Midnight's Children* in 1981, a new and ancient land has imposed itself on the world's literary consciousness, – a land whose language and concerns have stretched the boundaries of the possible in English literature. A generation of post-colonial Indian writers has brought a larger world – a teeming, myth infused, gaudy, exuberant, many-hued and restless world – past the immigration inspectors of English literature. Today it seems no year goes by without yet another Indian novel announcing its entry into the global canon. ("Soldiers")

One of the stated aims of Rushdie's and West's anthology is to "showcase the quality of a growing collective *oeuvre* whose status has been long argued over, but which has ... begun to merit a place alongside the most flourishing literatures in the world" ("Introduction" xi–xii). As demonstrated in the section "The Postcolonial Card" of the previous chapter, much of the desirability of IWE authors to western publishing houses in the 1990s, which drew them into the visibility of belonging to what Tharoor dubs the "global canon," was enhanced by Rushdie's commercial and critical success, the latter being inextricably connected to a bestowal of canonicity on the part of the western literary establishment. *The Vintage Book*, co-edited by someone who is, by many accounts, the most critically acclaimed and canonical postcolonial writer, was certainly one of the instruments that aided that "growing collective *oeuvre*," in Rushdie's phrasing, to enter the parameters of global circulation, further promoted by its accommodation in university curricula under the aegis of postcolonial studies.

---

[16] See back cover of the 1995 Vintage edition.

"Consecrated" texts, such as *Midnight's Children*, and "canonized" authors, such as Rushdie, display, as Huggan points out, "a simulacrum of scriptural authority," but both are inescapably "products of *secular* institutional processes" (*Postcolonial Exotic* 212). In this sense, Tejpal stresses that the post-*Midnight's Children* "flowering of talent" is also the outgrowth of the influence of "media and money" ("Rushdie"). While Rushdie has been an active stakeholder in the promotional circuit of postcolonial publishing, and his and West's anthology contributed to feed the burgeoning western interest in IWE, these were not the sole agents of legitimation involved in an intricate process wherein several stakeholders grant cultural authority and/or boost commercial success. Without question inspired by Rushdie's canonical aura, *The New Yorker* arranged for a family photo of "India's leading novelists" in a special fiction issue on the occasion of the fiftieth anniversary of the country's independence in 1997. *The New Yorker* was in this sense also responsible for regulating the establishment of a post-independence Indian literary star system in the late 1990s. With Rushdie strategically placed at the centre (because the literary star system, as any star system, involves a hierarchy), the photo (whose caption reads "A gathering of India's leading novelists") features, on the bottom row, Vikram Chandra, Rohinton Mistry, Arundhati Roy, and Anita Desai, and, on the top row, Kiran Desai, Ardashir Vakil, Vikram Seth, Amitav Ghosh, the Sri Lankan author Romesh Gunesekera, and Amit Chaudhuri. Because they followed in the writer's wake, these "leading novelists" had been dubbed by *The New York Times* as "Rushdie's Children" in 1991 (C. Singh 215). Alternatively (and belittlingly), Pankaj Mishra called this India-born literary elite a "set of defective clones" who imitate Rushdie (Schürer 84), and diagnosed these younger Indian authors as being afflicted with a "Rushdie-itis" infection, a "condition that has claimed Rushdie himself in his later works" (Rushdie "Introduction" xiii). The writer himself facetiously concedes to having been a victim of this spreading virus: "As to the claims of excessive Rushdie-itis, I can't deny that I've on occasion felt something of the sort myself. On the whole, however, it seems to be a short-lived virus, and those whom it affects soon shake it off and find their own, true voices" (xvi).

Rushdie, consecrated as a literary celebrity as early as the 1980s, is deemed responsible for the boom in IWE, while feeding upon this boom in a self-perpetuating process. An illustrative example of this is his endorsing of young authors such as Booker-prize winner Kiran Desai. If Anglophone western book publishers structure global tastes by setting trends and creating literary celebrities, fame in Rushdie's case was created by exploiting western institutions and global market forces. Indeed, the writer's symbolic power has been gathered through a "cumulative process of legitimation" (Huggan, *Postcolonial Exotic* 212) that involves, as seen in the previous chapter, different kinds of cultural currencies: the fame of the bestseller status, the prestige of the critical praise, the recognition of the literary prizes, and the legitimacy of academic consecration. This process of canonisation was built through the actions of diverse stakeholders – critics, prize juries, reviewers, and even PhD candidates – to be then used in the creation and marketing of cultural products such as *The Vintage Book*. Damrosch claims that, in "world literature" (which he defines as "works that are read and discussed beyond home-country and area-specialist audiences"), "as in some literary Miss Universe competition, an entire nation may be represented by a single author" ("World Literature" 48). Mishra's diagnosis of "Rushdie-itis" affecting not only IWE, but Rushdie himself, might then be understood as a backlash against the subsumption of the writer's work in the western canon – or, to use Damrosch's term, in a western-guided "hypercanon" – a subsumption assisted at least in part by the transnational response to the writer as a native informant or cultural representative of the Indian subcontinent.

Damrosch distinguishes between the "hypercanon" and the "countercanon," the first constituted by "the older 'major' authors who have held their own or even gained ground over the past twenty years," and the latter by "subaltern and 'contestatory' voices of writers in languages less commonly taught and in minor literatures within great-power languages" ("World Literature" 45), but which have nonetheless achieved a sizeable amount of cultural capital through critical recognition and commercial viability in the West. The idea of a "hypercanon" supplemented by the "countercanon" seems to be at the basis of Bloom's inclusion of *Midnight's Children* under the section "India (In English)" in his *The Western Canon*. Judging from the number of articles and books listed in the *MLA Bibliography* about postcolonial writers during the period 1964–2003, Damrosch notes that Rushdie "is by far the leader," followed by Chinua Achebe and Derek Walcott, of a group of authors belonging to a newfangled postcolonial hypercanon ("World Literature" 48). According to the critic's reasoning, because of Rushdie's current prominence in the postcolonial literary marketplace, authors such as R.K. Narayan are upstaged (48) and relegated to a "shadow canon" composed of "old 'minor' authors who fade increasingly into the background" (45).

In conclusion, both *The Vintage Book* and *The Picador Book* aim to re-present to their (western) readers previously overlooked Indian authors and texts. Examining the links these anthologies maintain to the process of canon-formation gives us a privileged glimpse into the wars raging on the Indian literature front. To compare and contrast different understandings of "Indian literature" is inevitable. Is there a way out of this impasse? One of the contenders in these canon wars offers what seems to be quite a sensible route: Indian literature "must be a continual work, and product, of the imagination; we must believe it when we encounter it, in the special way we believe in all fictions" (Chaudhuri, "Travels" 144–145).

Chapter 3
Film and Television:
Showcasing Pictures of India

During a conversation with filmmaker David Cronenberg, Rushdie, on one of the numerous occasions when he has reiterated the shaping influence cinema has had on his work, stated: "I've always said, and I think it's true, that movies had more impact on me than novels in a kind of formational way" (qtd. in Cronenberg 168). Cinema is thus in many respects central to the discussion of Rushdie's work. In the words of Vijay Mishra, "[a]ny study of Rushdie remains incomplete, indeed deficient, if not seen through the literature of migration and cinema" (11); Mishra further suggests that "[n]arrative as shooting script … holds the key to Rushdie's narrative technique" (19). As Rushdie confesses, watching Bombay-produced Hindi films "is entertainment of course, … but this also nourishes" (qtd. in Marzorati). The writer's employment of different cinematic intertexts has only recently begun to be addressed by critics who have however tended to focus on the Bombay cinema intertext.[1] Indian cinema, and in particular Bombay talkies, plays a major role in Rushdie's work. The author's engagement with a western cinematic intertext is no less extensive and its relevance to his work demands consideration. Indeed, in Rushdie's monograph on *The Wizard of Oz* he revealed that Fleming's 1939 film had been his first literary influence, not L. Frank Baum's 1900 novel *The Wonderful Wizard of Oz*, and went on to add that when he first saw the film it made a writer of him ("Short Tale" 18). As alluded to in the introduction, in the first case study of Rushdie's cultural brokerism, that screening inspired him, at the age of ten, to write his first story, entitled *Over the Rainbow*, which "was about a ten-year-old Bombay boy who one day happens upon a rainbow's beginning, a place as elusive as any pot-of-gold end-zone, and as rich in promises" (9). Moreover, the writer recalled, "when the possibility of going to school in England was mentioned, it felt as exciting as any voyage beyond rainbows. … England felt as wonderful a prospect as Oz" (9).

*****

The subject of this chapter is Rushdie's film and TV criticism, in particular his critique of what he labelled the "Raj revival." Ultimately, the present chapter is haunted by wondering how one would effectively ground political action towards collective change and cultural self-fashioning in a field of representation inexorably dominated by insidious and pervading media screens. On the whole,

---

[1] See Chordiya; V. Mishra; and Ramachandran; a notable exception is Thieme "Few Rainbows."

it looks at the roles films and TV series, included in or revisiting the Raj revival, play in the processes of an ever-increasing consumption of India-related images. It begins by probing the writer's critique of the 2008 film *Slumdog Millionaire* as a form of "slum tourism" and then returns to the essay "Outside the Whale" (1984), where Rushdie's arguments on the allure of the colonial Indian past for the British media in the 1980s – of TV series and films as "Raj tourism" – were initially penned. Against Rushdie's and Arundhati Roy's unfavourable reading of *Slumdog Millionaire* as a glamorized exhibition of Dark India – at times irrespective of a few subtleties – the following section considers if it might be possible to discern a self-ironic stance towards representations of the so-called Real India in Boyle's incorporation of Bollywood motifs into his film.

India Unshining[2]

> Our bars and city streets, our offices and furnished rooms, our railroad stations and our factories seemed to close relentlessly around us. Then came the film and exploded this prison-world with the dynamite of the split second, so that now we can set off calmly on journeys of adventure among its far-flung debris.
> —Walter Benjamin, "The Work of Art in the Age of Its Technological Reproducibility" 265

Danny Boyle's *Slumdog Millionaire*[3] adopts a multiple-choice question format as hook, acknowledging from the outset the quiz show *Who Wants to Be a Millionaire* as narrative backdrop. In the film's opening scenes, a series of cutaway shots from *Kaun Banega Crorepati* (the Indian version of the British format) are interspersed with a close-up of the protagonist's face as he is being tortured by the police on suspicion of fraud in the show. Jamal Malik, the lead character, who grew up as an orphaned street urchin in the slums of Mumbai, is at present an 18-year-old call-centre "assistant phone basher" competing on *Who Wants to Be a Millionaire*. In a nutshell, *Slumdog Millionaire* narrates how the incredible turns of the hero's life allow him to know nearly all the correct answers in the quiz show. At an early stage in the film, the viewer is approached as if she was herself a contestant and asked how Jamal, a "chai-wallah" with no formal education, could be one question away from winning twenty million rupees. According to the options provided, a) he cheated, b) he is lucky, c) he is a genius, or d) it is written. The motif of a multiple-choice question is replayed in the poster and trailer, and on the official website (where visitors could even create their own quiz) in taglines designed

---

[2] This section is a revised and expanded version of the article "Showcasing India Unshining: Film Tourism in Danny Boyle's *Slumdog Millionaire*," *Third Text*, 105, July 2010, published with the permission of Taylor & Francis.

[3] The global acclaim received by the film, a worldwide box-office and award success, is for the most part exclusively credited to the British filmmaker. Despite Loveleen Tandan's role as casting director and later co-director, *Slumdog Millionaire* is "a Danny Boyle film," as the closing credits make clear.

again as questions with a–d listed alternatives. Within an aggressive advertising campaign, this recurrent design is also used on the front cover of the Black Swan edition of *Q & A*, the 2005 novel by the Indian writer and diplomat Vikas Swarup on which the script for *Slumdog Millionaire* was based. *Q & A* was republished in late 2008 by Black Swan as a film tie-in and was then suitably retitled as *Slumdog Millionaire*; the revamped cover includes a picture of Jamal and Latika, the romantic couple from the film, showered with party confetti (instead of a young, apparently penniless waiter holding a tray in the 2006 edition), and Danny Boyle's name in block capital letters of nearly the same size as those used for the novelist's name.

The multiple-choice question is thus the visual clue that ties the film to the novel and assists in turning viewers into readers. In the film, through this device of the multiple-choice question purportedly similar to the structure underlying the quiz show *Who Wants to Be a Millionaire*, audiences are encouraged to engage actively in the viewing experience. Indeed, viewers are able to test their expectations regarding the film. Furthermore, the role of destiny – the fact that Jamal's saga might be "written" – is consistently highlighted throughout these different sites, despite slight variations in the alternatives provided (for example, the film poster poses the question "What does it take to find a lost love?" and the answers are: "A: Money / B: Luck / C: Smarts / D: Destiny"). By being the last option in the multiple-choice question, the relevance of destiny to the storyline leaves its imprint in the audiences' memory of *Slumdog Millionaire*. Viewers of quiz shows are, according to John Fiske, "positioned *actively* towards the text by its unwrittenness, its sense of a time span in which the present and future are equal for both characters and viewers" (273). Even if *Who Wants to Be a Millionaire* provides the structural inspiration for Boyle's film, the emphasis rests on the *writtenness* of Jamal's achievement, and by extension of his upward social mobility, as opposed to the *unwrittenness* that Fiske attributes to quiz shows.

In a parodic rewriting of the film's narrative hook, the critic Dennis Lim asks: "What, Exactly, Is *Slumdog Millionaire*?" He then proceeds to offer his own a–d alternatives: "a) a portrait of the real India, b) a Bollywood-style melodrama, c) a fairy tale, or d) a stylishly shot collection of clichés." This section borrows from Lim's multiple-choice question and his list of alternative answers to probe the critical reception of *Slumdog Millionaire* with particular emphasis on the unflattering reviews penned by Rushdie and Arundhati Roy, whose opinions roughly fall under Lim's last option. Interrelatedly, it then explores the use of Bollywood's staple techniques in the closing scene of *Slumdog Millionaire*. Boyle's film might be seen as "a Bollywood-style melodrama," as Lim has it in his second option. In the sense that the final song and dance tableau might be construed as a tourist showcasing of Bollywood suited to a western gaze, it is analized as exemplary of the tourist dynamics Rushdie detects in the film. Ultimately, cinematic representations of Indian poverty have been by and large open to allegations of aestheticising and showcasing squalor for artistic and commercial purposes. The concern in this section is not to reiterate these allegations in relation to *Slumdog Millionaire*, but to attempt a critical analysis of the film that reaches beyond the glamorized visual frame, an analysis that looks past its supposedly romanticized images of photogenic and picturesque poverty themselves to scrutinize the modes of circulation of these representations in the field of cultural production.

As Lim's answer options quoted above disclose, *Slumdog Millionaire* has been read in diverse and conflicting ways. In the midst of the near-unanimous praise of the film, quite a few discordant voices (the most audible at the time of the film's release being that of Bollywood's veteran celebrity Amitabh Bachchan, the original host of the Indian version of *Who Wants to Be a Millionaire*[4]) took issue with the exploitative "poverty porn" that exoticized and packaged Indian slum life for the consumption of voyeuristic western audiences. These criticisms directed at *Slumdog Millionaire* are very similar to those levelled earlier against Adiga's *The White Tiger*, as examined in the previous chapter. Both film and novel received mixed reviews and the most forceful critiques suggested that they replicated orientalist images of India – as an intensely poverty-stricken and corrupt country where impoverished but resilient locals fight for their lives among the corruption and the squalor. While some commentators read *The White Tiger* as part of a western conspiracy to curb enthusiasm about India's tiger economy (even if Adiga's satirical portrait also extends to China when his protagonist confronts the Chinese Premier thus: "I gather you yellow-skinned men, despite your triumphs in sewage, drinking water, and Olympic gold medals, still don't have democracy" [80]), others argued that Boyle's romanticisation of poverty was damaging the image of an emerging superpower (Kapur).

The India painstakingly represented by Adiga in *The White Tiger* and Boyle in *Slumdog Millionaire* is a jungle that can only breed "white tigers" and "slumdogs."[5] The print media in India was, on the one hand, the preferred site for the vilification of Boyle's allegedly inauthentic depiction of life in the squalid slums of Mumbai and, on the other hand, the ground for the discursive authorisation of an authentic portrait of Indian reality or, alternatively, of India as *Indians* perceive it. In this respect, Shyamal Sengupta bluntly states that *Slumdog Millionaire* is "not quite snake charmers, but it's close" (Magnier), while Tejpal, writing in the Indian magazine *Tehelka*, accuses Boyle of constructing "one more representation of India as the white man sees it, not as we do" ("Missionary Position"). Similarly to the protagonist Balram's rise from Darkness to Light in *The White Tiger*, *Slumdog Millionaire* depicts a rags-to-riches story, or "rags to raja," as Jason Solomons put

---

[4] Revealingly, Ramani's appearance in Rushdie's "The Free Radio" is compared to that of famous Bollywood actors such as Amitabh Bachchan: "Such a handsome chap, compared to you Shashi Kapoor and Amitabh (arguably two of the greatest Bollywood stars of the seventies) are like lepers only, you should go to Bombay and be put in the motion pictures" (22).

[5] "Dog," or "kutta," possesses a highly derogatory meaning in Hindi, and some slum residents have taken exception to being called "slumdogs" (Lim).

it in *The Observer*. The thematic affinities between novel and film extend to the fact that while Adiga's narrative was hailed as an heir to the novels of Dickens, Boyle's lead character was described by a reviewer from the *Washington Post* as "a young David Copperfield transported in time and place to the dizzying, impoverished, improbably beguiling city of Mumbai"; nonetheless, if the film "plays like Charles Dickens for the 21st century," there are still striking differences: "the stench and soot of Victorian England have been replaced by the Tata fumes and computer-screen glow that envelop a country in the throes of profound economic and cultural change" (Hornaday).

The hype around an increasingly affluent India and its booming high-tech industry – which has yet to result in a nationwide upgrade in most people's standard of living – has been almost entirely built around the slogan "India Shining." Through the eyes of Adiga's entrepreneur-narrator, the reader is taken on a tour of the many shadowy sides of the story of India Shining. This political motto was coined for the 2004 Indian general elections campaign by the then ruling nationalist Bharatiya Janata Party (BJP) to sell an idea of economic optimism and advertize the country's achievements abroad. India Unshining takes centre stage in *The White Tiger* – as Balram duly explains to the reader, his country, "though it has no drinking water, electricity, sewage system, public transportation, sense of hygiene, discipline, courtesy, or punctuality, *does* have entrepreneurs" (4). Balram remakes India Shining in his own criminal and corrupt image. Like Adiga's novel, *Slumdog Millionaire* brazenly displays India's underbelly – "the colossal underclass," in the novelist's words (qtd. in Datta) – as the reverse side of the much-vaunted India Shining. Most relevantly, these representations undermine a sanitized portrait of India's recent economic prosperity. In fact, the day after the film won four Golden Globe awards, *The Times of India* announced that India Shining was being replaced by the tagline "Indian Underbelly Shining" fashioned by Adiga's novel and Boyle's film. As Meena Iyer and Anubha Sawhney Joshi explain, "the unpalatable realities of asli [real] India are up there under the strobe lights for the world to gaze on. From snot-nosed children to the oppressive caste system, it's fodder that is being reloaded anew." *The White Tiger* strips away the veneer of India Shining not only by displaying, but also by unmasking the bleaker side of the country's rise as economic powerhouse. *Slumdog Millionaire* is, unlike Adiga's novel, ultimately an acclamation of India Shining despite its perceived engagement in a pornographic voyeurism of Indian poverty. In Roy's reasoning, the essentially upbeat portrait of the exhilarating life in the Mumbai slums projected by the film stems from the blatant commodification of India Unshining: "*Slumdog Millionaire* does not puncture the myth of 'India shining' – far from it. It just turns India 'not-shining' into another glitzy item in the supermarket" ("Caught on Film"). This much can be anticipated through the paradox contained in the film's title – after all, an underdog from a Mumbai slum manages to survive a childhood of destitution and abuse to become a millionaire, and in the process win nationwide fame and get his childhood sweetheart back, mirroring the narrative of India Shining.

Jamal's success is not predicated on murdering his employer and escaping with stolen money, as Balram's was in *The White Tiger*, but rather on excavating his poverty-stricken past, being persistent, competing on a quiz show, and being lucky. Unlike the protagonist of Adiga's novel who sees himself as the monstrous by-product of the crime and corruption afflicting Indian society, the resourceful Jamal rises up from misery morally unblemished with the help of *Who Wants to Be a Millionaire*. In this sense, Roy criticizes Boyle's film for failing to accurately portray the struggles of the Indian working class and instead "giv[ing] false hope to the poor that they too could become millionaires one day" (qtd. in Vohra). Tejpal unmasks likewise what he regards as "the carnival of implausibility" at the heart of the storyline: "The film tells a very big lie: that India's poor have a happy shot at leaping out of their misery into affluence and joy." The improbability of such a plot is also made apparent in Rushdie's "The Free Radio" through Ramani's fantasy of Bollywood fame and in Adiga's *The White Tiger*, whose lead character goes from rags to riches, but only through illicit means. Tejpal alludes to the inauthenticity of Jamal's voice, along lines similar to those used to attack *The White Tiger*: "you see the slum child Jamal grow into a refined public schoolboy who must surely be eating cucumber sandwiches for lunch. India's wannabe wealthy – billionaires among them – would slice their fingers to boast such a sophisticated son. For that accent alone, they would throw in their toes too" ("Missionary Position"). Both Tejpal and Roy accuse Boyle's rags-to-riches story of bypassing class politics given that, in the end, what *Slumdog Millionaire* is selling is, according to Roy:

> ... the cheapest version of the Great Capitalist dream in which politics is replaced by a game show, a lottery in which the dreams of one person come true while, in the process, the dreams of millions of others are usurped, immobilizing them with the drug of impossible hope (work hard, be good, with a little bit of luck you could be a millionaire). ("Caught on Film")

In keeping with this argument, the film's suggestion that destitution and child abuse can be overcome through perseverance, an international TV format, and "a little bit of luck" effectively cancels and settles an apparently dark picture.[6]

Similarly to the charges directed at Adiga, Boyle was faulted for framing *Slumdog Millionaire*, a low-budget transnational production financed by Hollywood's Fox Searchlight and British companies, "within the matrix of

---

[6] Fiske frames the discourse of luck within the hegemonic structure of capitalist (and of necessity competitive) societies: "The structure of such [capitalist] societies is necessarily hierarchical and elitist, they are like a pyramid with the mass of people at the bottom and very few at the top. Yet the dominant ideology insists that everyone has a chance to rise through the class, economic, and power systems. ... In the 'rags to riches' story which is such a potent myth in capitalist societies ..., hard work and luck are interdependent elements: work and dedication which make the most of 'natural' talents rely on the luck of being in the right place at the right time, or of a chance meeting with the right person, to provide the opportunities for that talent to flourish" (270).

Western lib-left perceptions of the Indian 'reality' which have little or nothing in common with the *real* India in which we [Indians] live" (Gupta). This comment can be seen as an iteration of the controversy surrounding the highly-regarded neorealist films of Satyajit Ray in the 1950s. Ray was then criticized in India for misrepresenting the "reality" of the country to cater to the expectations of western audiences in works such as *Pather Panchali,* or *The Song of the Little Road* (1955). Ray's debut arthouse film about an impoverished family from a Bengali village is the first part of *The Apu Trilogy* and portrays the childhood of the main character Apu in the rural Bengal of the 1920s. *Pather Panchali* is commonly regarded as the first film from post-independence India to garner major critical attention abroad and to throw into the spotlight the plight of India's poor. Even if this film faced severe opposition from some quarters within the West Bengal Government and the Government of India in Delhi because of its rendering of poverty in rural Bengal – and consequently because of the potential damage to India's international image – it was sent to the Cannes Film Festival in 1956, where it won the prize for Best Human Document (Robinson 104). Besides this accolade, *Pather Panchali* won the Indian President's Gold and Silver Medals in 1955, and another 10 prestigious international awards (Cooper 4).[7] At the time, some critics celebrated Ray's achievement with *Pather Panchali* as a window on to the real India, while others criticized what they took to be the peddling of deprivation to win foreign awards (Cooper 2).

Bollywood actress Nargis Dutt, who played the protagonist in the celebrated film *Mother India* (dir. Mehboob Khan, 1957) and who became a member of the Indian Parliament in the 1980s, was the most visible face of the resentment in some sections of Indian society concerning Ray's success in the West (Robinson 327–328). It is relevant to note that the film *Mother India* was seen as part of a nation-building project, as Rushdie observes:

> *Mother India* ... was the big attempt to make a kind of *Gone With the Wind* myth of the nation, and took the biggest movie star in India at the time, Nargis, and asked her, basically, to impersonate the nation. And the nation was invented as a village woman who triumphed over horrible hardships. (qtd. in MacCabe 215)

During an interview, quoted at length in Rushdie's essay on Ray, Nargis vehemently states that *Pather Panchali* did not accurately portray so-called "Modern India," if

---

[7] Likewise, Mira Nair's *Salaam Bombay!*, set in the squalid red-light district of Mumbai, received the Golden Camera and Audience Awards at the Cannes Film Festival in 1988, besides a nomination for the Academy Award for Best Foreign Language Film in 1989. Nair's directorial debut attempts to expose the hidden world of street urchins living on the pavements of Mumbai. More recently, *Born into Brothels: Calcutta's Red Light Kids*, directed by Ross Kauffman and Zana Briski in 2004, depicting the lives of the children of prostitutes who work in the red-light district of Calcutta, won the Oscar for Best Documentary Feature in 2005.

only because it did not echo the Nehruvian vision of dams as the temples of post-independence India:

> NARGIS: Why do you think films like *Pather Panchali* become popular abroad? ... Because people there want to see India in an abject condition. That is the image they have of our country and a film that confirms that image seems to them authentic.
>
> INTERVIEWER: But why should a renowned director like Ray do such a thing?
>
> NARGIS: To win awards. His films are not commercially successful. They only win awards ... What I want is that if Mr Ray projects Indian poverty abroad, he should also show 'Modern India'.
>
> INTERVIEWER: What is 'Modern India'?
>
> NARGIS: Dams ... ("Satyajit Ray" 108–109)

Nehru's vision led to the proliferation of dams in the country after independence (Varma 67). If dams embody post-independence Indian modernity, as they became a symbol of faith in India's technical progress, the railway is a symbol of pre-independence modernity brought by British colonial rule. Perhaps because the train is today an inescapable reality in India (and as such contributing to verify viewers' expectations regarding a film whose setting is India) there is a railway scene, important plot-wise, in which, to the sound of the music of British-born Sri Lankan superstar M.I.A., Jamal and his brother Salim try to make a living while riding on a train. One of the most celebrated sequences in *Pather Panchali* is precisely the train scene, where the lead character Apu and his sister Durga stare at a train in trepidation and awe.

Slumdog Millionaire is structured to be effortlessly decipherable by non-Indian viewers. A fast-paced editing, scored to A.R. Rahman's soundtrack, displays a readily identifiable landscape made up of recognisable images such as the labyrinthine slums, the skyscrapers, and the call centres of megalopolis Mumbai. The film also features cultural icons such as Victoria Station in Mumbai and the Taj Mahal in Agra. Rushdie unveils the exotic cachet of the latter thus:

> The trouble with the Taj Mahal is that it has become so overlaid with accumulated meanings as to be almost impossible to see. ... It sits at the top of the West's short list of images of the Exotic (and also Timeless) Orient. Like the Mona Lisa, like Andy Warhol's screenprinted Elvis, Marilyn and Mao, mass reproduction has all but sterilized the Taj. ("Taj Mahal" 186)

The fact that the Taj Mahal is the setting for swindling naïve western tourists might problematize the accumulated meanings of "the Exotic (and also Timeless) Orient" that the monument evokes according to Rushdie. Furthermore, such an unadorned portrait self-reflexively contributes to questioning the authenticity of western representations of India; indeed, the Germanic-looking tourists' failure to differentiate between a street urchin and a licensed guide discloses an ironic posture regarding such images. The issue of authenticity and its relationship with tourism is resumed when Jamal takes a couple of American tourists on a tour of the Mahalaxmi area known as Dhobi Ghat, the largest outdoor laundry in India, a tourist attraction in Mumbai. "Let's have a real look at this," one of the tourists says with self-satisfaction. Meanwhile, with Jamal's knowledge, their rental Mercedes is pillaged and stripped for parts. "You wanted to see a bit of real India? You're in it!" he shouts at the couple while he is being beaten by the Indian driver. Interestingly (self-ironically so), a reverse scene features the staff of the call centre where the protagonist works during a training session as they are being given an update on the Kat and Alfie storyline (named after fictional characters in the popular BBC soap opera *EastEnders*) while viewing a slideshow of iconic pictures of the UK. The purpose of this session focusing on various typified sights of Britain is, one suspects, to help the "phone-bashers" better visualize the landscapes of their customers' country, presumably Scotland, through stereotypical images such as kilts, Ben Nevis, the highest mountain in the British Isles, and "lochs," "their word for 'lakes'".

In the inaugural scene, depicting Jamal and his brother being chased by the police through the alleyways of a Mumbai slum, Boyle's seductive visual style and camera work, energized by the rhythmic pounding and drumming of the song "O… Saya" by Rahman and M.I.A., convey an exoticized spectacle of slum life as vibrant and enticing, but also chaotic, as well as dangerous and traumatic. The final aerial shot of the sun-soaked corrugated iron shacks of the Juhu shantytown in Mumbai contributes to this cinematographic fetishisation of slum experience. Through sound and sight – with a soundtrack flavoured with Indian melodies and intense filming resulting from the frequent use of the editing techniques of fast cutting, cross-cutting, cutaway, and cutback – images of the tightly packed spaces of a Mumbai slum are manipulated so that the gaze falls upon what the gazer expects to see. As Lim contends, "[i]f *Slumdog* has struck a chord, and it certainly seems to have done so in the West, it is not because the film is some newfangled post-globalization hybrid but precisely because there is nothing new about it. It traffics in some of the oldest stereotypes of the exoticized Other: the streetwise urchin in the teeming Oriental city." Using a double foreignising and domesticating process, *Slumdog Millionaire* projects the enticement of foreign, exotic difference as it domesticates it by incorporating this now known other into the circuits of image consumption through film tourism.

Walter Benjamin's fascination with the art of film is partially based on his perception that the cinema screen permits audiences (in particular the flâneur) to access diverse and often distant geographical spaces without leaving the comfort of their seats and, one might add, facing the potential perils of travel. Departing from Benjamin's contention that the filmic image facilitates a virtual sense of travel, Anne Friedberg discusses "the imaginary flânerie of cinema spectatorship" (3) and argues for the centrality of a *"mobilized 'virtual' gaze"* as a feature of cinematic and televisual apparatuses (2). Friedberg further sustains her use of the compound term "*mobilized 'virtual' gaze*" by explaining that the "*virtual gaze* is not a direct perception but a *received* perception mediated through representation," whereas the roots of the mobilized gaze lie in "cultural activities that involve walking and travel" (2). Not unrelatedly, a reviewer includes "The Tourist Factor" in the list of what he identifies as the "six secrets of 'Slumdog' success":

> For those whose only exposure to India might have been phone calls to customer service and the odd curry dinner, "Slumdog" is an eye-opener. Boyle resisted stepping back and shooting the movie like a travelogue. Instead, he thrusts the audience into a street-level view of the sights and sounds of India – from the slum's crowded back alleys to the new gleaming towers of Mumbai, from the Taj Mahal to a stomach-churning outhouse. When you watch "Slumdog," *you feel like you've been to India*. (Crow; emphasis added)

As such, the experience of viewing *Slumdog Millionaire* might be construed as a form of armchair tourism where audiences engage in tourist "window shopping" without moving from their seats. For example, the idea of travelling to India through the consumption of cultural commodities recurs in the trend-setting list "Haute List: Yay Bombay" published in *The New York Post* in April 2008: "For spring/summer 2008, the Subcontinent and its neighbors might be the hautest place on Earth. ... O.P.I.'s spring/summer collection ... "India" – come in colors like "Royal Rajah Ruby," "Curry Up, Don't Be Late" and "I'm Indi-A Mood for Love". ... At the Hermes store ... catch "The Home and the World," a collection of photographs from Indian photographers Raghubir Singh and Dayanita Singh. ... *It's cheaper than a flight to Mumbai* – just" (Mirchandani and Lo; emphasis added). Besides the blatant commodification of India, and notwithstanding the orientalist references to rajahs and curry used as inspiration for glamorous nail-polish colours, where different shades function as a metonym for consumable exotica, the underlying message reads that it is possible for the westerner to travel to India via the photographs of Raghubir Singh and Dayanita Singh.

The critical term "mobilized 'virtual' gaze" can adequately describe the film spectator's gaze as she embarks on a virtual journey provided by Boyle's film, "a gaze that travels in an imaginary *flânerie* through an imaginary elsewhere and an imaginary elsewhen" (Friedberg 2). The connection between this film and tourism also extends, as Rushdie stresses in his essay on adaptation published in the *Guardian*, to a peculiar form of film tourism: poorism, or slum tourism. Film tourism is sometimes called movie-induced or film-induced tourism and has been defined as "tourist visits to a destination or attraction as a result of the destination being featured on television, video or the cinema screen" (Busby and Klug 317). Part of the critical reception of *The Beach* (2000), one of Boyle's earlier films, also framed it within the thematic of film tourism and analysed it as being itself inextricably related to tourist practices (see Law et al.). Whereas *The Beach* quite infamously engaged in actual physical impact upon the filming location, altering landscapes to suit the production's needs, in *Slumdog Millionaire* Boyle had his filming crew sneak through crowds and shoot a large part of the film in digital video with handheld cameras that made them look more like tourists than a film crew.

Despite Lim's argument that *Slumdog Millionaire* retreads old clichés, Rushdie identifies a significant difference in the object of film audiences' interest about India in the 1980s and now. The writer describes the plots of films belonging to what he dubbed the "Raj revival" in England in the 1980s as displaying an unflinching interest in issues of gender and sexuality, in particular inter-racial sexual adventure and romantic enterprise overseas:

> It used to be the case that western movies about India were about blonde women arriving there to find, almost at once, a maharajah to fall in love with, the supply of such maharajahs being apparently endless and specially provided for English or American blondes;[8] or they were about European women accusing non-maharajah Indians of rape, perhaps because they were so indignant at having being approached by a non-maharajah;[9] or they were about dashing white men galloping about the colonies firing pistols and unsheathing sabres, to varying effect. ("Fine Pickle")

The thematic recurrence of literary and cinematic representations of British India as a gendered space, where native and European women were ascribed pre-determined roles, was part of the cultural construction of Empire. The leitmotif of European women in India where permanently in danger of being either seduced by maharajahs or raped by non-maharajahs, as Rushdie puts it, undeniably exerted an exotic appeal for western audiences in the 1980s, a point that will be further developed in the last section of this chapter. As the writer notes during a 1982 interview, "Britain's always had a great fondness for exotic things – what it defines as exotic things – and that's because it's a cold, grey northern country, rather small, in which the horizons are relatively narrow" (qtd. in Dube 11). He expands on his reasoning:

> The British have always had a kind of fantasy about themselves as being glamorous, adventuresome, risk-taking daredevils you see, and they have relatively little grounds for thinking this. One of the reasons that the Empire was wonderful for the British is because it gave them a chance to behave like that. Suddenly they had this enormous canvas that was Africa, India, America, gigantic places that they – very small groups of them – were gloriously running. It gave them the chance to be heroes on a large scale. ... And suddenly these little figures from minor provincial regions of England who would never have a chance to be anything other than minor provincial figures, were suddenly given a chance to exist in cinemascope. I think it fulfilled a great national longing, to be like that. (qtd. in Dube 11).

---

[8] A likely reference to the Merchant-Ivory film *Heat and Dust* (1983), with a screenplay by Ruth Prawer Jhabvala based on her Booker-prize-winning novel.

[9] Rushdie might be alluding to both David Lean's film *A Passage to India*, whose screenplay is based on the 1924 novel of the same name by Forster, and to the British television mini-series *The Jewel in the Crown*.

In a coetaneous essay on Richard Attenborough's film *Gandhi* (1982), Rushdie recounts being asked in India: "why should an *Englishman* want to deify Gandhi?" To this query, the writer adds one of his own: why "should the American Academy wish to help him, by presenting, like votive offerings in a temple, eight glittering statuettes to a film that is inadequate as biography, appalling as history, and often laughably crude as a film?" In this 1983 review of Attenborough's film, Rushdie argues that *Gandhi* "satisfies certain longings in the Western psyche" and hence one of the main reasons behind the award success of this film lies in the gratification of "the exotic impulse, the wish to see India as the fountainhead of spiritual – mystical wisdom" (102). In the early 1980s, the casting of Gandhi as "celluloid guru" was consistent with the idea of a Spiritual India in the western imaginary because it "follow[ed] in the footsteps of other pop holy men"; in fact, as Rushdie phrases it, the "Maraharishi [Mahesh Yogi] blazed this trail" (102). With eight Academy Awards of its own, including one for Best Picture, Boyle's *Slumdog Millionaire* demonstrates that not only the Raj period, but also the idea of a Spiritual India, have lost exotic cachet in the twenty-first century. This, of course, relates to Adiga's staging of a Dark India in *The White Tiger* and the novel's de-exoticising of the river Ganges.

More than two decades after the Raj revival on film and television, audiences now crave for "enough grit and violence to convince themselves that what they are seeing is authentic; but it's still tourism" (Rushdie "Fine Pickle"). To Rushdie the idea of tourism is indeed central to the success of Boyle's film: "If the earlier films were raj tourism, maharajah-tourism, then we, today, have slum tourism instead." In keeping with this reading, the popular appeal of *Slumdog Millionaire* is fuelled by two of the desires that lie at the root of tourism: fantasy and escape. In effect, the influence of film on tourism, especially in the case of feature films seen by mass audiences, is evident at film sites mainly through an increase in visitor numbers following a film's release. As the tourist industry, both at a domestic level and abroad, has increasingly been focusing itself on the consumption of experiences and on the marketing of countries as commodities *per se*, tourists as consumers are approached through exoticist discourses of otherness and thus impelled to engage in these.

It should come as no surprise then that after the worldwide commercial success of Boyle's film Indian slums began to appeal more visibly to consumers as new exotic tourist destinations, away from the well-trodden path of so-called conventional tourism. In the midst of this burgeoning interest in this controversial slum tourism, Ganesh Tikonkar, a guide for the Mumbai-based Reality Tours and Travel company, asserts at the time of the release of Boyle's work that "[e]verybody [was] talking about *Slumdog*" and that these film tourists "want[ed] to see *the real thing*" (Blakely; emphasis added). The "real thing" that Tikonkar is referring to is Dharavi, famously Asia's largest shantytown and widely assumed to be the setting for Boyle's film; nonetheless, *Slumdog Millionaire* was actually shot in the slums of Juhu and Versova in northern suburbs of Mumbai (Iyer and Joshi). Ultimately, these "Slumdog tours" problematize even further the already problematic notion of an authentic landscape. In this sense, the unflinching quest for the "real" that is attached to a tour in Dharavi by these film tourists is doomed from the start – the quest is, as the tourists themselves may be well aware, for a constructed and fetishized location that could not be replicated in real experience. The allure of India Unshining as depicted in *Slumdog Millionaire* is definitely a pull factor for such film-induced slum tourism. This can be seen as part of a broader process by which exotic landscapes are staged to meet the tourist gaze given that, as John Urry theorized in *The Tourist Gaze* (1990), tourists' images of real locations and their desire to visit them are shaped and validated through non-tourist practices:

> Places are chosen to be gazed upon because there is anticipation, especially through daydreaming and fantasy, of intense pleasures, either on a different scale or involving different senses from those customarily encountered. Such anticipation is constructed and sustained through a variety of non-tourist practices, such as film, TV, literature, magazines, records and videos, which construct and reinforce that gaze. (3)

In the early 1990s, at the time of the first edition of Urry's influential work, the relationship between film and tourism was a relatively new area of academic inquiry, which accounts in all probability for the inclusion of film in the above list of "non-tourist practices" that influence tourists' behaviour. The fact is that *Slumdog Millionaire* not only boosted slum film tourism, but also presents itself as a virtual slum tour; as such, following Urry's arguments, tourists travelled to Dharavi to experience the virtual landscapes of Mumbai's slums as fabricated and reinforced by Boyle's cinematic images. Apparently, some western tourists wanted to discover and explore these images, regardless of their authenticity. India Unshining is hence the object of product placement; in other words, a romanticized version of Indian poverty, skillfully depoliticized, is packaged for consumption and promoted through embedded marketing in the film as if it were, in Roy's phrase, a "glitzy item in the supermarket" ("Caught on Film"). As Roy further expounds, "the film de-contextualises poverty – by making poverty an epic prop, it disassociates poverty from the poor. It makes India's poverty a landscape, like a desert or a mountain range, an exotic beach, god-given, not man-made." She critiques the sensationalisation of poverty in Boyle's film – as, similarly, the critic Shyamal Sengupta dismisses it as a mere "poverty tour" (Magnier):

> People are selling India's poverty big time both in literature and films. As they say, there is lots of money in poverty today. I am not against showing slums, but depicting them in a depoliticised manner, as has been done in the film, is quite unfortunate. Films do not show the real poor. Even if they are depicted, it's not the true picture. The real poor are not shown in films because they are not attractive. Poverty sells but the poor do not. (qtd. in Vohra)

Judging from the box-office results and the prizes Boyle's film garnered, this depiction of India's poverty (or of India as a poor country) has unmistakably mass appeal. Despite this appeal, one should not be too quick in assuming viewers' passivity in this process. In fact, it is feasible that the viewer might sense a participation in the power structures sketched out by the film and a certain uneasiness at what she is viewing.[10]

In an interview, Swarup attributes the success of the filmic adaptation of his novel in part to a "global hunger" for India: "The world is curious about India – what is powering this nine percent growth rate, how is India combining tradition with modernity" (qtd. in Osaka). Still, Roy argues that Boyle's film projects an image of "the exotic poor": "The stockpiling of standard, clichéd horrors in Slumdog are, I think, meant to be a sort of version of Alice in Wonderland – 'Jamal in Horrorland.' It doesn't work except to trivialize what really goes on here. The villains who kidnap and maim children and sell them into brothels reminded me of Glenn Close in *101 Dalmatians*" ("Caught on Film"). A scene in the film depicts the procedure whereby children are blinded to increase their profitability as street beggars. According to Roy, mixing the reality of the forced recruitment of children for begging and prostitution, and the practice of blinding and disfiguring them with hyperbolized horror results in the political de-contextualisation and hence trivialisation of the experience of child poverty in India. In her argument, such reality is presented to the film's viewer as a mere plot contrivance that will lead to knowing the correct answer in a quiz show. Swarup presents the scenes of horror in his novel in a different light, one that Roy might characterize as resulting from a de-contextualized outlook on Indian social reality:

> This isn't social critique .... It's a novel written by someone who uses what he finds to tell a story. I don't have firsthand experience of betting on cricket or rape or murder. I don't know if it's true that there are beggar masters who blind children to make them more effective when they beg on the streets. It may be an urban myth, but it's useful to my story. (qtd. in Jeffries)

The increasing popularity of slum tourism in developing countries is consistent with a voyeuristic fascination with the spectacle of poverty. In Rushdie's essay on cinematic adaptation – which he entitled "A Fine Pickle" using the word "pickle" not only in the sense of an edible product that has been preserved and flavoured, but also in its informal use of predicament – he describes Boyle's film as "[a] feelgood movie about the dreadful Bombay slums, an opulently photographed movie about extreme poverty, a romantic, Bollywoodized look at the harsh, unromantic underbelly of India." Even before the Oscar-related hype surrounding Boyle's film, Swarup was referred to in the press as having received "the supreme

---

[10] In connection to the advertising industry, Adorno and Horkheimer similarly state: "The triumph of advertising in the culture industry is that consumers feel compelled to buy and use its products even though they see through them" (167). Elsewhere, Adorno contends: "we cannot content ourselves with merely stating that spontaneity has been replaced by blind acceptance of the enforced material. Even the belief that people today react like insects and are degenerating into mere centers of socially conditioned reflexes, still belongs to the façade" ("Popular Music" 47).

accolade" of an onslaught from Rushdie (McCrum). The writer takes issue first and foremost with the literary merits of the work adapted, Swarup's novel *Q & A*. He contends that Swarup's narrative displays an outlandishly contrived plot that overuses the device of analepsis and, in the end, defies logic. Given that the creative team behind *Slumdog Millionaire* transposed this plot device to the film, the latter "too, beggars belief" ("Fine Pickle").

Boyle was directly inspired by Bollywood films, as Amitava Kumar demonstrates in the article "*Slumdog Millionaire*'s Bollywood Ancestors" (2008) published in the magazine *Vanity Fair*. In this respect, *Slumdog Millionaire* is a hybrid film because it blends distinctly different cinematic styles together, using a range of techniques and perspectives which merge Indian cultural influences with the formulas and devices of western cinema. In effect, the most recognisable features hybrid films share are that they mix classical western narratives with the forms of culturally different cinematic codes, and that their subject matter regularly dwells on the juxtaposition of cultural frameworks, often as a legacy of a colonial past. Boyle made no attempt to conceal the constructed nature of his film. Still, the suspension of disbelief demanded from audiences by the film's several plot contrivances (for instance, when Hindi-speaking street urchins metamorphose into English-speaking teenagers) might betray a deliberate overplay with implausible coincidences, as well as a partial embracing of Bollywood-style storytelling.

Admittedly, the film capitalizes on the crossover appeal of the exotic that is associated with Bollywood; however, Boyle uses some of the popular patterns of popular Hindi film strategically and self-consciously. As such, the film plays with (while not necessarily transcending) such appeal. *Slumdog Millionaire* closes with a Bollywood-style finale – a dance sequence that Rushdie ironically qualifies as "nifty" because "[i]t's probably pointless to go up against such a popular film" – which is but one example of a western cultural artefact drawn to the visual richness of the Mumbai-based Hindi film industry. In the 2000s western cinema began pastiching Bollywood and this was instrumental in the renaissance of the western musical film genre. For instance, Baz Luhrmann's *Moulin Rouge* (2001) refashioned Bollywood cinematic stylistics: in the song "Hindi Sad Diamonds," *Moulin Rouge* reworks the music piece "Chamma Chamma" from the Bollywood film *China Gate* (dir. Rajkumar Santoshi, 1998); Luhrmann's version is a pastiche of this Hindi film song and of "Diamonds Are a Girl's Best Friend," the song popularized by Marilyn Monroe. Conversely, Gurinder Chadha's film *Bhaji on the Beach* includes in its soundtrack a Punjabi version of Cliff Richard's song "Summer Holiday." This 1950s song was, Chadha soon realized, an icon of Englishness ripe for subversion; nonetheless, South Asianness is also questioned, as the filmmaker discloses:

> A straight Bhangra song was too schmaltzy in the film and "Summer Holiday" in its original form was too predictable, but the way I did it in Punjabi it became a warm inviting metaphor for the whole film, taking Englishness and Indianness and remodelling both ... and wrong-footing people at the same time. (Bhattacharyya and Gabriel 61)

The final Bollywood number in *Slumdog Millionaire* turns out to be one of the film's trademarks: for the closing credits, the protagonists, accompanied by a group of dancers passing as train passengers, perform a dance routine on a railway platform to the sound of the Oscar-winner song "Jai Ho." The closing song and dance sequence assumed an independent agency beyond *Slumdog Millionaire*. The American pop band Pussycat Dolls performed an English remix version of A.R. Rahman's Oscar-winning song "Jai Ho" ("You Are My Destiny") in a talk show within less than a month of its winning of the Oscar for Best Song. The official video clip features the singers in a packed train and at a bazaar, dressed Indian-style; besides, the final train scene from the film is re-enacted. Against the backdrop of the booming mainstream-western success of the Bollywood film industry, what might be the narrative purpose of the Bollywoodized choreography in Boyle's film? To signal the narrative closure of Jamal and Latika's fairy tale and shatter the suspension of disbelief? To make perfectly clear that *Slumdog Millionaire* is, in the end, a fantasy in true Bollywood fashion? Or rather to provide relief for the tensions raised by the film? Might this be a critical pastiche?

The blatant artificiality of such a staged ending, and most importantly the pastiche of Bollywood motifs, discloses the intention to present Jamal's life story as fabrication. The Bollywood finale is in fact self-consciously framed and interspersed by the credits. As the multiple-choice question introduced at the beginning of the film anticipates, "it is written." In fact, the Bollywoodized dance routine betrays the film's self-conscious framing as fantasy (made even more forceful earlier by the initial multiple-choice question) and foregrounds its strategic inauthenticity as it transfers Indian slum experience visually across linguistic, geopolitical, and cultural boundaries onto the screen. The displacement that Boyle's strategic inauthenticity renders visible assists in puncturing the understanding of the film as a guided tour to an Indian slum, against Rushdie's contention that the blockbuster really does no more than reduce India's slums to an exotic spectacle and merely cash in on the idea of Poor India. In other words, the film is saved from lapsing into a mere rehearsal of poorist clichés and does manage to go beyond the illusion the viewer might have, as Jonathan Crow suggested in his inventory of the secrets of the film's success, that she has been to India.

Return of the Raj (With a Twist)[11]

> Outsider! Trespasser! You have no right to this subject! … Poacher! Pirate! We know you, with your foreign language wrapped around you like a flag: speaking about us in your forked tongue, what can you tell but lies?
> —Rushdie, *Shame* 28

---

[11] This section is a revised version of the chapter "Heritage Revisited: The Cultural Politics of Heritage in *Goodness Gracious Me*," included in Cláudia Álvares (ed.), *Representing Culture: Essays on Identity, Visuality and Technology*. Newcastle upon Tyne: Cambridge Scholars Publishing, 2008, 119–129, published with the permission of CSP.

In the essay "Outside the Whale" Rushdie locates a "revisionist enterprise" at the heart of Margaret Thatcher's Britain, the aim of which is the "refurbishment of the Empire's tarnished image" (91). While debatable, Rushdie's arguments draw attention to the cultural implications of the commercial success of contemporary revisionist narratives of imperial themes. Focusing on the interplay between revision and revival, and using the terms of Rushdie's critique of Raj revivalist products, the exoticisation of colonial history that he discerns in films such as *A Passage to India* (dir. David Lean, 1984) and TV series such as *The Jewel in the Crown* (1984) is examined in this section as it is played out in reverse in *Goodness Gracious Me* (1998–2001), a BBC comedy series written and performed by British-born artists of South Asian descent. Drawing primarily on the second series of the show and Rushdie's essay "Outside the Whale," the focus rests on the satire of the allure of the past for the British visual media.

*****

In the 1984 essay "Outside the Whale" the author posits the existence of a pernicious Raj revival. Incorporated in this commercial venture are films and TV programmes exploiting Raj nostalgia: *The Far Pavilions*, *The Jewel in the Crown*, *Gandhi*, and *A Passage to India*. In these "phantom twitchings" of what Rushdie identifies as the "amputated limb" of Empire he discerns a fantasy which "encourages many Britons to turn their eyes nostalgically to the lost hour of their precedence" (92). The writer is indisputably correct to draw a connection between Raj nostalgia and the ideological framework of Thatcher's Britain; however this correlation may involve not only a determination to breathe life into former achievements, but also an apparently morbid fascination with current decline (Huggan *Postcolonial Exotic* 114). Paul Gilroy accounts thus for such regressive and post-imperial melancholic tendencies acted out in popular media:

> These popular works may salve the national conscience, but they compound the marginality of colonial history, spurn its substantive lessons, and obstruct the development of multiculturalism by making the formative experience of empire less profound and less potent in shaping the life of colonizing powers than it actually was. This popular, revisionist output is misleading and dangerous because it feeds the illusion that Britain has been or can be disconnected from its imperial past. (2)[12]

---

[12] As Martin Hipsky observes, unlike the British, the North American audience may enjoy heritage films' spectacular rendition of history guilt-free: "In many ways, these historical films function to efface the very social history they purport to portray; they provide North American viewers with a kind of sanitized, guilt-free nostalgia. It is, after all, the historical landscape of our trans-Atlantic cousins there on the screen, and while we are aware of empire and class injustices hovering somewhere beyond the movies' immediate social landscape, they trouble us not, as they do not signify any dirty historical laundry of our own" (106).

By the end of the Thatcherite decade, the term "heritage" had been tainted by a negative connotation since most studies of British film connected the industry and its re-enactment of the past with the preservation of national identity promoted by the New Right regime. While generally admitting the important role heritage films played in the revival of British cinema, critical surveys of British culture in the 1980s such as John Corner's and Sylvia Harvey's edited volume *Enterprise and Heritage: Crosscurrents of National Culture* (1991) emphasize a certain contamination of heritage culture by conservative ideology. One crucial point critics make in *Enterprise and Heritage* is that heritage films became part of the decade's marketing craze, turning the British past into a commodity to be sold as a sightseeing attraction in organized tours of old architectural landmarks and as a cultural product in films and television. The associated recreation of Britain's colonial past in film and TV or, in other words, the exoticisation of colonial history has also been looked at as suggestive of a loss-of-identity feeling generated by the continuing trauma of the break-up of empire and translated into aggressive nationalism and an increased sense of isolation from the rest of the European Community. Analysing the nostalgia for an idealized, counterfeit British past, Tana Wollen voices the general opinion that the increasing ethnic and cultural diversity characterising post-World War II Britain, in exile from its most important colony, India, generated a need among conservative elements of the British population to look at history as the preserver of national identity: "the Right has had a singular project: to incorporate everyone under the same category, to render multitudes as one and the same, not as a straggled set of others. History is to be about nationhood" (181). Wollen further stresses the status of Raj screen fictions as consumer commodities in the early 1980s by relating them to the growing interest in museums and to the increase of tour operators offering package holidays to India (192).

Along the same line, Cairns Craig wrote that the success of heritage films such as *A Passage to India* is "symptomatic of the crisis of identity through which England passed during the Thatcher years" (3). Entitled "Rooms Without a View," Craig's essay suggests that despite most of these films' dealing with the crossing of borders between cultures, in the end, the main characters always withdraw into the "barricaded room" of their own English upper-class identities. As the critic notes, the negative effect of this phenomenon is twofold: if "for an international audience, the England these films validate and advertize is a theme park of the past, then for an English audience they gratify the need to find points of certainty within English culture" (4). Thus, the films become marketable both internationally – due to their apparent ethnic openness – and nationally, due to their final validation of Englishness. The English past is, on the one hand, ruthlessly objectified for the international market; on the other hand, it is ethnically purified to encourage identification with mainstream culture for an increasingly diverse audience in post-imperial Britain. Nonetheless, if the Raj revival was promoting nostalgia for a lost imperial prestige, it was doing so, like the heritage film more generally, in an ambivalent way. As John Hill argues, films such as *Heat and Dust* "do not straightforwardly endorse the empire but reveal a liberal concern to show up its idiocies, injustices, and, to a limited extent, even its brutalities" (99). While (sometimes ostensibly) debunking imperial glories and being evidence of an ironic awareness of their own belated status,[13] these fictions are in the end accused in Rushdie's "Outside the Whale" of being little more than "artistic counterparts to the rise of conservative ideologies in modern Britain" (92), marketing money-making imperial myths (Huggan, *Postcolonial Exotic* 112).

One of those myths, as Rushdie exposes, is that the British Empire was "in spite of all its flaws and meanness and bigotries, fundamentally glamorous" ("Outside" 101). This view was taken up in sketches from the BBC satirical series *Goodness Gracious Me*. This TV series is part of a body of diasporic South Asian, or Br-Asian, cinematic and televisual productions which have been, since the early 1990s, increasingly visible in the cultural industries, both British and worldwide, contributing to what Moya Luckett designated the "Britasian renaissance" (403). Before proceeding, a note on terminology is due regarding the terms "diasporic South Asian," "British Asian," "British-Asian," "Br-Asian," and "Britasian." Raminder Kaur and Virinder S. Kalra argue that the label "Asian" "has no consistent historical or global use" (218). According to this reasoning, the term "British Asian," commonly used to refer to British citizens who descended from South Asia, "essentialises both terms" while "hierarchizing the former against the latter"; as such, the alternative "Br-Asian" is "forwarded as an analytical tool from which it is possible to consider identity formations in the particular locality of Britain" (221). In its eliding of the letters "–itish" in "British" and its use as a prefix separated from "Asian" by a hyphen, the term "Br-Asian" starkly highlights the multiple identifications and decentred sense of belonging that result from inhabiting both British and South Asian cultures, and as such better accounts for the sort of compound cultural affiliations that this book is concerned with.

Arriving first on BBC Radio 4 in 1996, the crossover comedy series *Goodness Gracious Me* later had three successful seasons running from 1998 to 2001 on BBC Two, signalling the restructuring of the broadcasting corporation to include more diverse markets. Indeed, breaking out from its initial target area and reaching out to a non-Asian audience, the comedy show promptly achieved cult status in Britain and widespread commercial success, with the first series escalating up to an estimated 85 per cent white audience (Malik 102–103). Looking at similar audience statistics which reportedly attribute to the show a massive white spectatorship, Luckett questions "how white is white?" (407). Meera Syal, one of the multitalented performers of the show, was not surprised by the numbers: "I suppose that would make sense because only five per cent of the population is Asian. But I hope people now see it as *a* comedy show rather than *an Asian*

---

[13] Demonstrating that the construction of Englishness as an all-encompassing identity is consistently undermined in British heritage productions which recast imperial themes is outside the reach of this subchapter and has already merited sustained critical attention. For that purpose, see, for example, M. Berger; Muraleedharan; and Shailja Sharma.

comedy show" (qtd. in Gould 15; emphasis added). In this sense, Alison Donnell reported that "[w]hen the audience majority was thought to comprise Asians, *Goodness Gracious Me* was considered an 'Asian comedy' yet when found to be 80 per cent white it became 'mainstream'" (128).

The Times, heralding the programme as "the oil of race relations" in 1998, credited its achievements to a post-imperial "happy multiculturalism," a notion borrowed from Zadie Smith's satirical picture of "Cool Britannia" in her novel *White Teeth*, where the narrator denounces the deceptive rhetoric of immigrants in Britain "merrily weaving their way through Happy Multicultural Land" (398). Such critical and commercial success led to a national theatre tour and to the sitcom being exported to countries in and outside Europe, even though it never aired on the wider audience catcher BBC One. With Syal starring, the sketches in *Goodness Gracious Me* featuring intertextual parodies of Raj revival television formats strategically disrupt narrative characteristics of heritage works, such as nostalgic feelings, thematic emphasis on setting, and the splitting of stories between the moment chronicled and the narration. The comic effect of parodic sketches based on *The Jewel in the Crown* relies on the audience's familiarity with heritage visual and thematic features. The intertextual critical play with the Raj revival that *Goodness Gracious Me*'s team takes on can be traced back to the pioneering Asian comedy show *Tandoori Nights* produced by Channel Four in 1985–87, and in which Syal was likewise involved. This programme played out the competition between two restaurants: the *Jewel in the Crown* and the *The Far Pavilions*, named after the popular 1980s television serials adapted from Paul Scott and M.M. Kaye's novels set in the British Raj.

In the second series, episode three, of *Goodness Gracious Me*, a group of four sketches depict an interview conducted by a British journalist with an elderly Indian woman – a character significantly named Lady Chatterjee and performed by Syal – on her experience of growing up as a little girl in colonized India. Through the comic technique of role reversal, contrary to the general practice of Raj fictions according to which Indians "get walk-ons, but remain, for the most part, bit-players in their own history" (Rushdie, "Outside" 90), the main part is seized by one of those who are usually extras or perform minor parts. The character of Lady Chatterjee makes a revisionist comeback as leading figure by the hand of Syal. It is relevant to note here that Zohra Sehgal is one of the Indian performers who actually gets a walk-on in *The Jewel in the Crown*, playing precisely Lili Chatterjee. Sehgal's very own career – ranging from acting parts in the blatantly crude and stereotypical misrepresentations of the 1970s sitcoms *Mind Your Language* and *It Ain't Half Hot Mum* to the radical *Bhaji on the Beach* and the queer film *Chicken Tikka Masala*, directed by Harmage Singh Kalirai in 2005 – illustrates the increased opportunities for minority acting in Britain.

In the first of four sketches of *Goodness Gracious Me* under scrutiny here, describing her near-death beating at the hands of young British fusiliers whilst chained to a gate, Lady Chatterjee cannot help but seek recourse in images reminiscent of the seductive visual style typical of heritage conventions:

beautifully kept gardens, well-groomed officers, and glittering parties at the governor's residence (to which she was denied entrance being an Indian) featuring lavish decorations and illustrious people wearing striking outfits. In her words, these were "wonderful days" regardless of the "hullabaloo" made by the founding fathers of the modern Indian subcontinent, Gandhi and Jinnah, who, in her perspective, seem to be responsible for a moment of unity gone astray.[14] The British interviewer feels manifestly troubled and helpless when faced with Lady Chatterjee's bizarre longing for colonial times, in particular by the end of the third sketch when she confesses to her romantic excitement when a handsome British general came to execute her auntie.[15] In the fourth and final sketch, Chatterjee overturns the rape-plot current in Raj revival narratives, according to which "frail English roses were in constant sexual danger from lust-crazed wogs" (Rushdie "Outside"), by depicting the assault of Indian women as a spare time occupation for British army officers in perfectly creased trousers.[16] In Raj screen fictions, British Indian heterosexual relationships are repeatedly depicted as the outcome of the fascination of the white British woman towards the exoticism and mystery of India, which presumably makes middle-class English domesticity seem by contrast dull and unappealing. Lady Chatterjee's sketch in *Goodness Gracious Me* reverses the typical romantic scene between the eastern man and the western (white) woman visible in films such as *Shakespeare Wallah* and *Heat and Dust*, as well as in the TV series *The Jewel in the Crown*. "If rape must be used as a metaphor of the Indo-British connection," as Rushdie questions, "then surely, in the interests of accuracy, it should be the rape of an Indian woman by one or more Englishmen of whatever class" (89). The creative team behind *Goodness Gracious Me* seems to have followed up on his reasoning.

By subsuming physical cruelty and sexual assault into elements of setting which characteristically constitute visually pleasing heritage iconography, attention is drawn to the absurdity of a wistful longing for the glamour of the British colonial past. In the end, this group of sketches reasserts that, as Rushdie put it, "the jewel in the crown is made, these days, of paste" (92). As previously mentioned, this humorous parody of *The Jewel in the Crown* succeeds due to the viewers' acquaintance with the specific style of filmmaking characteristic of Raj screen fictions. Strategically, it invokes and suspends the audience's knowledge, inviting their nostalgic and revivalist reading of Raj narratives, which it rewrites as parody. The comic sketches enact the perceived behaviour of a nostalgic individual: facing estrangement, disruption, and alterity in the present, ruptures that fracture her identity, she begins to bracket "wonderful days" together with the past, that is, with a vanished moment of equilibrium. Such a revivalism of a colonial past has been seen by Gilroy as resulting, on the one hand, from the ambivalence of "postcolonial melancholia" structuring British political institutions and culture,

---

[14] Series 2, episode 3, 0:04:20–0:05:51.
[15] Series 2, episode 3, 0:16:50–0:17:20.
[16] Series 2, episode 3, 0:19:02–0:19:43.

the outcome of a refusal to come to grips with the break-up of Empire, and, on the other, by a surfacing "unkempt, unruly and unplanned multiculture" (x). Such a sense of lost unity and departed imperial glory can also translate into objects, such as the well-trimmed gardens, the impeccably creased trousers, and the polished boots celebrated by Syal's Lady Chatterjee.

Throughout the sketches, the interview is structured as a narrative reconstruction of a tale featuring an Edenic moment and its loss; however, a mix of comic strategies and intertextual ironic operations turn the nostalgic past into a disruptive one, opening it up to other histories told from the perspective of the colonized. In the second sketch, Chatterjee's recollections include a train journey where a crowd of chattering elderly women and bubbly children meet, as they arrived at the station, the deadly bullets coming from dashing British fusiliers.[17] As the blood trickles down the aisle during the attack, she cannot help noticing how brightly polished the officers' boots are. Her somewhat pathetic attempts to displace the focus away from the turbulent days of the Raj only lead to the reinforcement of the real turmoil of these "wonderful days." Chatterjee's outlandish longing is throughout set alongside the shock and embarrassment of a white British journalist, whose discomfort is apparently the result of having to face up to colonial oppression and brutality. Chris Weedon finds representational problems in the structure of these sketches, repeated throughout several others in *Goodness Gracious Me*, since the viewer might identify more easily with the "normal" white English character against which the Indian character is unfavourably measured (267). Weedon asks us to consider if the audience laughs *with* or *at* the Indian character. On a related level, the viewer might also be asked to sympathize with the (white) British as at present "victims" of their imperial past.

Regardless of a predictable redeployment of colonial fictions in a more appealing and mainstream-friendly way, this alternative comic portrayal disturbs beyond repair the apparent harmony of time and place of the "wonderful days." In a challenging and empowering way, imperial nostalgia is made to re-signify and is turned around for subversive effect, talking back against the "refurbishment of the Empire's tarnished image" (Rushdie, "Outside" 91). Even if Rushdie's critique, written in 1984 during Thatcherism and its distrust of difference, might come across as slightly outdated, it did maintain its relevance in the new context of Tony Blair's "Cool Britannia" of the late 1990s and early 2000s. Indeed, shortly after the airing of this episode, *The Jewel in the Crown* peaked at number 22 on a list of the 100 Greatest British Television Programmes drawn up by the British Film Institute in 2000. Aided by this expanded space for Br-Asian cultural production in mass mediated forms, nostalgic Raj fictions are returned to the cultural location where they surfaced in the past – the TV medium – replayed as oppositional practice to a hybrid audience, Br-Asian and white British, challenging nostalgic screen narratives with empowered representation. Furthermore, the sketches' satirical edge lies as well in the recognition of heritage narratives as ambivalent

---

[17] Series 2, episode 3, 0:11:47–0:12:37.

and marked by fracture. In fact, Andrew Higson considers that several heritage films stage an unsettled conflict between a safe, traditional, and elite Englishness and a more unstable concept of national identity which is presented to us through the experiences of marginalized social groups, perceived as simple "footnotes of history" (*English Heritage* 28). Although framed and mediated, thus limited, media representation of otherness has been crucial in articulating narratives of resistance. In the sketches, Lady Chatterjee begins by pointing to a crack between the post-imperial present and the wished-for colonial past. However, the absurdity of her nostalgia underscores that the present is in fact located in that distant past and that those who were considered "mere footnotes of history" now demand to be incorporated into the narrative.

Chapter 4
Music and the Brown Culture Industry

Focusing on the western-based music industry, this chapter puts forward a reading of the novel *The Ground Beneath Her Feet* that demonstrates the potential of critical theory to address the entanglement of postcolonialism and postcoloniality in Rushdie's literary and critical writings. An update of Adorno's and Horkheimer's 1940s concept of culture industry, the "brown culture industry" is suggested as a variation of Ellis Cashmore's notion of a "black culture industry" (1997) that accounted for the surfacing of a black culture industry in the North American context. After tracing the "Koolisation" of South Asian-influenced popular culture and analysing the tangled web of commodification of brown difference in the first section of this chapter, in the second section Rushdie's novel *The Ground Beneath Her Feet* is examined in its connection with the idea of a brown culture industry.

The Business of Culture

> Nothing remains as of old; everything has to run incessantly, to keep moving. For only the universal triumph of the rhythm of mechanical production and reproduction promises that nothing changes, and nothing unsuitable will appear.
> —Max Horkheimer and Theodor Adorno 134

Bringing Adorno's and Horkheimer's observations into a contemporary frame, the revamped conceptual category "brown culture industry" allows for a fusion between one of the foundational theories in the study of popular culture, related to the political economy of the culture industry, and a burgeoning concern of postcolonial critiques regarding the commodification of difference in the cultural industries. As such, this concept aims to reconjugate critical theory and a postcolonial studies approach, drawing on the analytical and critical power of the category of "commodification" for a broader and more complex view of postcolonial cultural production.

*****

As highlighted by Huggan's *The Postcolonial Exotic*, so far one of the most influential materialist theorisations of the imbrications of postcolonial literary production, the university, and the marketplace, developments in metropolitan institutions such as academia and its associated publishing sector have led over the last decades to the foregrounding of cultural difference within the fields of cultural and postcolonial studies. While the general purpose of the present chapter is to introduce and extend discussion on the exoticisation and commodification of postcolonial culture in recent years, this first section employs the concept "brown culture industry" so as to handle the specificity of South Asian diasporic formations, in particular concerning Br-Asian politics of postcolonial representation. It is crucial to acknowledge the theoretical space that frames the cultural practices under examination here, all of which are involved in the workings of the global markets in a post-Fordist era and their cashing in on a fascination with cultural difference. Indeed, a return to Horkheimer's and Adorno's theoretical model provides a productive basis for critically assessing the cultural politics surrounding the marketing of cultural difference, against the backdrop of a growing awareness in the cultural industries of the potential marketability of exotica.

Despite the remarkable value that the critical theory of the Frankfurt School holds, it requires updating to account for the accrued complexity of present-day cultural practices. As Rupa Huq points out, Adorno's model "was of a general nature and is now woefully outdated" (*Beyond Subculture* 55) which makes the arguments of the German theorist "an easy target when writing from the standpoint of the twenty-first century" (46). Critical theory has not wearied of its own paradigm, but times of transition demand new analytical tools and Adorno's and Horkheimer's theories need to be mediated through an emerging tradition of recent readings. Considering that, more than ever before, cultural difference has been commodified and marketed accordingly, and in the light of the renewed interest in Horkheimer's and Adorno's theorisations on the political economy of the culture industry on the part of those involved in a critique of postcolonial cultural production (as referred to in the introductory chapter to this book), the concept of a brown culture industry seems as adequate to describe the predicament of South Asian diasporic culture as Cashmore's model was when it accounted for the surfacing of a black culture industry in the North American context.

In the opening pages of *The Black Culture Industry*, the critic forcefully states: "It is time for black culture to be examined with the same cynicism that Theodor Adorno brought to American culture in general" (3). Cashmore explains how blackness had been seized by capital in the late 1990s, transformed into a marketable commodity and rehabilitated in a profit-making marketing move in the interests of white-owned multinational entertainment corporations that carefully planned and controlled production and consumption. Following previous marketing practices involving jazz, disco, and rap music, such repackaged black experience was seen as commercially viable as long as it echoed and thus reinscribed stereotypical representations. For instance, Cashmore alleges that black performers such as Michael Jackson and "the artist formerly known as Prince" consented to being promoted and marketed in the mass entertainment industry according to the regimes of representation in commodity capitalism, i.e. racialized for white Euro-American audiences. They were fixed and essentialized as black artists in order to be better managed for commercial ends. Cashmore contends that the mainstream visibility of black culture in the 1990s US was far from emancipatory given that the existing power relations remained, in the end, essentially unscathed. This corporate-sponsored essentialized blackness, wholly contained within the commodity system, fits the scenario Horkheimer and Adorno described when they provocatively linked culture and industry.

Addressing the British context, Hutnyk similarly observes in the case of "new Asian dance music" (Sanjay Sharma et al. 1996) a co-optation by the market which eventually compromised the music's oppositional politics. In his words, "[t]he visibility of some South Asian stars in the Culture Industry is, in itself, potentially useful but not guaranteed progressive — a favourite trick co-opts a few high profile names to foster the illusion that everyone else is ok" (8). Cultural difference fuels and drives the market, so Horkheimer and Adorno argued, and in the UK difference also rose to prominence in the 1990s as a built-in element of New Labour's "Cool Britannia" focused on projecting a national image of multicultural conviviality. Whereas difference was crucial for understanding the political arena of Thatcherite Britain in the 1980s, as the 1990s progressed it was increasingly distributed and exchanged in order to fit the demands of post-Fordist capitalism. Then, as Gilroy put it, a "pastiche of multiculture," facilitated by an increasing media interest in Br-Asian popular culture, was "manipulated from above by commerce" (163). This was especially the case with music: Madonna and Boy George, as well as he bands Bananarama, Erasure, and Siouxsie & the Banshees have all released songs with South Asian instrumentation. This is not new though when one recalls the use of sitars by the Beatles.

There has indeed been a rising awareness of how the marketing of hybridity – and alterity in general under the headings of "difference" and "ethnicity" – has become a core tactic of post-Fordist cultural industries. The Br-Asian playwright, screenwriter, actress, and novelist Meera Syal outlines the hypervisibility of cultural difference in the arts in general in 1990s Britain in the following terms:

> Artists appeared like Anish Kapoor and Chila Kumari Burman, musicians like Nitin Sawhney, Talvin Singh and Black Star Liner, the fusion-wallahs coexisting with the ever thriving Bhangra and Dub scenes, Asian fashions swept the catwalk; every North London home sported Rajasthani cushion covers and Tibetan wall hangings. Madonna did Mendhi and yoga, Jamima Kahn became Pakistani aristocracy, Indian women kept sweeping the board at beauty competitions and any club worth their salt flocked to Asian fusion nights in London's hippest venues, wearing their bindis with pride. ("Last Laugh")

In the case of cinema, it is possible to identify a significant increase of films from and about the "Brown Atlantic," that is, South Asian diasporas in the United States, Canada, and Britain (J. Desai ix), initiated by Gurinder Chadha's 1993 *Bhaji on the Beach*. This film, it can be argued, is the precursor of "The New Asian Kool," a marketing label devised in the mid-1990s which heralded the hypervisibility of South Asian diasporic cultural production within mainstream culture. Screenwriter-filmmaker Chadha was the first Br-Asian woman to be granted access to mainstream media production in the 1980s through state-supported funding, and was in the vanguard popularising "Asian Kool." According to Jigna Desai, today's diasporic South Asian films are most frequently integrated into the canons of national cinemas through the logic of cultural hybridity (36). This signals a transformation when compared with Br-Asian films of the 1980s which were "neither easily incorporated into the national cinema as the films openly challenged national narratives and identification processes nor were able to enter the film industry without intervention from social movements" (54). As the critic puts it, the emphasis is now on profit (65). Since the 1990s, the British film industry, powerless to compete with Hollywood, has found itself ambivalently recognising the role that Br-Asian filmmaking has played both as a potential site for revenue and in the promotion of its international image (39). *Bhaji on the Beach* can thus be regarded as an ambivalent text, simultaneously central to a new canon of British cinema and re-appropriated into the multicultural heritage industry as the cult film that put South Asia on the map of British popular culture and that had a decisive impact on opening up of the definition of a British (post) national cinema.

As Higson remarks, cinema is one of the most dynamic sites of cultural negotiation and one should take into account that in recent decades "new types of film-making have embraced multiculturalism, transnationalism and devolution," thus making up for "a powerful critique of traditional ideas of Britishness and consensual images of the nation" (35). Underscoring the constitutional fuzziness of national cinemas (O'Regan 139), Higson puts forward a postnational model for British cinema, able to accommodate the permeability of borders and of the fluidity of identification, and to integrate ambivalent representations of national identities in postwar Britain, such as those featured in filmic narratives such as *My Beautiful Laundrette* (dir. Stephen Frears, 1985) and *Trainspotting* (dir. Danny Boyle, 1996), both produced by Channel Four. Higson's postnational model for British cinema hence challenges monolithic understandings of nationhood and gestures to a transnational ethos. The critic elaborates on a move from "a British cinema of consensus to one of heterogeneity and dissent" (40). Highlighting the complexity implicated in the notion of British cinema, Chadha wants her films to be representative of the "new" national cinema: "What I'm trying to say is that Britain isn't one thing or another. It isn't just *Howard's End* or *My Beautiful Launderette*. There are endless possibilities about what it can – and is – already" (qtd. in S. Street 107). In an interview given in 2000 she had already stated that *Bhaji on the Beach* was about "opening up what we mean about British cinema" since it was "a very British film, made in a very British way, with Indians" (qtd. in Chhabra). The interstitiality of Br-Asian films prevents assimilation and full co-optation; furthermore, the project of Br-Asian filmmaking has not simply been about the contestation of Britishness as a singular and unified concept, but equally about the diversity and intrinsic dynamic that constitute diasporic South Asian identities.

Bearing out the fact that the cinema of the South Asian diaspora has become the object of close critical attention and that it has acquired the potential to appeal to British mainstream audiences is the fact that the image selected for the cover of one of the most influential analyses of modern British filmmaking – Higson's

Dissolving Views: Key Writings on British Cinema (1996) – was a still from *Bhaji on the Beach* depicting a middle-aged English actor in a colonial panama hat engaged in a lively conversation about Bollywood films with a diasporic Indian woman in a traditional sari, against the backdrop of the English seaside resort Blackpool. All the while, one must be attentive to the fact that Chadha's award-winning debut feature film was produced with funding from Channel Four Television in the UK as part of the scheme "Film On Four." Unsurprisingly, *Bhaji on the Beach* – as other Asian Kool films – was (and still is) consumed mainly by British and Br-Asian elite audiences (Werbner 903).[1] Nevertheless, films such as Chadha's have the power to heighten reflexivity in the face of essentialized renderings of ethnic difference, the kind which the "international difference machine" (Hutnyk 123) has had a hand in producing and perpetuating. Within this context, which includes an escalation in hate crimes and restrictive immigration policies, Hutnyk's words published in 2000 still resonate today: "[d]espite the effervescent cultural industries, the 'hybrid' visibility of Asian cultural forms has not yet translated into any significant socioeconomic redress of multi-racial exclusions within Fortress Europe" (4). Even if, as Hutnyk highlights, it still remains to be seen if the increased profile of a Br-Asian cultural presence is an indisputable political achievement, difference is more visible in popular culture than in the past due to the restive production of hybrid commodities such as the ones described a few paragraphs back by Syal. In fact, the visibility of Br-Asian representation in the public sphere depends on the political economy of the cultural industries. Following Desai's theorisation, this hypervisibility has been integrated into the mainstream through the rhetoric of cultural hybridity, since late capitalist diversification supports "plurality in constructing and penetrating its differentiated target markets" (66). As Desai puts it, "visibility can become a way to spice up culture without a compensatory interrogation or shift of values and epistemologies" (62).

Such logic parallels the focus on hybridity discernible in the field of postcolonial and cultural studies during the last three decades. A disputed and contested concept, but nevertheless a key one, "hybridity" refers to "the creation of new transcultural forms within the contact zone produced by colonisation" (Ashcroft et al. 118). The current prominence of this concept and its, at times, glorification as an emancipatory wellspring of creative expression, which have turned hybridity into a fashionable academic commodity in recent years, have not failed to summon negative reactions from critics. For instance, Annie E. Coombes and Avtar Brah note that the deployment of hybridity has "resulted in an uncritical celebration of the traces of cultural syncretism which assumes a symbiotic relationship without paying adequate attention to economic, political and social inequalities"; in their

---

[1] Gayatri Gopinath includes Chadha in "a new crop of Indian diasporic feminist filmmakers" who "are in no small part responsible for this translation of Bollywood into Hollywood, in that they act as modern-day tour guides that in effect 'modernize' Bollywood form and content for non–South Asian audiences" (162).

reading, a "potentially transgressive power" has been attributed to the concept "which might seem to endorse the celebration of its traces as transgressive *per se*" (1). Hutnyk's *Critique of Exotica*, focusing on the central issues of hybridity and authenticity, also questions optimistic readings of crossover, hybrid projects within contemporary cultural studies. Hutnyk argues that hybridity-talk is altogether contained by the commodity system; as he reminds us, "a pro-hybridity stance does not seem ... to offer any guarantees of a revolutionary project, since the place for articulation of hybridity is also a space which already seems all too easily articulated with the market" (36). Hybridity-talk might not act as a disturbance of capitalist structures and hence can run the risk of keeping them essentially unimpaired (31–32). Likewise, Huggan recognizes that his own academic output in the field of postcolonial studies is inextricably "bound up in a late-capitalist mode of production ... in which such terms as 'marginality', 'authenticity' and 'resistance' circulate as commodities available for commercial exploitation" (*Postcolonial Exotic* xvi). Being "bound up with" one another, "postcolonialism and its rhetoric of resistance have themselves become consumer products" (6). Acknowledging and critiquing this hybridity turn of cultural studies as somewhat empty of its professed political impact, Sanjay Sharma, John Hutnyk, and Ashwani Sharma reacted as early as 1996 to a rising commodification of "Asian Koolness" when they applied the notion of selling difference to popular music production in Britain. On the first page of the introduction to their collection *Dis-Orienting Rhythms*, the editors state: "Ethnicity is in. Cultural difference is in. Marginality is in. Consumption of the Other is all the rage for late capitalism. Finally, it appears that the 'coolie' has become cool" (1).

Looking back at the developments in the field of cultural studies during the last decades, a growing plethora of criticism has devoted itself to assessing the ways the cultural industries have been cashing in on a fascination with difference within a global commodification of exotica. "Capital has fallen in love with difference," noted Jonathan Rutherford in 1990, because "cultural difference *sells*" ("Place" 11). In Stuart Hall's words on the relation between ethnic difference and capitalism, "in order to maintain its global position, capital has had to negotiate," that is, "it had to incorporate and partly reflect the differences it was trying to overcome" ("Local" 182). In effect, according to Gilles Deleuze and Félix Guattari, postmodern capital "does not proceed by progressive homogenization, or by totalization, but by the taking on of consistency or the consolidation of the diverse as such" (481). In line with this "isomorphic" power of postmodern capital, the capitalist axiomatic "tolerates, in fact it requires, a certain peripheral polymorphy, to the extent that it is not saturated, to the extent that it actively repels its own limits" (482). Capitalism allows differences to become visible as long as they are controlled and sanitized. Capital must ensure the existence on some level of that which stands as its other, that which opposes it; capital accommodates cultural difference by neatly circumscribing and marketing alterity. The disparaging implication of this emphasis upon the cultural production of newness is that postmodern capitalism not only finds value, but also *stimulus* in its most radically other. Ultimately, capitalism must enable radical opposition to continue to go about its business if capital is to have anything left to incorporate.

"What parades as progress in the culture industry, as the incessantly new which it offers up," writes Adorno, "remains the disguise for an eternal sameness" ("Culture Industry" 100). Elsewhere, Horkheimer and Adorno further contend:

> The constant pressure to produce new effects (which must conform to the old pattern) serves merely as another rule to increase the power of the conventions when any single effect threatens to slip through the net. Every detail is so firmly stamped with sameness that nothing can appear which is not marked at birth, or does not meet with approval at first sight. (128)

According to these arguments, products in the culture industry are pre-digested and demand little categorisation from the individuals who consume them. Cultural products have already been put into pre-existing categories and hence classified and packaged for easy and immediate consumption. It might be tedious to reassert that even though the make-up of the cultural industries in their transition to a post-Fordist era differs to a great degree from how it was at the time when Horkheimer and Adorno were writing, the logics presiding over them seem to have remained unchanged. The fact is that the cultural industries continue to rely on progress disguised as difference (based on the relationship of an other to a dominant self) to prove their own newness and diversity. Cultural difference, functioning within a global cultural economy, is thus part of the marketplace and becomes *itself* a marketable commodity. This is obvious in the surfacing of a market for so-called "world music"[2] in the late 1980s followed by the trend of Asian Kool music in early 1990s Britain. The Asian Underground scene reached the threshold of crossover reputation in the early 1990s partly as the result of the visibility of the British bhangra scene in the 1980s. Nonetheless, while the success of Br-Asian artists such as Talvin Singh, Cornershop, Asian Dub Foundation, Fun-da-mental, Bally Sagoo, Apache Indian, and Nitin Sawhney was hailed as a significant step towards the establishment of a South Asian space within mainstream British culture, their breakthrough to crossover acceptability was also regarded as being part and parcel of the brown culture industry rising to prominence around that time, and that has since continued apace.

The ethnically-oriented labels "world music," "Asian Underground," and "new Asian dance music," umbrella terms firmly stamped on diverse musical expressions at the point of production, act as the pre-digestion Adorno identifies in the culture industry. As the German critic argues:

---

[2] "World music" is a marketing term that refers to a diverse range of non-western musical expressions and, as Huq observes, it "can be seen as politically suspect for engaging in the neo-colonial practices of appropriation and domination" (*Beyond Subculture* 67). Huq further adds that this is "a problematic descriptor with distinct echoes of colonial relationships in 'othering' and exoticising non-western mainstream pop music" (88).

> The entire practice of the culture industry transfers the profit motive naked onto cultural forms. ... The autonomy of works of art, which of course rarely ever predominated in an entirely pure form, and was always permeated by a constellation of effects, is tendentially eliminated by the culture industry, with or without the conscious will of those in control. ("Culture Industry" 99)

According to Adorno, consumers are provided by the culture industry with pre-packaged products that have already been conceptually managed and classified for effortless and immediate processing. In his words in the essay "On Popular Music":

> The composition hears for the listener. This is how popular music divests the listener of his spontaneity and promotes conditioned reflexes. Not only does it not require his effort to follow its concrete stream; it actually gives him models under which anything concrete still remaining may be subsumed. The schematic build-up dictates the way he must listen while, at the same time, it makes any effort in listening unnecessary. Popular music is "digested" in a way strongly resembling the fad of "digests" in printed material. (22)

In this way, it is not necessary for the listener to impose labels on films, television programs, or popular music, trying to fit them into open conceptual frameworks.

By the same token that cultural products have increasingly become pre-digested, it seems there is no escape from the process whereby ethnic alterity is commodified and repackaged by western market forces. Notwithstanding the fact that postcolonial cultural products springing from areas as diverse as literature, theatre, film, and visual arts are inescapably affected by some degree of commodification, music, with its predisposition to and reliance on mass circulation, plainly illustrates the tie between ethnic alterity and capitalist consumption. The next section focuses on this connection between difference and consumption with reference to Rushdie's novel *The Ground Beneath Her Feet*.

"Not 'goods from foreign' but made in India"[3]

> This is the tale of Ormus Cama, who found the music first.
> —Rushdie, *The Ground Beneath Her Feet* 99

The Ground Beneath Her Feet is framed in the context of a struggle between the worldwide circulation of media images emanating from an ever-growing global market, specifically a western-based music industry, and the subjects of these representations, in this case, Ormus and Vina, who have risen to superstardom from

---

[3] This section is a substantially revised version of the chapter "Orpheus and Eurydice as Indian Rock-and-roll Superstars: Salman Rushdie's *The Ground Beneath Her Feet*," printed in Cristina M. Gámez-Fernández and Antonia Navarro-Tejero (eds), *India in the World*, Newcastle upon Tyne: Cambridge Scholars Publishing, 2011, 203–210, published with the permission of CSP.

Bombay to "Rio, Sydney, London, Hong Kong, Los Angeles, Beijing" (559). This section draws its attention to Vina's and Ormus's negotiations in the context of the political economy of international rock music. It concludes by demonstrating that the novel self-consciously takes part of the world of international celebrity and globalising forces, demonstrating Rushdie's acute sensitivity to the contradictions and possibilities that permeate the experience of global celebrity.

*****

Against the backdrop of interconnected flows of globe-spanning migration, economic globalization, and large-scale corporate media that transfigure both the West and "the back yards of the world" (419), this novel is Rushdie's self-professed first move into an "American" fictional territory:

> The country that has mattered the most to me with this book has been the US. ... [*The Ground Beneath Her Feet* is] my first American novel. I mean, not just because a lot of it happens in America, but because rock and roll is a thing that came from America. And so one of the things that I was writing about was how the rest of the world has responded to American culture, and how America has responded to the rest of the world. (qtd. in Kadzis, "Salman Speaks" 223–224)

Attesting to the writer's cultural magpie tendency, the narrative is rooted both in Greek mythology and in popular culture. Rushdie recasts the mythical figures of Orpheus and Eurydice as the rock superstars Ormus Cama and Vina Apsara, and this postmodern retelling of Greek mythology is set against the background of twentieth-century stardom. The many-layered construction of the novel, particularly its interweaving of rock-and-roll lyrics and mythology, defies any attempt to offer the reader a simple, straightforward outline of its plot. The narrative spans the lifetime and afterlife romance between two singers of South Asian provenance who become purveyors of much-celebrated transcultural music. Vina, of Indian and Greek descent, born in the US and later "returned" to her motherland India, is a contemporary mix between the Greek myth of Eurydice, the Mexican myth of the snake god Quetzalcoatl, and the Hindu goddess of passion and lust Rati. Ormus, her co-vocalist in the famous rock band VTO, is a Bombay-born Parsi Zoroastrian composer and guitarist, and a mythological hybrid as well, resulting from the juxtaposition of the Greek poet and musician Orpheus with the Hindu god of love, Kama, who was rescued from the underworld by his consort, Rati. Besides this intertextual connection to Orpheus and Kama, Ormus Cama – "quiffed, sideburned and pelvis-swivelling Ormus" (91) – has likewise echoes of Elvis Presley and Bob Dylan.

Rock-and-roll, acting as the prime structural underpinning of the novel, is presented as the new global virus which allows the protagonists to cross all frontiers and thereby overcome the East-West divide. In an interview conducted by Peter Kadzis around the time of the novel's release, Rushdie posits rock music as the unifying "language of cultural reference" of our times; besides, on a personal note, it provided the soundtrack for his childhood in Bombay:

> [Rock] was a language of cultural reference that I could use which people all around the world would easily get, just in the same way that people once might have got a range of classical or mythological reference. Rock is the mythology of our time. It was interesting to contrast it in the novel with that older mythology .... I wanted to write about rock and roll partly because it's the music of my life. When I was young, it was young. We've more or less grown up and grown old together. It feels as if rock music is the soundtrack of my life.[4] As if I could associate all kinds of moments in my life with songs, and songs would evoke memories that otherwise might have been lost. (qtd. in "Salman Speaks" 222–223)

In this interview, Rushdie speaks of listening to rock as a child on the radio, but not on the state-controlled All India Radio, which did not allow the playing of western music because "in that post-colonial moment, it was thought to be culturally unsound." Even so, he managed to tune in to "a few hours of a Western hit-parade kind of program" on the more tolerant Radio Ceylon and, given that Bombay "was so international," he heard this type of music at his friends' houses. "It wasn't easy for that music to arrive, given these constraints," he stresses, "[a]nd yet it did arrive, and we all heard" (219). Because of its ability to penetrate borders, rock music became, in the writer's words, "the first globalized cultural phenomenon" (219). In another interview, he reiterates that rock-and-roll "must have been a phenomenon of extraordinary force to have managed to have spread around the world at a time when it was so difficult for that to happen" (qtd. in Nagarajan).

In the Bombay of the time, according to the version of the narrator of *The Ground Beneath Her Feet*:

> ... communications technology was in its infancy. There was no tv and radios were bulky items under strict parental control. Also, the state broadcasting corporation, All-India Radio, was forbidden to play Western popular music, and the only Western records pressed in India, at the Dum Dum factory in Calcutta, tended to be selections from Placido Lanza,[5] or the sound-track music from the MGM movie *Tom Thumb*. Print media were likewise parochial. I cannot remember seeing a single photograph of American singing stars in any local showbiz magazine, let alone the daily papers. (91)

Said, discussing the effects of cultural encounter and exchange, writes that "[t]he history of all cultures is the history of cultural borrowings. Cultures are not impermeable. Culture is never just a matter of ownership, of borrowing and

---

[4] This idea finds resonance in the novel through the narrator's memories: "Rock music, the music of the city, of the present, which crossed all frontiers, which belonged equally to everyone – but to my generation most of all, because it was born when we were children, it spent its adolescence in our teenage years, it became adult when we did, growing paunchy and bald right along with us" (96).

[5] Obviously, "Placido Lanza" (Mario Lanza) exemplifies Rushdie's cultural fictionalisings across the text.

lending with absolute debtors and creditors, but rather of appropriations, common experiences, and interdependencies of all kinds among different cultures" (*Culture and Imperialism* 261–262). Countering the perceived trend whereby the values of cultural imperialism are exerted, for instance, through the exportation of western rock music, *The Ground Beneath Her Feet* instead emphasizes rock-and-roll's protean hybridity and dynamics. Besides, an overt defence of the musical genre's productive impurity and counter-hegemonic potential is presented in the novel when, after dissecting the meaning of the word "culture" as a "squirm of germs on a glass slide ..., a laboratory experiment calling itself a society" (95), the narrator Rai Merchant (a.k.a. Umeed Merchant) proceeds to ask rhetorically:

> In India it is often said the music I'm talking about is precisely one of those viruses with which the almighty West has infected the East, one of the weapons of cultural imperialism, against which all right-minded persons must fight and fight again. Why then offer up paeans to culture traitors like Ormus Cama, who betrayed his roots and spent his pathetic lifetime pouring the trash of America into our children's ears? Why raise low culture so high, and glorify what is base? Why defend impurity, that vice, as if it were a virtue? (95)

Rushdie capitalizes on the subversive and anti-establishment quality of music by selecting the workname "Rai" for the narrator, a name which echoes a variety of Algerian music known as "raï." This music has been the target of religious fundamentalism in recent years, as the narrator realizes: "in another part of the world, Rai was music. In the home of this music, alas, religious fanatics have lately started killing the musicians. They think the music is an insult to god, who gave us voices but does not wish us to sing, who gave us free will, *rai*, but prefers us not to be free" (19).

In the novel, music is not seen as a commodity "through and through" (Adorno, "Culture Industry" 100), a commodity whose sole function is being traded for profit, but is instead presented as contrapuntal. In musical terminology, "counterpoint" refers to the connection between two or more voices concurrently autonomous in rhythm and interrelated in harmony. Said resolutely refused to privilege either side of the encounter that comprises contrapuntal reading, a reading that is called into being by a series of oppositions. In contrapuntal reading, as in music, "various themes play off one another, with only provisional privilege being given to any particular one" at any given time; contrapuntal reading, Said adds, opens all texts up for the ways in which their premises, themes, and even styles "brush up unstintingly against" the counter-texts to which they are opposed (*Culture and Imperialism* 51). A contrapuntal reading must then take into account disparate social processes, "each with its particular agenda and pace of development, its own internal formations, its internal coherence and system of external relationships, all of them co-existing and interacting with others" (36). In the case of the protagonists of *The Ground Beneath Her Feet*, these opposing social processes are that of complicity with the brown culture industry and that of resistance to it. Reading contrapuntally thus involves extending our thinking through texts to encompass simultaneously "the metropolitan history that is narrated" and "other histories against which (and together with which) the dominating discourse acts" (Said, *Culture and Imperialism* 51).

In Rushdie's work, a provocative repatriation of the quintessential western musical genre of rock-and-roll as "not 'goods from foreign' but made in India" (96) invests it with a subversive edge. Such a fantastical origin attributed to rock in the novel's "variant version of history" allows for the refashioning of a West that is "exotic, fabulous, unreal" (260). Rushdie ironizes further this "amazing proposition" using an empire-writing-back stance: in their colonising efforts, "maybe it was the foreigners who stole it from us [Bombayites]" (96). This reversing of the origins of rock-and-roll goes against an assimilationist understanding of globalisation and instead posits its diversification potentialities. This shift allows for a nuanced critique in the novel of globalising forces in such a way that the cracks and contradictions within power structures are exposed and explored through Rushdie's rendering of the workings of the music industry. The rewriting of rock-and-roll's history does not end with its geographical relocation: in Rushdie's version Simon and Garfunkel are women whose first names are Carly and Guinevere (156), Lou Reed is also female, Elvis Presley turns out to be Jesse Garon Parker, the legendary line from Bob Dylan's song "Blowin' in the Wind" is misappropriated as inter alia "[t]he ganja, my friend, is growing in the tin" (141), John Lennon instead of the Rolling Stones performs the major hit song "Satisfaction," whereas *Rolling Stones* is one of the magazines the musical critic Madonna contributes to. Other instances of this rewriting of recorded history abound in *The Ground Beneath Her Feet* and the author refers to this "variant or parallel version of the world" in an interview as an attempt to "blur the edges between the fictional world and the real world" (qtd. in Nagarajan).[6] Admittedly, the most powerful inversion of this imaginary world is having rock-and-roll start off in Bombay around 1960. The narrator's outrageous suggestion is that Ormus knew the lyrics of Elvis and Dylan first hand, even before these artists did, given that the lyrics were channelled through his psychic underworld one thousand and one days before their manifestation in the West. "From the beginning," Ormus

---

[6] For instance, in this version of history, John F. Kennedy survives his assassination attempt in 1963 because Lee Harvey Oswald's rifle jammed (185). Bobby and John F. Kennedy eventually die in a double murder (225). Ormus later gets in touch with an alternative dimension which comes to resemble "reality": "John Kennedy got shot eight years ago. Don't laugh, Nixon's President. East Pakistan recently seceded from the union. Refugees, guerrillas, genocide, all of that. And the British aren't in Indochina, imagine that; but the war's there all right, even if the places have different names. I don't know how many universes there are but probably that damn war's in every one. And Dow Chemicals and napalm bombs. *Two, four, six, eight, no more naphthene palmitate*—they've got another name for that too, but it burns little girls' skins the same way. Naptate. ... [T]here's a ton of singers in sequins and eyeliner, but no trace of Zoo Harrison or Jerry Apple or Icon or The Clouds, and Lou Reed's *a man*" (350).

"claimed that he was literally years ahead of his time" (89). The narrator describes the link between Ormus and Elvis thus:

> if I mention, as I must, the grinding rotation of his hips as he moved through the apartment on Apollo Bunder, and the increasing explicitness of his pelvic thrusts and the dervish thrashings of his arms; if I linger upon the baby-cruel curl of his upper lip, or the thick black hair hanging in sensual coils around his brow, or the sideburns that were straight out of a Victorian melodrama – if, above all, I attempt to reproduce the few strange sounds he was managing to produce, those *unnhhs, uhh-hhhs*, those *ohhs* – then you, stranger, might excusably write him off as a mere echo, just another of that legion of impersonators who first rejoiced in, and afterwards rendered grotesque, the fame of a young truck driver from Tupelo, Miss., born in a shotgun shack with a dead twin by his side. (89)

Ormus and his deceased twin brother Gayomart developed a telepathic connection which allowed the musician to access, by way of dreams, western rock-and-roll songs prior to their performance at "the Sun Records Studio or the Brill Building or the Cavern Club" (96). The apparent absurdity of attributing an eastern origin to rock music is somewhat dispelled in the narrative by making the West an inherent part of the East. By the same token that Bombay is not wholly East because the West has always been present in this city – indeed, from its inception – Ormus belongs neither to East nor West, but rather, to "West, East, North and South":

> This is what Ormus and Vina always claimed, never wavering for a moment: that the genius of Ormus Cama did not emerge in response to, or in imitation of, America; that his early music, the music he heard in his head during the unsinging childhood years, was not of the West, except in the sense that the West was in Bombay from the beginning, impure old Bombay where West, East, North and South had always been scrambled, like codes, like eggs, and so Westernness was a legitimate part of Ormus, inseparable from the rest of him. (95–96)

Vina's and Ormus's status within the political economy of international rock music is an integral part of their characterisation: even if these pop music icons eventually become "deracinated" (426), they "'[go] political,' organizing the Rock the World charity concerts, meeting world leaders to demand action on global famine, protesting the cynicism of international oil companies in Africa," and so forth, to such an extent that "the same commentators who had abused them for their superficiality now berated them for pomposity, for stepping out of their playpen to argue with the grown-ups" (425). While in the mainstream rock music of VTO's glory days any Indian musical input is negligible,[7] Vina's music later evolves into

---

[7] Still, the narrator ponders: "Sometimes I try to imagine how she [Vina] would have sounded singing ghazals. For even though she dedicated her life to another music entirely, the pull of India, its songs, its languages, its life, worked upon her always, like the moon" (124).

a more hybrid form after the break-up of the band. Similarly, Ormus's solo stage of his career, after Vina's death, bears a resemblance to world music when he begins to fuse "un-American sounds" into his musical production, such as "the tabla rhythms and sitar and yes vina riffs pushed through his sequencers along with pure synthesised sound" (546), developing towards an avowedly transnational music. To this Indian-western music also contribute "the sexiness of the Cuban horns, the mind-bending patterns of the Brazilian drums, the Chilean woodwinds moaning like the winds of oppression, the African male voice choruses like trees swaying in freedom's breeze, the grand old ladies of Algerian music with their yearning squawks and ululations, the holy passion of the Pakistani *qawwals*" (379).

Christopher Rollason detects in Rushdie's text a failure to engage creatively with world music and looks at this in extensive detail in his study "Rushdie's Un-Indian Music" (2001). Rollason has problems with the world-music turn in the novel, which he finds underdeveloped, being too superficial to function as anything more than as an interesting prospect, and concludes:

> Rushdie has missed a golden opportunity, fluffing the challenge of a sustained literary engagement with the world music phenomenon. We could have had an Indian Buena Vista Social Club; what we get is VTO, playing born-in-the-USA rock'n'roll while laying claim to an Asian "authenticity" that derives from literary sleight-of-hand alone. (114)

He finds this aspect so significant that in his view it "cast[s] doubt on the validity and usefulness of Rushdie's social critique" (117). Granted, such criticism is sensible; yet, this world-music twist to the plot is vital because it provides Rushdie with yet another opportunity for panning re-orientalism. At one point, the narrator urges young Americans "in search of new frontiers" to "board VTO's Orient Express" (379). The writer demonstrates that Indian culture is exoticized as economic strategy and sold as Indo-chic to feed an ever-expansive global market. Epitomising the blind consumption of the exotic other, a secondary character by the name of Goddess-Ma acts as a spiritual guru, transmitting a trendy – and profitable – "Wisdom of the East" to the élite of New York society:

> India-blah, Bharat-burble, the so-called Wisdom of the East is definitely back in fashion. In fact, India in general is hotter than ever: its food, its fabrics, its doe-eyed dames, its direct line to Spirit Central, its drums, its beaches, its saints. (When India explodes a nuclear device, the notion of Holy Mother India takes a few dents, but it is quickly agreed by *le tout* Manhattan that in this matter India's unwise political leaders have betrayed the land's true spirit. The valuable Oriental Wisdom concept suffers little lasting damage, unlike the much-shaken planet.) (496)

This section has not intended to engage with the protagonists' music in a celebratory tone, as if their hybrid music instantaneously amounts to being progressive and politically emancipatory, and, equally, it does not wish to condemn it as a mere commodity, the end product of skilful marketing strategies used by transnational entertainment corporations. The purpose of this section is instead to draw attention to the extent to which their music embodies and enacts in an interdependent fashion both complicity with neo-colonial cultural industries *and* resistance to it. These hybrid interactions should not, despite the fact that they take place within a brown culture industry, be reduced either as offspring of cultural diversity or as the end product of sheer commodification. Vina's and Ormus's fusion music is not wholly generated by the machinery of the brown culture industry, but rather reclaims its contrapuntal potential as a medium of creative expression. Rushdie's approach to popular music in this novel not only explores the paradoxes that result from the cultural commodification of difference, but also considers the transformative potential of ideological subversion and social critique contained within those paradoxes. Even if the protagonists' music is compatible with and even functional for the brown culture industry, and hence does not act as an irreversible disruption of that industry, it does exhibit some degree of autonomy, critical acumen, and emancipatory possibility that manage to escape the dominance of commodity fetish forms. In other words, their music might be a site for resistance to capital even as it is produced by way of and advances the interests of corporate profit.

The novel mirrors an age in which power lies more in regulating images than administering territories. In this respect, Jean Baudrillard has influentially theorized the politically disempowering "precession of simulacra" in the postmodern world where the cultural terrain is created and regulated by the spectacle. Baudrillard's work on simulation conveys how, in an age in which the simulacrum no longer refers to an original, but has become the original – a "hyperreal" – the representation predates and predetermines the real. A possible alter ego of the French philosopher makes its appearance in Rushdie's text as the cultural theorist Rémy Auxerre, who draws the reader's attention to the fact that we are living in a surrogate reality created by televisualisation (484). "Once it's been on tv," Auxerre argues, "people are no longer acting, but *performing*," prey to the trap of the televized "real" and its "*feedback loop*" (484–485). There is no difference between reality and its "immediatization," the sound and its echo, the event and the media response to it (485) – what remains is simulacra. Thus, Rushdie devises a fictional world, echoing Baudrillard's realm of simulacra, where "[o]nly the show [or the spectacle] was real," where "outside that fiction, the cosmos was a fake" (559), and where Ormus and Vina, and consequently their transnational rock band VTO, had ceased to be "real."

To illustrate this non-existence of "reality," after Vina's death in an earthquake in Mexico, on Valentine's Day 1989 (3) (interestingly enough, the same day of Rushdie's personal earthquake following the fatwa), the female rock star resurfaces in an unprecedented "impersonation craze" as numerous Vina look-alikes perform "the underground, heavy-metal and reggae Vinas, the rap Vinas, the Vina drag queens, the Vina transsexuals, the Vina hookers on the Vegas strip, the Vina strippers ..., the porno-Vinas" (490), and so on. The deceased celebrity "*Vina Divina*" is caught by the trap of the simulacrum, subjected to the demands of capital enhancement strategies and forced post-mortem to cater for the artificial needs of a postmodern consumer culture. In addition to Vina look-alike Quakette dolls, the offspring of her death in the earthquake, "there will be video games and CD-ROMs and instant biographies and bootleg tapes" (486). As the narrator despondently remarks, "[i]t seems that all the cascading emotion of the Vina phenomenon will end in the slave market of capital. One minute she's a goddess, and the next she's *property*" (486). Vina's and Ormus's actions mirror a larger dilemma faced in the context of the oppositional politics of postcolonial cultural production, namely, the unfeasibility of postcolonial strategies of resistance in the context of globalized multinational corporations, such as those lurking behind the western-based music industry. The narrative of *The Ground Beneath Her Feet* is indeed framed against the background of a struggle between the worldwide circulation of media images emanating from an ever-growing global market and the subjects of these representations coming from marginal nations. Ultimately, Rushdie places the stress on the ambiguity residing between the resistance of the megastar protagonists to that global power structure, and their capitulation to the seductiveness of US mass culture.

While *The Satanic Verses* was flavoured with countless sarcastic observations on the Americanisation or "Coca-Colonization of the planet" (406), *The Ground Beneath Her Feet* self-consciously takes part in the world of international celebrity and global culture it chronicles. In this novel, Rushdie brings into play the icon of the deceitful Trojan Horse to satirize America's cultural imperialism. The narrator Rai, who is a news photographer, offers the following comments when he describes his *The Trojan Horse*, a book of pictures taken in Indochina:

> My idea was that the war in Indochina hadn't ended at the time of the ignominious U.S. withdrawal. They'd left a wooden horse standing at the gates, and when the Indochinese accepted the gift, the real warriors of America – the big corporations, the sports culture of basketball and baseball, and of course rock'n'roll – came swarming out of its belly and overran the place. Now, in Ho Chi Minh City and Hanoi, too, America stood revealed as the real victor. ... Almost every young Indochinese person wants to eat, dress, bop and profit in the good old American way. MTV, Nike, McWorld. Where soldiers had failed, U.S. values ... had triumphed. (441)

In a sense, by incorporating rock-and-roll into the American "Cultural Revolution" (441), the author interrogates this musical genre as another corporate marketing tool – consequently, as an agent of neo-colonial practices – and not solely as an anthem for democratic principles and a vehicle of social protest, or, in other words, a medium to bring to light and condemn what artists perceive as injustices. Notwithstanding the potential of rock music to cut across all frontiers – a latent possibility which Rushdie indeed validates – the alter ego stalking Ormus (his resentful brother, Cyrus Cama) overtly denounces the artist's transcultural musical fusions as not symbolising global unity, but instead of partaking of "the arrogance of the West" and, as a result, of being complicit with discourses of neo-expansionism: "We must not take Ormus Cama at his own low estimate, as a mere troubadour or popster; for his self-hating, deracinated music has long been at the service, I would even say at the very heart, of the arrogance of the West, where the world's tragedy is repackaged as youth entertainment and given an infectious, foot-tapping beat" (556).

In spite of this alleged connivance with western ideals, rock is, ultimately, the driving force that boosts the protagonists' self-fashioning, or "auto-couture" (95). Although rock-and-roll is, according to common knowledge, an American invention, it does not stand for (American) standardisation in the novel, but rather invokes creative processes of cultural hybridisation. As Mariam Pirbhai notes, in Rushdie's fictional world, even the homogenising forces of globalisation – decried as akin to the Americanisation of culture – are permeated with ambiguity, if we consider that American culture is itself blatantly hybrid (57). All cultures are the result of intermingling, always made up of endless appropriations and criss-crossings, and the US emerges in *The Ground Beneath Her Feet* as the contemporary symbol of the heterogeneity of origins. The present-day US is particularly suitable as the centripetal focus for Ormus and Vina to be drawn to, having "generated a powerful fable of itself as a land of immigrants" (Appadurai, *Modernity* 173). When Rushdie rewrites the history of rock-and-roll as beginning in India, he seems to intend more than just presenting a "magic gift" to the subcontinent (141). He appears to ironize the extent to which one can trace any singular point of origin or ascertain authenticity in a globalized world. Cultural hybridity puts into question, from the outset, the direction in which cultural exchanges and influences flow. As such, Rushdie ridicules the notion of one pure, uncontaminated origin in a shifting, globalized world, and his example is a musical genre whose origins may be found not only in the West, but also in the East.

Chapter 5
Rushdie, the Public Intellectual

In a 2008 interview with Boyd Tonkin, Rushdie states that "how the world adds up, and how this part connects to that part, is something [he had] been trying to explore for a really long time"; he adds: "*The Satanic Verses* is a novel about migrations, but in the last three or four books, [he had] been trying to write about how over here connects to over there" ("Salman Rushdie"). At a post-panoptical juncture dominated by the shifting dynamics of the internet and large-scale global travel, many of the writer's essays included in *Step Across This Line*, as well as his novels *The Ground Beneath Her Feet*, *Fury*, and *Shalimar the Clown* set the stage for the writer's "American turn." In line with the extant circulation of the post-national paradigm, these essays and novels remind us of the intensifying inadequacy of institutional borders as boundary markers. The aim of this chapter is to tease out an interrelated set of elements that have contributed to shaping the discursive predicament in which Rushdie has been trapped for a couple of decades. Its purpose it not to attach a one-dimensional "American" label to Rushdie's post-fatwa and post-9/11 literary production and politics, which some critics even claim effectively advance US economic and political interests. North America is not only a site of enunciation for Rushdie, but, with particular reference to the post-9/11 geopolitics of terror, is, also and most importantly, a site of cultural critique.

Outside the Whale[1]

> The truth is that there is no whale. We live in a world without hiding places; the missiles have made sure of that. ... Outside the unceasing storm, the continual quarrel, the dialectic of history. Outside the whale there is a genuine need for political fiction, for books that draw need and better maps of reality, and make new languages with which we can understand the world.
> —Rushdie, "Outside" 99–100

---

[1] This subchapter combines revised and expanded sections of the previously printed essays "'Artworks, unlike terrorists, change nothing': Salman Rushdie and September 11," in Cara Cilano (ed.), *From Solidarity to Schisms: 9/11 and After in Fiction and Film from Outside the US*, Amsterdam and New York: Rodopi, 2009, 93–114, and "'Beware Behalfies!': Contradictory Affiliations in Salman Rushdie's *Step Across This Line*," in Manuela Sanches et al. (eds), *Europe in Black and White: Immigration, Race, and Identity in the "Old Continent,"* Bristol and Chicago: Intellect, 2011, 67–76, published with the permission of Rodopi and Intellect.

Rushdie states that "works of art, even works of entertainment, do not come into being in a social and political vacuum; ... the way they operate in society cannot be separated from politics, from history. For every text, a context" ("Outside" 92). In addressing the writer's shifting positions as a public intellectual, expressed in both his more recent essays and in the novels *Fury* and *Shalimar the Clown*, the purpose of this section is not to appraise what has been called (most of the times derogatorily) Rushdie's "American turn," nor to ascertain the inconsistencies of his ideological standing with reference to the cultural authority and military power of the US in general, and to the aftermath of September 11, 2001 in particular. A focal intention of this section is to undermine the idea that the writer manifests, or did indeed manifest, a clear-cut pro-US government position in support of the "war on terror."

*****

According to Said, the attention of contemporary secular criticism is engaged by the twin "temptations" of vertical *filiation*, wherein critical consciousness is inextricably connected "by birth, nationality, profession" to a stable place of origin, and horizontal *affiliation*, in which newfangled critical solidarities are formed "by social and political conviction, economic and historical circumstances, voluntary effort and willed deliberation" (*World* 24–25). Not unrelatedly, a review by Randy Boyagoda of *Step Across This Line* underscores the "dizzying" outcome of the "contradictory affiliations" resulting from Rushdie's self-pledged multipositionality in and out of the discourse of politics. "Over the course of the collection," Boyagoda notes, the writer presents himself as "a Muslim, Indian, New Yorker, Briton, European, American, trans-nationalist, post-nationalist, internationalist, immigrant, exile, emigrant, migrant" (48). The reviewer recognizes that such apparent changeability of social, cultural, and political affiliations – notably regarding the 9/11 attacks and their aftermath in US foreign policy – is defensible in Rushdie's fictional writing, where his characters exhibit hybrid selves and are thus far from lending themselves to unitary categorisation. In Rushdie's fiction, generally speaking, identities are fluid and always incomplete. Boyagoda considers nonetheless that in a cultural critic this multipositionality results in an unavoidable inconsistency and turns this anthology of essays and newspaper columns into a sort of "postmodern chutney" most likely to cause "an unfortunate indigestion" to its readers (49). What this section sets out to demonstrate is that rather than being an instance of fission, Rushdie's most recent non-fiction, as well as his novels *Fury* and *Shalimar the Clown*, are the ultimate product of fusion in the way that they result from the synthetic encounter – not disintegration – of contradictory states of affiliation.

In an interview with the British newspaper *The Daily Telegraph*, the writer comments on how individuals are being pigeonholed into circumscribed categories: "People are being invited to define themselves increasingly narrowly .... They're either Muslim, or Christian, or British, American, or whatever. ... The truth, of course, is that we're not just one thing, or another; we're all these little clouds of contradictions" (qtd. in Preston). In another interview, he likewise observes:

> I've never had an identity crisis. Ever. People keep telling me that I should have. But I've never had one. I mean, there're all kinds of dislocations. There's not just that. There's much more than that. First of all, as you say, I live in England and I've written about India. That's one dislocation. Secondly, my family went to Pakistan, so that's three countries anyway. Two legs and you have to have your feet in three countries. So that's a problem. Then Bombay is not like the rest of India. People who come from Bombay anyway feel different from the rest of India and quite rightly. On top of that, my family comes from Kashmir and Kashmir is not like the rest of India. So that's four or five separate dislocations. And I mean, it doesn't seem to me to be a problem. It seems to me to be quite enjoyable. (qtd. in Dharker 50)

On the one hand, Boyagoda seems to confirm the trend Rushdie discerns whereby individuals are being narrowly categorized and, on the other hand, he sidesteps an essential prerequisite of Rushdie criticism in the twenty-first century: as an Indian-born British citizen, New York resident, secular humanist Muslim, postcolonial writer, global literary celebrity, and transnational polemicist, Rushdie must of necessity experience some degree of paradox in his geopolitical ties. In the early 1980s, he had already been confronted with the difficulty faced by other diasporic individuals when trying to define his nationality: "I have constantly been asked whether I am British, or Indian. The formulation 'Indian-born British writer' has been invented to explain me. ... You see the folly of trying to contain writers inside passports" ("Commonwealth" 67). In 2003, Boyagoda outwits all of the above not by underlining the fault-lines within the writer's affiliations, but rather by emphasising how they seem to *threaten* his integrity as cultural commentator.

Throughout Rushdie's career he has always favoured the unencumbered subject, but his conceptualisation of "home" and the broader interrelated idea of geopolitical space have subtly changed over the years. In his earlier writings, migrancy constituted "a *political* act with political implications" (Mondal 180). Conversely, the writer espouses a "new thesis of the post-frontier" in the essay "Step Across this Line" (425), delivered at Yale University in February 2002 under the heading *The Tanner Lectures on Human Values*, and which provides the title for Rushdie's eponymous collection, appearing as the final piece in it. In view of this, de-territorialisation – a process in which stable frames of reference have been diluted by "the emergence, in the age of mass migration, mass displacement, globalized finances and industries, of this new, permeable post-frontier" (425) – has resulted in the transcending of formerly given territorial boundaries. This conceptual move to a post-national understanding of social and economic processes, consistent with Rushdie's career-long interests in migrant identity, verifies David Morley's and Kevin Robbins's assertion that "globalization is like putting together a jigsaw puzzle: it is a matter of inserting a multiplicity of identities into the overall picture of a new global system" (116). Ensuing from the escalating import of mobile capital, instant communication, and global travel in flexible capitalist societies, the permeability of frontiers is hence "the distinguishing feature of our times" (Rushdie, "Step Across" 425). *Shalimar the Clown*, postulating likewise a new age of the post-frontier, where "[e]verywhere was now a part of everywhere else. Russia, America, London, Kashmir" (37), highlights the way transnational terrorist networks and fundamentalist movements have assisted in the weakening of territorial borders. As a result of this "glocal" interconnectedness, "[o]ur lives, our stories, flowed into one another's, were no longer our own, individual, discrete. This unsettled people. There were collisions and explosions. The world was no longer calm" (37). Three years after the publication of *Shalimar the Clown*, sensitive about the uncritical celebration of mass migration experience today, Rushdie voices his concerns in an interview:

> [It used to be] easier to imagine mass migration as a positive force, a liberating force, both for the migrant and the culture into which the migrant came. … Now, I think there are big question marks around that idea because people are scared. The element of fear has arrived in a way that wasn't there before, because of the violence of the age. (qtd. in Tonkin, "Salman Rushdie")

In effect, in the 1985 essay "The Location of *Brazil*," the author had adopted a more celebratory tone when discussing migration: "To be a migrant is, perhaps, to be the only species of human being free of the shackles of nationalism (to say nothing of its ugly sister, patriotism). … To see things plainly, you have to cross a frontier" (125). As Yumna Siddiqi notes of this development in Rushdie's literary work, *Shalimar the Clown* articulates a cosmopolitan standpoint in the framework of post 9/11 terrorist and counter-terrorist practices – instead of "present[ing] private individual destinies as allegories of the situation of the nation, the novel symbolically maps geopolitics in relation to its protagonists' lives" (294).

Rushdie's latest de-territorialized exilic narratives bear out Zygmunt Bauman's analysis of the ongoing liquefaction of modernity – what the critic dubs "liquid modernity" – wherein fluid and seamless power structures are displacing those once perceived as fixed and stable (3–6). Rushdie's recent work rehearses this melting of previously "solid" modernity into liquid modernity: whereas his earlier writing dealt predominantly with the individual's relation to the materiality of territorial figurations, now it is the non-physicality of the globe and the ultimate discarding of frontiers that appeal to him. If, as the author argues, in "our deepest natures, we are frontier-crossing beings" ("Step Across" 408), then it seems that what used to be considered a political act – such as the traversing of borders – is turned into an innate one (Mondal 180), or one which might lead to an emptying of the potential transgressiveness of migrancy. Said's concept of "worldliness," understood as the intellectual's critical engagement with contemporary politics, implies the eradication of the strictures involved in "[n]ationality, nationalism, nativism" (*Culture and Imperialism* 277). To a certain extent, Rushdie embodies this worldliness in his professed anti-nationalist politics of non-alignment, as well as in his own uncompromisingly secular cosmopolitanism of which his voluntary exile in Britain and later in the US is part and parcel. Yet, by proposing the thesis of a post-frontier world, he has taken Said's model of worldliness to the extreme, potentially draining away the emancipatory potential of the crossing of borders, national or otherwise.

The reconfiguration of Rushdie's cultural geography has led critics to address what they see as a shift of political positioning in the writer's non-fiction. In this respect, Mondal argues that such change betrays "in effect if not intent, ... an endorsement of the status quo" (182). It should follow that the writer's texts have of late betrayed an opposition to Said's understanding of the public role of the exilic intellectual as "outsider, 'amateur,' and disturber of the status quo" (*Representations* x). Mondal interrogates the political significance of Rushdie's stance and proceeds to conclude that "[a]t best it has none, save for a residual rhetorical value that attempts to outmanoeuvre the politics of fear promoted by the US administration's 'war on terror', for which the permeability of borders represents a national security threat" (181). Has Rushdie indeed abandoned an earlier Saidean aspiration of speaking truth to power? Has his pen lost the ability to be provocative and incendiary, to excite debate in the way that both the front and back covers of the Vintage edition of *Step Across This Line* would have us believe it still can?[2] If we follow Mondal's argument, the writer's latest work is non-adversarial. In fact, according to this critic, Rushdie as a public intellectual seems to represent an updated, post-9/11, "war on terror" version of the professionalized and co-opted intellectual class of the cold war period that Said condemned.

While in the 1980s Rushdie's writings, in particular his 1987 travelogue *The Jaguar Smile*, the novel *The Satanic Verses*, and the essays assembled in *Imaginary Homelands*, reflected a distinctive left-liberal political stance, the articles collected in *Step Across This Line* have been, for the most part, the object of (mostly left-wing) disapproval and unprecedented controversy. For example, Ziauddin Sardar in an article entitled "Welcome to Planet Blitcon" (2006), published in the left-leaning British weekly *New Statesman*, includes Rushdie in a triumvirate of writers, along with Martin Amis and Ian McEwan, who "are the vanguard of British literary neoconservatives." To describe what Sardar perceives as the neoconservative political affiliations of these three prominent writers, he coins the acronym "Blitcons" (from *B*ritish *lit*erary neo*cons*ervatives). He expands on their "project" thus:

> The Blitcon project is based on three one-dimensional conceits. The first is the *absolute supremacy of American culture*. Blitcon fiction is orientalism for the 21st century, shifting the emphasis from the supremacy of the west in general to the *supremacy of American ideas of freedom*. ... The second Blitcon conceit is that Islam is the greatest threat to this idea of civilisation. ... The third Blitcon conceit is that *American ideas of freedom and democracy are not only right, but should be imposed on the rest of the world*. The extent to which this conviction has become central to these writers' thought can be traced by

---

[2] Both the 2003 and 2007 editions use the same image of the pencil-cum-match.

Rushdie's surprising progression, over the past 20 years, from political left to centre right. (emphases added)

Sardar exemplifies the second Blitcon conceit with "Rushdie's suspicion of and distaste for Islam" which for the critic is patent in four of his novels: *Midnight's Children*, *Shame*, *The Satanic Verses*, and *Shalimar the Clown*. In the latter, Sardar draws the reader's attention to a questionable chain of events wherein Shalimar "turns from a loveable clown and tightrope walker into a fuming terrorist"; he proceeds to question: "But what motivates his fury? The sexual betrayal of his wife and the fanatical zeal of an 'Iron Mullah' who forces people to build mosques and shroud their women in burqas." Sardar hence concludes that "[i]n Rushdie's world, a humane interpretation of Islam is a total impossibility." Despite Sardar's sweeping description of Amis's, Rushdie's, and McEwan's "project," and his exaggerated contention about the writers' shared "clear global political agenda" promoted by their celebrity status, his observations on the role of writers as "global pundits" today, which echo earlier arguments of this book regarding the branding of writers, are nonetheless perceptive and undisputed:

> The names of the most famous contemporary writers have become international brands. When they speak, the world listens. And increasingly, they speak not just through their fiction, but also via newspaper opinion pages, influential magazines, television chat shows and literary festivals. Novelists are no longer just novelists – they are also global pundits shaping our opinions on everything from art, life and politics to civilisation as we know it.

This section will now focus on Sardar's third Blitcon conceit – that Rushdie espouses the opinion that "American ideas of freedom and democracy are not only right, but should be imposed on the rest of the world." The writer's engagement as elite transnational intellectual with the issues arising from the events of September 11 appeared, in the words of Sabina and Simona Sawhney, "to join, rather than interrupt, the chorus on the street" and was perceived to be "surprisingly indistinguishable, in ... tone and argument, from many mainstream [US] media responses" (433). In an attempt to assess the verifiability of these words, the remainder of this section focuses on the development in Rushdie's positioning from the pre-9/11 novel *Fury* to his post-9/11 non-fiction and novel *Shalimar the Clown*. Mita Banerjee argues, with reference to *Fury* and also Hanif Kureishi's *Gabriel's Gift* (2001), that this traumatic event "could well be considered not only the ground zero of American literature and the American nation, but also the ground zero of the very paradigm of postcolonial studies" (309). Banerjee clarifies that even if "these two novels cannot be literal reactions to September 11, they nevertheless react to a political climate out of which September 11 arose" (313). This date acted as a conceptual turning point for the writer. Shortly after 9/11, Rushdie declared in an interview given to Sue Ellicott that because of this event we "need a new picture of the world," if only because "all the things we thought were true, turned out not to be"; September 11, he added, "was a new fictional moment" (qtd. in Manus). This reasoning is consistent with arguments voiced during the series of lectures given at Yale in the aftermath of 9/11:

> Like every writer in the world I am trying to find a way of writing after 11 September 2001, a day that has become something like a borderline. Not only because the attacks were a kind of invasion, but because we all crossed a frontier that day, an invisible boundary between the imaginable and the unimaginable, and it turned out to be the unimaginable that was real. ("Step Across" 436–437)

The perception of a turnaround in Rushdie's political affiliations can be traced back to one of his newspaper pieces written prior to the traumatic events of September 11. In the column "Globalization" (1999), first published in the *New York Times* where he was a regular commentator, Rushdie sustains the "authority of the United States" as "the best current guarantor," in the face of "tyranny, bigotry, intolerance, fanaticism," of the universal value of "freedom" (297). This standing sharply differs from his earlier critique of US foreign policy and the war in Nicaragua penned in *The Jaguar Smile*. In this travelogue of Rushdie's three-week stay in that Central American country in 1986, the writer compares the then Reagan administration in the US with "the bandit posing as the sheriff" (40). Here, one of his roles as a writer included "the function of antagonist to the state" (50). More than a decade later, while disapproving of the facile debunking of "the spread of American culture" – "[s]neakers, burgers, blue jeans and music videos aren't the enemy," he writes – Rushdie seems to support the role of the US as "world policeman" ("Globalization" 296). He contends that instead of seeing the US as the oppressor, we should "keep our eyes on the prize" since "[o]ut there are real tyrants to defeat" (298). These are the foes, not the dissemination of American culture we tend to slight "with our cultural hats on" whilst "shelter[ing] under the *pax Americana*" (296–298). Relatedly, Morton posits that Rushdie's "recent fiction and essays seem to suggest a resignation to, and even at times a tacit approval for, America's unilateralist foreign policy in the early twenty-first century, and in particular the Bush administration's war on terrorism" (117). Such an interpretation of the writer's post-9/11 work as apologetic for a US project of worldwide hegemony is irrespective of, for instance, the critique of the US government's rhetoric on the war against terror that Rushdie offered in an interview with François Armanet and Gilles Anquetil published in the French weekly *Le Nouvel Observateur* in 2006. Here, the writer argues that the word "freedom" has different senses and that his own concept of freedom is not that of George W. Bush, as, similarly, it was used in totally different senses by Ayatollah Khomeini and John Stuart Mill.

Looking at these apparent paradoxes in Rushdie's politics, Brennan states that "the evolution of Rushdie's public persona is more clearly understandable in the framework of professional pressures than diasporic insights (his need, that is, to find a space in the op-ed columns of the New York establishment, which considers itself at war)" (92). It is within these contradictions that one must critically scrutinize the writer's role as a public intellectual. Regardless of Rushdie's current self-positioning as a New Yorker and as an "American" writer, he has certainly not turned into an uncritical, flag-waving enthusiast of the US administration under Bush, which he portrays as a "hard-line, ideologue right-wing regime" ("Grand Coalition?" 361). On the contrary, he posits that "it is America's duty not to abuse its pre-eminence, and our right to criticize such abuses when they happen"; in fact, in a note added to the article afterwards, he asserts that "[i]n spite of all Bush's attempts to turn the USA into a pariah state, however, it remains the case that American culture isn't the enemy. Globalization isn't the problem; the inequitable distribution of resources is" ("Globalization" 298).

The post-9/11 Rushdie has sharply criticized any endeavours by the intellectual left to draw simplistic connections between US foreign policy and the terrorist attacks in New York. In the article "Anti-Americanism," published in February 2002, he manifests his indignation at what he perceives as the anti-American offensive led by a left-liberal faction. In the militaristic aftermath of September 11, this is "an ideological enemy [of America] that may turn out to be harder to defeat than militant Islam" (398). Rushdie notes that one of "the most unpleasant consequences of the terrorists' attacks on the United States" has been, as he puts it in another article, "the savaging of America by sections of the left" ("Attacks" 392). One might recall how the narrator of *Fury* affirms that anti-Americanism buttresses US-centred exercise of global power, seeing it as "Americanism in disguise, conceding, as it did, that America was the only game in town and the matter of America the only business at hand" (87). Commenting on the US-led conflict in Afghanistan, an ongoing military operation which began on 7 October 2001, Rushdie argues that "America did ... what had to be done, and did it well" ("Anti-Americanism" 399). He adopts a liberal defence of the invasion, dubbed "Operation Enduring Freedom" in response to the September 11 attacks, justifying it in entirely humanitarian terms. As one knows with hindsight, he was proven mistaken. "Great power and great wealth are perhaps never popular," the writer points out, but continues to stress that "more than ever, we need the United States to exercise its power and economic might responsibly" (400).

Even considering that this newspaper piece was penned within months of the 9/11 attacks, and well before both the Abu Ghraib prisoner abuse scandal in 2005 and the massive civilian casualties in Iraq, and that Rushdie has withdrawn his support for the US government's so-called "war on terrorism" – for example, as Abdulrazak Gurnah notes, the writer took part in protests against the detention centre at Guantanamo Bay in 2005, where suspects classified by the United States as "enemy combatants" were held (7) – a few questions are still in order. What to make of this accolade of the present-day geopolitical pre-eminence of America? Should we take the writer's words at face value? As Sabina and Simona Sawhney note, "Rushdie is certainly not the first writer to present us with a set of political writings incongruent with the general trajectory of his work" (437). Entertaining the expectation that the writer should be an unequivocal supporter of a predetermined political agenda might well be one of the pitfalls of reading Rushdie as "political event" (Muir). To Rushdie, any writing is a political act and is developed in an ineradicably political context. The writer certainly did not mince words in condemning British policies in the 1980s, and speaking truth to power did invest him with leftist credentials at the time.[3] One might argue that he himself created the above pitfall into which critics frequently stumble upon when, in 1982, he wrote:

> redescribing a world is the necessary first step towards changing it. And particularly at times when the State takes reality into its own hands, and sets about distorting it altering the past to fit its present needs, then the making of the alternative realities of art, including the novel of memory, becomes politicized. ... Writers and politicians are natural rivals. Both groups try to make the world in their own images; they fight for the same territory. And the novel is one way of denying the official, politicians' version of truth. ("Imaginary" 14)

How are we to interpret Rushdie's more recent inner dialectic between the author's political and literary sensibilities? Even conceding that such distinction between the literary and the political is artificial – in the sense that Rushdie offers critiques of the status quo, openly and through literary subversion – how is the reader to balance, on the one hand, his vilification of an increasing anti-American sentiment and, on the other hand, his scathing critique in *Fury* of US strategies for legitimising a neo-imperialist project? It should be noted that in this novel, published just within a week of 9/11, its New York-based protagonist Malik can be heard pondering:

> Might this new Rome actually be more provincial than its provinces; might these new Romans have forgotten what and how to value, or had they never known? Were all empires so undeserving, or was this one particularly crass? ... Who demolished the City on the Hill and put in its place a row of electric chairs, those dealers in death's democracy, where everyone, the innocent, the mentally deficient, the guilty, could come to die side by side? Who paved Paradise and put up a parking lot? Who settled for George W. Gush's boredom and Al Bore's gush? (86–87)

Yet, a month after the terrorist attacks, in a newspaper article the writer seems to call forth a "secret war" against those who had assaulted his new adopted home:

> They broke our city. I'm among the newest of New Yorkers, but even people who have never set foot in Manhattan have felt her wounds deeply, because New York in our time is the beating heart of the visible world. ... To this bright capital of the visible, the forces of invisibility have dealt a dreadful blow. ...

---

[3] This overtly political stance was chastised by Daniel Pipes in 1990: "Rushdie is a disaffected intellectual who criticizes or makes fun of nearly everything. One book attacks the Gandhis and modern India [*Midnight's Children*]; another reviles the leadership in Pakistan [*Shame*]; a third takes on American foreign policy [*The Jaguar Smile*]; the fourth one blasts fundamentalist Islam and Britain [*The Satanic Verses*]. The assault comes easily" (49).

Yes, we must send our shadow warriors against theirs, and hope that ours prevail. ("Attacks" 391–392)

Rushdie's texts not only reflect anxieties which result from the vexed positionality of the US in "cultural globalization and its military-political sidekick, intervention" ("Globalization" 296), but also ponder over the cultural significance of 9/11. In this respect, W.J.T. Mitchell (2005) reads the devastation of the World Trade Center on September 11 as "a new and virulent form of iconoclasm" (13) or "iconoclash" (11). Mitchell contends that "the moral imperative is to offend the images themselves" – such as those of the twin towers of New York – "to treat them as if they were human agents, or at least living agents of evil, and to punish them accordingly" (15). Thus, the "real target [of the 9/11 attacks] was a globally recognizable icon, and the aim was not merely to destroy it but to stage its destruction as media spectacle"; iconoclasm was accordingly "rendered as an icon in its own right" (13–14). Mitchell's reading echoes the description of the collapsing of the towers in Mohsin Hamid's 9/11 novel, *The Reluctant Fundamentalist* (2007), whose protagonist Changez depicts the instant of the attack thus: "my thoughts were not with the victims of the attack … no, I was caught up in the symbolism of it all, the fact that someone had so visibly brought America to her knees" (73). In a remarkably prescient manner, Rushdie anticipates both Hamid's literary portrayal and Mitchell's theorisation when he digresses in the essay "Step Across This Line" on 9/11 as artistic text, on the symbolic relevance of the destruction of the towers, and on the responsibilities of novelists after these harrowing events:

> Murder was not the point. The creation of a meaning was the point. The terrorists of September 11, and the planners of that day's events, behaved like perverted, but in another way brilliantly transgressive, performance artists: hideously innovative, shockingly successful, using a low-tech attack to strike at the very heart of our high-tech world. In dreams begin irresponsibilities, too. …
>
> In the aftermath of horror, of the iconoclastically transgressive image-making of the terrorists, do artists and writers still have the right to insist on the supreme, unfettered freedoms of art? Is it time, instead of endlessly pushing the envelope, stepping into forbidden territory and generally causing trouble, to start discovering what frontiers might be necessary to art, rather than an affront to it? (436–440)

The writer's declared answer to the above question was in the negative mode, although he provocatively goes on to assert that "[a]rtworks, unlike terrorists, change nothing" (441), seeming to downplay the transgressive potential of art, again baffling the reader. He emphasizes instead the political ineffectualness of artistic creation,[4] while prior to the events of September 11 his defence of art was far from muted. In fact, the debate over artistic political responsibility is often woven into Rushdie's fictional narratives. For example, in *The Satanic Verses* the

---

[4] Rushdie seems to reiterate W.H. Auden's despondency regarding the apparent uselessness of poetry in the 1939 elegy dedicated to W.B. Yeats (66–67).

poet Baal presents a writer's work as possessing the symbolic power "[t]o name the unnameable, to point at frauds, to take sides, start arguments, shape the world and stop it from going to sleep" (97). Similarly, in *Haroun and the Sea of Stories* the author has one of the characters, the sceptical son Haroun Khalifa, ironically question his storytelling father Rashid about the usefulness of *"stories that aren't even true"* (22). While Rushdie's fiction and his critical writing should not be correlated in any simplistic or reductive fashion, in the lecture "Is Nothing Sacred" (1990), in memory of Herbert Read, the writer states that novels claim *"the right to be the stage upon which the great debates of society can be conducted"* (420), and cautions in the essay "Outside the Whale" that if "writers leave the business of making pictures of the world to politicians, it will be one of history's great and most abject abdications" (100). Furthermore, in the 1997 essay "Notes on Writing and the Nation," he argues:

> In the aftermath of Empire, in the age of super-power, under the "footprint" of the partisan simplifications beamed down to us from satellites, we can no longer easily agree on *what is the case*, let alone what it might mean. Literature steps into this ring. Historians, media moguls, politicians do not care for the intruder, but the intruder is a stubborn sort. In this ambiguous atmosphere, upon this trampled earth, in these muddy waters, there is work for him to do. (66–67)

In a 2002 interview with Dave Weich, Rushdie confides that his own reading of *Fury* had changed to the extent of becoming nostalgic after September 11. While he was structuring the novel, the author felt "a sense of urgency about getting it down," as if he had been motivated by "some kind of prescience or foreknowledge" that the world would "change fast" (and in fact it would alter dramatically within a year from the time he finished writing it). Referring to the "sense of infinite possibility" brought about by an economic boom as a bubble that was inevitably "going to burst," Rushdie notes that even though he "didn't foresee calamity," he "did see that these moments in a city, or in a society, are usually pretty brief." As the writer puts it, the novel is a response to the climate out of which 9/11 arose as well:

> [I]f I want to capture *this* moment, I better do it fast because any second now it isn't going to be here to capture. I think September 11 in a way underlined and dramatized that change .... I always thought the book [*Fury*], if I did it right, could at some later point—which we're already at, as it turns out—be a kind of evocation of an age. ... Sometimes literature is the way in which the past can really be captured and held, in such a way that we're able to enter it. I hoped the book would be that. I still hope the book will be that; it's just shocking how rapidly the future has arrived. (qtd. in Weich)

Despite his intention that *Fury* might be truly evocative of the *Zeitgeist*, on the release of *The Enchantress of Florence* in 2008, Rushdie argued in an interview at the City Arts & Lectures in San Francisco that so-called post-9/11 fiction has yet to inaugurate new ways of representing the attacks and their after-effects.

In spite of Rushdie's contention, post-9/11 novels have become a highly marketable commodity: September 11 is a central trope in several bestsellers, such as Ian McEwan's *Saturday* (2005), Jonathan Safran Foer's *Extremely Loud and Incredibly Close* (2005), Jay McInerney's *The Good Life* (2006), Ken Kalfus's *A Disorder Peculiar to the Country* (2006), John Updike's *Terrorist* (2006), Don DeLillo's *Falling Man* (2007), and Joseph O'Neill's *Netherland* (2008). Notwithstanding this flood of post-9/11 novels (with *Shalimar the Clown* contributing to the deluge), Rushdie feels that September 11 still needs to "return and be assimilated as art," perhaps because one is too close to the events themselves. Thus, the traumatic events of that particular day, as well as their aftermath, have yet to be fundamentally rethought and significantly worked into the fabric of fiction and therefore affect cultural practice in a truly groundbreaking fashion. "Maybe another generation has to look at it from a greater distance," the writer argues, so that fresh ways of extracting meaning and rendering aesthetically this unique *Zeitgeist* can be successfully forged (qtd. in Krasny[5]).

Like some post-9/11 literature, the novel *Shalimar the Clown* delves into the making of geopolitical strife, global terrorism, and Islamic militancy and apparently fits into the conventional and reductionist "clash of civilizations" plot line. Nonetheless, in initially upholding, yet ultimately undermining the "hyperdiscourse" that contributes to set up the dichotomy West/Islam (Salvatore 9), Rushdie fashions a novel that subverts the reader's expectations – which heavily influenced the reception of the novel – of what a 9/11 literary text is or should be like. What at first appears to be the political assassination of the Jewish-American Max Ophuls, head of US anti-terrorism operations, by the Kashmiri born Muslim fundamentalist Shalimar – formerly a tightrope walker, born as Noman Sher Noman, and, by a calculated turn of fate, later Max's chauffeur in the US – reveals itself in due course to be passionately personal. When India Ophuls, the illegitimate offspring of the ambassador's affair with Shalimar's wife Boonyi Kaul, discovers her father dead on her doorstep in Los Angeles, assassinated by his Kashmiri chauffeur, the police and she suppose at once that the murder is terrorism-related and not the result of a personal quest for vengeance. Max had a past as "America's best loved, then most scandalous Ambassador to India" (5) – scandalous because romantically involved with Boonyi in Kashmir. Later on, the police, when they become aware of this back-story, conclude that Max's death is not politically motivated:

> The crime, which had at first looked political, turned out to be a personal matter, insofar as anything was personal any more. The assassin was a professional, but the consequences of U.S. policy choices in South Asia, and their echoes in the labyrinthine chambers of the paranoiac jihadi mind, these and other related geopolitical variables receded from the analysis, could with a high percentage of probability be eliminated from the equation. The picture had simplified, becoming a familiar image: the cuckolded and now avenged husband, the disgraced and

---

[5] 0:10:43–0:12:50.

now very nearly decapitated philanderer, locked in a final embrace. The motive, too, turned out to be conventional. *Cherchez la femme*. (338)

Even if Shalimar has indeed been trained to be a terrorist, his quest is to take vengeance on the man who so deftly seduced his wife. Siddiqi contends that Rushdie's depiction of "jihadist" violence in the novel is not apolitical but rather "a gendered politics of wounded masculinity" (303). Accordingly, the motif of dishonoured manhood attains political significance given that it is allegorical of the exploitative geopolitical effects of American neo-imperialism on the Indian subcontinent and Kashmir in particular. While Max stands for western economic and political influence, Shalimar personifies a kind of postcolonial grievance against such global power. By the same token, Boonyi's later dependence on drugs and food, when Max takes her as his mistress after seducing her, degrades her body, making it in her own words hideous and monstrous (*Shalimar* 205). This Siddiqi again reads allegorically as "globalized concubinage, one which destroys the national romance," that is, "as criticism of post-era liberalization, consumerism and cupidity: The East is seduced by the Western promise of limitless wares" (305). Alternatively, the narrative can be interpreted as *purportedly* avoiding any causal engagement with the transformation of the title character Shalimar into one of the "mujahedeen." This happens while *ostensibly* failing to contextualize how American neo-imperialism and the current globalized Islamic terrorist movements (with their iron mullahs and fundamentalist messages) are both actors playing out their roles within the same scenario.[6] Besides baffling some of the assumptions haunting post-9/11 debates about terrorism, *Shalimar the Clown* confronts the reader with her prejudgements about 1) a post-September 11 novel and 2) a post-fatwa novel penned by an author notorious for his own experience of Islamic fundamentalism and also for his fiery public statements, as a polemicist, after the 9/11 attacks and the 7/7 London underground bombings.

Concerns about Rushdie's conflicting political affiliations have at times implied that his work as postcolonial author should necessarily serve political goals. Understanding the writer's work as a "political event" accounts for the critics' stupefaction at Rushdie's perceived endorsement of the values of the western establishment. This tendency is manifest in Sabina and Simona Sawhney's foreword to the special issue of *Twentieth Century Literature* devoted to "Reading Rushdie After September 11, 2001." The editors' introduction discloses their bafflement in the face of the writer's "shift in [political] approach": "Part of the perplexity arises from a sudden onrush of doubt: did we misread the earlier texts, overlook the clues that would explain this surprising volte-face? Were those who had always dismissed Rushdie as another panderer to Western tastes for the colonial exotic right after all?" (435). As if aware of the "chronic ambivalence" (Mondal 174) and "contradictory affiliations" (Boyagoda) critics notice in Rushdie's current positioning, it seems that in the 2000s he defended a conceptual detachment between

---

[6] Interestingly, Siddiqi herself fears that such reading runs "the risk of being crude" (304).

writing and political commitment. Morton finds evidence in *Fury* of the author's progressive "withdrawal from the political" (117). A 2008 interview published in *The Times* to promote *The Enchantress of Florence* reflects precisely this intended distancing. Although the writer is metonymically referred to as "walking political symbol," he is portrayed in the opening remarks of the interview as being, nearly twenty years after the fatwa, "tired of politics" and not willing "to talk about current affairs." Having been a forceful defender of the political responsibilities of the writer, he now presents himself as an unlikely proponent of an apolitical vision. He justifies his position in the following statements:

> I'm feeling less political than I used to .... I've spent so much of my life talking about these issues which take on the times we live in very directly. I've had enough of that for a bit. ... I feel I have been damaged as a writer by the way people perceive my work *as part of a political event*. It is seen as a political entity rather than an artistic one. When *Midnight's Children* and *Shame* were published, people responded quite differently to my writing. Then there was a real shift in tone, when they said: 'Oh that was what he was really trying to do!' I am still a fiction writer underneath all that mess. (qtd. in Muir; emphasis added)

During another interview, Rushdie confesses that the experience of the fatwa did not affect his writing, but had transformed "the kind of writer people thought [he] was"; in his own words, "[p]eople began to think of me as non-fictional. People asked me to comment on events, and for a while I fell into that trap. As if I were to become a rent-a-quote. So I decided I've got to go back to why I started writing in the first place" (qtd. in Freeman). In an earlier interview, the writer had already commented on the construction of "Rushdie" as public figure:

> I think the worst damage that the fatwa did to me was ... [that] it gave people a very false sense of who I was and what my writing was like and what kind of reading experience it might be to open a book of mine. Attacks on my personality were also violent – and the great, famous thing about mud is that it sticks. Some of it did in some parts of the world, and I've been trying since to clean it off and to get people to see who's really here. (qtd. in Nagarajan)

Similarly, in the third page of his memoir *Joseph Anton*, written in the third person, he recounts:

> He was the person in the eye of the storm, no longer the *Salman* his friends knew but the *Rushdie* who was the author of *Satanic Verses*, a title subtly distorted by the omission of the initial *The*. *The Satanic Verses* was a novel. *Satanic Verses* were verses that were satanic, and he was their satanic author, 'Satan Rushdy', the horned creature on the placards carried by demonstrators down the streets of a faraway city, the hanged man with protruding red tongue in the crude cartoon they bore. *Hang Satan Rushdy*. (5)

In interviews, Rushdie recurrently voices his desire to be regarded first and foremost as a writer, not a symbol nor a political cause. References to the fatwa, inevitable as they may be, provoke weariness in the writer, as worded in an interview with John Preston: "All I'm hoping is that I can say to people [on the twentieth anniversary of the religious edict], 'Look, you've had 20 years of talking about this stuff, please can I have the rest of my life?' ... The whole thing has been an albatross around my neck in so many ways. ... All I want is to be seen as someone who writes books." He similarly observes in yet another interview: "Because of all the things that happened to me, there are people who think of me primarily as some kind of political animal. I began to feel it was getting in the way of people being able to read my books as books should be read" (qtd. in Tonkin, "Salman Rushdie"). The writer remarks in the lecture "Step Across This Line" that the transgressive qualities of his work – its unwavering "crossing of borders, of language, geography and culture" and its "lowering of the intolerable frontiers created by the world's many different kinds of thought policemen" – are part of "the literary project that was *given* to [him] by the circumstances of [his] life, *rather than chosen* by [him] for intellectual or 'artistic' reasons" (434; emphasis added). The somewhat crude irony is that in 2012, when Rushdie in fact went ahead with his declared intention to write a book about his experience of the fatwa, *Joseph Anton*, that memoir of life under duress proved a commercial success.

In "Outside the Whale" Rushdie argues that artists have an unavoidable political power and therefore should make "as big a fuss, as noisy a complaint about the world as is humanly possible" (99). In this essay of 1984 – whose title derives from George Orwell's "Inside the Whale" (1940) – he claims that "there can be no easy escapes from history, from hullabaloo, from terrible, unquiet fuss" (101) given that "we are all irradiated by history, we are radioactive with history and politics" (100). Arguing that "politically committed art can actually prove more durable than messages from the stomach of the fish" (96), he objects thus to Orwell's contention that the artist should recede into "the whale's belly" and concentrate on her own inner existence as subject matter (95). If, as he notes in 2002, "[t]he journey creates us" and "[w]e become the frontiers we cross" ("Step Across" 410), what are we to make of this further tension of political multipositionality originating from someone regarded by many as a cultural critic and, more relevant still, as a *political* writer? Frederic Jameson has famously elaborated on the significance of third-world literature as national allegory; third-world texts, he notes, "necessarily project a political dimension in the form of national allegory" in the way that "the story of the individual destiny is always an allegory of the embattled situation of the public third-world culture and society" (69). Notwithstanding the limitations of Jameson's theoretics, which have been extensively pointed out by A. Ahmad and others, his argument assists us in comprehending, at least in part, the phenomenon of reading Rushdie's work as political. In his contentious career, the writer has thrived on contradictions, personal and political. Even if Rushdie has professed of late his detachment from politics, the persistent ambivalence of his stance remains and, to the reader's puzzlement, despite all the rationalisation he provides, in the course of his 2008 interview with Kate Muir for *The Times*, he does not altogether close the door on politics. "[N]ever say never," he states after a pause, and we can almost see him grinning.

Cultural Warfare Redux[7]

> I'm certainly going to somewhat find myself resisting the idea of being called a representative British figure. I think I'm flattered, but ... I think there are certain British figures who would contest quite seriously the idea that I represented anything British.
> —Rushdie, qtd. in W.L. Webb 93

The following reading of Rushdie's knighthood is grounded in the assumption that postcolonial authors necessarily inhabit a provisional position, always prone to revision due to the dynamic interdependence between margins and centres. Rushdie's own standing in the field of postcolonial cultural production cannot be adequately charted on an exhausted two-dimensional map which relies on centre/periphery and left-wing/right-wing dichotomies. Beyond a consideration of how *The Satanic Verses* controversy was reignited by the awarding of the knighthood, this section addresses the potential of the "Rushdie affair part II" for questioning such binary oppositions.

*****

On 16 June 2007, on the occasion of Queen Elizabeth II's eightieth birthday honours, it was announced that Rushdie was to be made a Knight Bachelor of the Order of the British Empire by the reigning monarch for his "services to literature" – thus officially metamorphosing into Sir Salman Rushdie. This rank is part of the British honours system, under which titles and decorations are awarded for multiple forms of public service, in a twice-yearly ritual. The bestowal of this honour upon the writer in recognition of his outstanding achievement in the field of literature incited, without delay, widespread outrage in countries with Muslim majority populations. Public outcry swiftly ensued in Iran and Pakistan, with hostile demonstrations and effigies of the author burnt on the streets, while government officials accused Britain of insulting Islam and requested an apology from the cabinet of the then Labour Prime Minister Gordon Brown. In the row over the honour – or Rushdie affair part II, as it was labelled in the print media – Pakistan's hard-line religious affairs minister went as far as to suggest that the knighthood was justification enough for suicide attacks (Batty and Walker). In the meantime, Britain's first Muslim peer, Lord Nazir Ahmed, in statements to the French newspaper *Le Figaro*, drew a comparison between Rushdie's knighthood and the hypothetical granting of a formal commendation by the Afghan or Saudi governments to the 9/11 suicide hijackers (Godeau). In the eyes of irate Islamists, Britain's decision to honour the so-called "blaspheming apostate" could only be

---

[7] This section is a revised version of the chapter "Cultural Warfare Redux: Salman Rushdie's Knighthood," in Helena Gonçalves da Silva et al. (eds), *Conflict, Memory Transfers and the Reshaping of Europe*, Newcastle upon Tyne: Cambridge Scholars Publishing, 2010, 218–230, published with the permission of CSP.

a jingoistic ploy, coldly calculated to incite antagonism in the Muslim world. Such resentment provided the inspiration behind an art installation exhibited in September 2008 at the Imam Khomeini grand mosque in Tehran as part of the International Koran exhibition. Hinting at Rushdie's perceived Americanisation and endorsement of the "war on terror" in the aftermath of the September 11 attacks, a fake coffin bearing a US flag was on display, featuring skulls instead of the customary stars, as well as an Israeli flag accompanied by images of the writer, one with him behind bars and fittingly dressed in an American flag, and the other with him holding up a copy of *The Satanic Verses*.

Frow observes that "no object, no text, no cultural practice has an intrinsic or necessary meaning or value or function; and that meaning, value, and function are always the effect of specific social relations and mechanisms of signification" ("Economies" 61). As Michael Fischer and Mehdi Abedi note, *The Satanic Verses* "has become a highly charged social text, a lightning rod or projective screen against which contemporary cultural and social conflicts are drawn, enacted, and elaborated" (385). The knighthood provoked nearly as much outrage as had the Rushdie affair part I nearly two decades before, when Khomeini issued a fatwa against the writer for supposedly blaspheming Islam in his novel. On 19 June 2007, only three days after the news of the honour was released, Mohammad Reza Bahonar, first deputy speaker of Iran's parliament, declared:

> Salman Rushdie has turned into a hated corpse which cannot be resurrected by any action. The action by the British queen in knighting Salman Rushdie, the apostate, is an unwise one. The British monarch lives under this illusion that Britain is still a 19th century superpower and that bestowing titles is something still deemed important. (Spencer)

Bahonar raises a valid question regarding the cultural meanings attached to an awards system that is conditioned by its institutional dynamics and, most importantly, by Britain's imperial past. Seen by many as a quaint remnant of a defunct era in the context of a post-imperial society, the honours system has been at the centre of a debate over the urgency of its reform or even complete eradication. Bahonar's inflammatory statement discloses one of the issues this section focuses on – if only incidentally – namely, the function and significance of the British honours system today. Indeed, given its colonial connotations, this system has been included in a broader agenda for institutional reform. The purpose of this section is not to delve into the furore in the Islamic world over the awarding of a knighthood to Rushdie, nor to address its impact on global politics; in other words, it does not intend to deal with the worldwide political and religious storm brought about by the knighthood. The central aim of this subchapter is rather to examine the antagonism stirred up in the British press by Rushdie's honour and to present an alternative approach to this polemic from the one outlined by commentators in the print media. The focus on the cultural warfare provoked by the Rushdie affair part II is limited to examining how it operated on a domestic level and specifically how complex power struggles played out in the British media. It is significant in this respect that the first negative reactions to *The Satanic Verses* at the time of its publication happened not in Iran, but in India and Britain. In fact, copies of the novel were publicly burned on 14 January 1989, in Bradford, England. Beyond a consideration of how the *Satanic Verses* controversy was reignited by the awarding of the knighthood, this subchapter addresses the liberating potential of the Rushdie affair part II in terms of questioning and exposing such binary oppositions. The issue is then how to bypass this cultural warfare, lest it inhibit critical analysis of the questions at stake.

In a 1982 essay Rushdie bluntly remarks that four centuries of loot and plunder, of assuming superiority to "the Fuzzy-Wuzzies and the wogs," must of necessity have left their imprint on British society ("New Empire" 130). He quotes E.P. Thompson's description of Britain as the last remaining colony of the British Empire to sustain the argument that the country was in the early 1980s a "new colony" with Asian and black immigrants as colonial subjects and the British police force as colonising army (130–132). "This is how," Rushdie contends, "the new Empire was imported" (133). In an interview from the same period, the writer maintains the above reasoning:

> I think the trauma in England over the withdrawal from Empire has been not entirely economic, not just to do with the fact that they have lost their position geopolitically and they are no longer as rich as a nation. I think it has just as much to do with the fact that their cultural horizons have come back around them and locked them back into this island. (qtd. in Dube 11)

As has been shown in detail in the previous chapter of this book, while the Indian-born writer sees the popular appeal of "television series, films, plays and books all filled with nostalgia for the Great Pink Age" ("New Empire" 130) as an incontrovertible evidence of a nostalgic longing for a "new Empire," Gilroy detects in the early 2000s an analogous postcolonial melancholia, which manifests itself in an incapability or unwillingness to accept the demise of the British Empire (116). This section is built on the premise that Rushdie's knighthood itself can be addressed within the framework of a renewed nostalgia for an imagined British community and hence construed as a symptom of postcolonial melancholia. Borrowing Bahonar's statements, one of the after-effects of what Gilroy identifies as postcolonial melancholia might well be the "illusion that Britain is still a 19th century superpower and that bestowing titles is something still deemed important." This brings us to the diverse, yet related, critical reactions to Rushdie's knighthood, coming mostly from left-wing intellectuals in Britain, centred on these thorny questions: Why would a postcolonial author, committed to undermining imperial hegemonies, accept a royal accolade? How could he be, in his own words, "thrilled and humbled to receive this great honour," and "very grateful that [his] work has been recognised in this way" (Dugan)? Does such excitement and appreciation betray the writer's conversion to establishment values? Why would a self-styled leftist be so willing to accept an honour that annihilates his "leftist credentials"? This subchapter poses a few interrogations of its own: After all, what compels critics to feel they have constantly to comment on Rushdie's political views (misinterpreting, most of the time, their marked complexity)? How could his acceptance of a knighthood, apparently validating the status quo, be explained? Has Rushdie indeed shifted from a position of detachment to one of subordination vis-à-vis the British establishment, or is this act in any way subversive?

For some detractors of Rushdie's knighthood, the authoritative precedent of the Indian author Rabindranath Tagore stands as a reminder that the bestowal (and repudiation) of a British knighthood is not exempt from political implications. Writing in Bengali during the period of the British Raj, Tagore was awarded the Nobel Prize for Literature in 1913 and was knighted in 1915 by King George V but, following the Jallianwala Bagh, or Amritsar massacre four years later, he renounced his knighthood in protest against colonial repression in India.[8] In a letter published in the reputed English-language Indian newspaper *The Statesman*, addressed to the then Viceroy, Lord Chelmsford, and dated 3 June 1919, Tagore asks to be "relieve[d]" of the title and explains his reasons at length:

> The enormity of the measures taken by the Government in the Punjab for quelling some local disturbances has, with a rude shock, revealed to our minds the helplessness of our position as British subjects in India. ... The time has come when badges of honour make our shame glaring in the incongruous context of humiliation, and I for my part, wish to stand, shorn, of all special distinctions, by the side of those of my countrymen who, for their so called insignificance, are liable to suffer degradation not fit for human beings.

Besides the authoritative example of Tagore, a more recent high-profile case of a prospective recipient of an award under the British honours system who publicly turned it down concerns the Afro-Caribbean British activist and poet Benjamin Zephaniah, in 2003 (he had been awarded the "ordinary" decoration or OBE, rather than the knighthood that later accrued to Rushdie). Following the example set by Tagore, who returned his knighthood through an open letter published in the Indian press, Zephaniah made public his reasons for refusing to accept the honour from Elizabeth II in a polemical article – with the suggestive title "'Me? I Thought, OBE Me? Up Yours, I Thought'" – published in *The Guardian* in November 2003. The Rastafarian poet justifies his attitude, describing the OBE as a legacy of the inhumanity of colonialism. The declared intention behind declining the OBE is to protest against the monarchy, an institution "that still refuses to apologise for sanctioning slavery." Furthermore, the poet's attack is also directed at British government policies, including the pro-US stand on the war in Iraq, and in particular at then Prime Minister Tony Blair whom he deems accountable for "pour[ing] the working-class dream of a fair, compassionate, caring society down the dirty drain of empire." Zephaniah jokes that "[w]hoever is behind this offer can

---

[8] There is a reference in Rushdie's essay on Attenborough's film *Gandhi* to Tagore's returning of his knighthood on account of his being "disgusted by the British reaction to the [Amritsar] massacre" (103).

never have read any of [his] work," or his name would not have been submitted to the Queen for approval. He even suggests that, instead of the knighthood, he be given "some of those great African works of art that were taken in the name of the empire and let [him] return them to their rightful place."

More than two years previous to his rejection of the OBE, Zephaniah had already repudiated such practices. In the aptly-entitled poem "Bought and Sold," formerly published in his 2001 poetry collection *Too Black, Too Strong* and reprinted in his Guardian article, he denounces black writers who compromise their work by accepting "smart big awards and prize money" and who consent to being decorated at Buckingham Palace:

> It's not censors or dictators that are cutting up our art.
> The lure of meeting royalty
> And touching high society
> Is damping creativity and eating at our heart. ...
> The empire strikes back[9] and waves
> Tamed warriors bow on parades
> When they have done what they've been told
> They get their OBEs.

Refusing to join what he dubs "the oppressors' club," the poet chastizes fellow writers who, in his view, have sold out their artistic integrity by accepting such accolades. Zephaniah regards the bestowment of honours upon black artists as part and parcel of Blair's "Cool Britannia" that "gives OBEs to cool rock stars, successful businesswomen and blacks who would be militant in order to give the impression that it is inclusive."

Besides the ambivalent nature of the honours system itself, under the perception that postcolonial artists might at times be co-opted by the establishment there lies a persistent anxiety. Zephaniah himself confesses to having been "called a sell-out for selling too many books, for writing books for children, for performing at the Royal Albert Hall, for going on Desert Island Discs, and for appearing on the Parkinson show." In the self-reflexive shift of the last decades, postcolonial critics have denounced the progressive evacuation of resistance to renovated forms of western imperialism in postcolonial cultural artefacts. These have become not only institutionalized, but also inescapably commodified and some have even been turned into multicultural staples. For instance, Banerjee contends that September 11, 2001 marks the emergence of the "postethnic postcolonial" (313) and that, in a related conservative turn, postcolonial literature has been converging with "post-leftist politics"; in this context, she asks whether the post-9/11 Rushdie might adequately be regarded as "the Tony Blair of postcolonial studies" (321). Against this backdrop, it should come as no surprise that Rushdie should have been on the receiving end of fierce attacks when he accepted the knighthood. Indeed, leftist critics felt that the ideologically oppositional agenda of postcolonialism was

---

[9] "The empire strikes back" was an expression famously reappropriated by Rushdie.

necessarily compromised when one of the most high-profile – and much defamed – British postcolonial authors chose to accept the honour.

As Tonkin notes, "[m]ore than any other writer alive," Rushdie "has found himself transformed into a character – ogre, joker, beast and, just occasionally, hero – in other people's scripts and stories" ("Salman Rushdie"). Even for a polemic writer, he has been for an uncommonly long time the object of controversy on both left and right. Throughout the Thatcher era, the writer was a renowned adversary – and definitely not a supporter – of the British establishment. At the time, both Rushdie's fictional work and essays castigated the policies of the then Prime Minister and leader of the Conservative Party and exposed the pervasiveness of British institutional racism, as when he pronounced that "British thought, British society, has never been cleansed of the filth of imperialism. It's still there, breeding lice and vermin, waiting for unscrupulous people to exploit it for their own ends" ("New Empire" 131). To some right-wing commentators, Rushdie was and is an ungrateful rabble-rouser who, by vilifying Thatcher – or "Torture. Maggie the Bitch," as one of the characters calls her in *The Satanic Verses* (269) – bit the hand that during the Rushdie affair part I provided him with costly police protection, estimated to amount to £1 million a year (Womack). The debate around Rushdie's police guard and his ingratitude is still resurrected on a regular basis. As quoted in an article by Sarah Womack in *The Daily Telegraph*, in 2001 the Labour peers Lord Nazir Ahmed and Lady Manzila Pola Uddin called for the removal of the protection on the grounds that the writer was obsessed with egocentric self-promotion, "whether it's with a model [Padma Lakshmi, who later became his wife] or saying his life is in danger." In the same article, according to Baroness Uddin, "[p]ublic money should be used for someone who is grateful. We should not pay for this protection when he has so little gratitude. It is a mockery of democracy." In an indirect response to these accusations, Rushdie declares in 2008: "It's been a decade now since I had any police protection, since all those things that I'm supposed to be guilty of. That the country spent so much money protecting me and so forth. Well, the country hasn't spent any money on me in the last 10 years, during which I've faithfully paid my taxes. So it's possible that I have paid it back. In a way it's been a good investment – keep me alive and my taxes will pay for it" (qtd. in Preston). As expected, after his polemic non-refusal of the knighthood nearly two decades after the Iranian fatwa, conservatives blamed again the self-centred troublemaker for allegedly threatening Britain's internal security (P. Cohen).

Some leftist critics have seen Rushdie's caustic comments on press freedom in Denmark or Islamic dress as treason to the tenets of cultural relativism and these controversies were only to be reinforced in light of the knighthood the writer was "thrilled and humbled to receive" (qtd. in P. Cohen). The award did not sit well with some parts of the British press, with some commentators labelling it a reward for Rushdie's apparent backing of the Iraq invasion and his pro-establishment attitude towards the US-British "war on terror." Previous to this acceptance, left-wing commentators had already claimed the writer had gone right-wing – they had taken issue with his "American turn" in both his cultural criticism and literary practice, and with his apparent endorsement of US foreign policy. Journalists and editorialists alike were swift to offer their insights on the political implications of a postcolonial writer accepting an award bestowed by the reigning monarch of Britain and head of the Commonwealth. Rushdie was expected to refuse the knighthood, following the examples of Zephaniah and Tagore; instead, he accepted it and the consequences of the writer's apparent realignment – or perceived ideological repositioning vis-à-vis his stance of the 1980s and early 1990s – are put forward in various comments in the print media, by and large to the left of the political spectrum. A few reactions published in the newspaper *The Guardian*, the self-described "world's leading liberal voice,"[10] are significant in this respect: on the same day of the announcement of the knighthood, Esther Addley, a senior reporter on the broadsheet newspaper, comments that the honour "signals a belated endorsement by the British establishment"; a few days later, Michael White, a former political editor of The Guardian, confesses his perplexity in the face of the writer's actions: "I still don't understand why a leftie like Salman Rushdie, who abandoned Britain for New York in a huff, would want an honour from the British establishment." These reactions somehow replay the earlier furore in the British press over *The Satanic Verses*. In the late 1980s, as Subrahmanyam recalls in an article marking the twentieth anniversary of Khomeini's fatwa, "Rushdie-bashing was ... a low form of journalistic sport, including unpleasant puns on his name ('Salmonella' Rushdie and so on)" ("Angel").

The most heavily quoted and extensively reprinted piece from *The Guardian* in the aftermath of the writer's award was penned by Priyamvada Gopal. From a position Rushdie might well characterize as "sanctimonious moral relativism" and regard as representative of "a *bien-pensant* anti-American onslaught" ("Attacks" 392), Gopal reads Rushdie's acceptance of the knighthood as the culmination of a career trajectory that began with radical opposition to the British establishment, with work imbued with an "uncompromising ethical vision," and then slid into conservatism. She states that the writer's honour is "a reward for abandoning the anti-establishment stance he once espoused." Gopal contrasts what she perceives to be Rushdie's current right-wing political positioning with his prior critique of "tyrannical forces in both west and non-west," a recognition of these forces "as twinned," and a pronouncement of "a plague on both their houses." The writer is seen as the unthinking spokesperson for US political, military, and cultural domination. Gopal charges Rushdie with ideological betrayal and concludes the article lamenting: "the mutation of this relevant and stentorian writer into a pallid chorister is a tragic allegory of our benighted times, of the kind he once narrated so vividly." She notes the irony of accepting an award from the queen regnant of a nation which Rushdie had once symbolized in the image of a kipper, "a peculiar-tasting smoked fish full of spikes and bones" (*Satanic* 44). In an (autobiographical) episode in *The Satanic Verses*, the young Saladin, just sent by his father to an elite

---

[10] See the official website of *The Guardian* (http://www.guardian.co.uk/).

boarding school in England (a stand-in for Rushdie's own alma mater, Rugby School), is, after only a few days in his new adoptive country, presented with a kipper when he comes down for breakfast. Unacquainted with grilled herring, Saladin "sat there staring at it, not knowing where to begin" (44). He eats it whole, including the tiny bones, while his fellow students watch him in silence without any intention of helping him. This adventure teaches Saladin a valuable lesson, and, being "a bloody-minded person," he sets his mind to conquer England: "'I'll show them all,' he swore. 'You see if I don't.' The swallowed-up kipper was his first victory, the first step in his conquest of England. William the Conqueror, it is said, began by eating a mouthful of English sand" (44).

In targeting inconsistencies in the ideological stance of the post-fatwa and post-9/11 Rushdie, commentators risk diverting attention from the bigger picture. To assert that the writer *should* and *must* be an unequivocal standard-bearer of a fixed and unchanging political agenda, of the left or of the right, only serves to prove how he has been trapped in a discursive dilemma for the last decades. Critics should instead be concentrating on moving the debate forward: what is needed here is to displace the primacy of the fatwa years, by drawing attention to this predicament. English and Frow argue that the Rushdie affair part I was sparked by "the attempted conversion" of the writer's pre-existent literary capital in the early 1980s, "by means of the whole apparatus of his celebrity, into a special kind of political standing"; this ignited controversy in Britain because it was, "from the standpoint of the local religious leaders who first attacked the novel [*The Satanic Verses*], a threat and an affront" (54). Likewise, the left-liberal onslaught, or Rushdie affair part II, that the writer faced in the British media following his non-refusal of the knighthood seems to be motivated by feelings of "threat and affront." Ever since the fatwa descended on his head in 1989, his name has been a political battleground, a site of conflict where commentators on the left and on the right struggle over the label – either progressive or conservative – to attach to the writer's shifting ideological positions. As Tonkin asserts:

> Symbol, victim, blasphemer, target – Salman Rushdie, it seems, is anything people need him to be. ... Everyone, fan or foe, invokes their own imaginary Rushdie. We dream him up, and he duly takes shape: as blaspheming apostate for many still-outraged Muslims; as cocky subcontinental pseud for old-school British racists; as martyr to free speech for liberal literati. With the announcement of his knighthood ..., this parade of straw men swelled to a seething carnival of prejudice and projection. ("Salman Rushdie")

Even if Gopal is one the "kneejerk-leftist haters" in this "seething carnival of prejudice and projection" (Tonkin, "Salman Rushdie"), she is correct in pointing out that what is ultimately at stake in the issue of the knighthood is not "one man's oddly bathetic 'gratitude' or even the meaning of being knighted in this day and age." Conceptualising Rushdie as a liminal cultural actor allows for a fresh understanding of his seemingly paradoxical acceptance of a knighthood. His position as postcolonial fiction writer should not be grounded in a terrain artificially constructed around a centre/margin binary. Following the logic of the centre/margin dichotomy, his acceptance of the knighthood might well be construed as an example of the numerous symbolic ways in which Rushdie has written himself into the metropolitan centre – or, alternatively, as a critical intervention from the margin. Both of these have proven to be incorrect readings, because partial and incomplete. The line dividing centre and periphery – upon which commentators in the British print media relied for guidance in their analyses of the knighthood polemic – has been blurred by globalisation and postcolonialism. In the end, the binary centre/margin should be construed as relational. Any such dichotomy had already been disturbed and dismantled through the postcolonial performative act of eating a kipper on the part of the Indian-born writer, then a pupil at Rugby School.

Conclusion

> The way in which art changes society is never in a broad sweep, you know – you write a book and governments fail – that never happens. What matters most is the way in which the book acts on the people who really read it and connect to it. It is then that it can make an absolutely irreversible shift in the way they see things – even some very small thing. I'm aware that once you read *Ulysses* or *Moby Dick* or whatever that you're not the same person you were before. There's been some tiny shift in your perception of the world which sticks and never shifts back. That's why I write fiction.
> —Rushdie, qtd. in John Mitchinson 97

Rushdie's aptitude to apprehend experience from an array of transient positionings is rooted in the belief that creative writers should identify themselves with a cosmopolitan ideal and steer clear of any explicit parochial agenda. In reality, his defence of IWE in his introduction to the co-edited anthology *The Vintage Book* is based on the conviction that "parochialism is perhaps the main vice of the vernacular literatures" (xv). The writer's call to detachment in the context of contemporary anxieties over the ever-increasing fluidity of boundaries testifies to the inoperability and even outmodedness of the notion that "home" constitutes a binding filial connection which subjects are expected to experience in relation to a homeland. Likewise, Said censures anti-colonial nationalist models such as Frantz Fanon's, underscoring that fetishized allegiances of "[n]ationality, nationalism, nativism" might be just as constraining to the individual as colonialism (*Culture and Imperialism* 277). Said's secular ideal is, at its core, both a form of exilic displacement and an adversarial critical exercise grounded in opposition to what he perceives as the near-dogmatic tenets of national alliances. Along similar lines to Said's secularism, in the essay "Notes on Writing and the Nation" Rushdie updates the argument presented in the introduction to *The Vintage Book*, dubbing the sort of parochialism entailed in "writing nationalistically" (xv) as "New Behalfism." The writer expresses his contempt for "behalfies" and warns against their self-enforced role as cultural representatives: "Beware the writer who sets himself or herself up as the voice of a nation. This includes nations of race, gender, sexual orientation, elective affinity. This is the New Behalfism. Beware behalfies! ... Seeing literature as inescapably political, it substitutes political values for literary ones. It is the murderer of thought" (66).

According to Bhabha, culture is a transnational and translational strategy of survival (*Location* 172).[1] Not unrelatedly, Huggan sees postcolonial cultural

---

[1] Bhabha reasons: "the borderline work of culture demands an encounter with 'newness' that is not part of the continuum of past and present. It creates a sense of the new as an insurgent act of cultural translation. Such an act does not merely recall the

producers as "both aware of and resistant to their interpellation as marginal spokespersons, institutionalized cultural commentators and representative (iconic) figures"; furthermore, "they make their *readers* aware of the constructedness of such cultural categories; their texts are metacommentaries on the politics of translation, on the power relations that inform cross-cultural perception and representation" (*Postcolonial Exotic* 26). Rushdie's role as cultural broker – more than that of a "cultural mulatto" who is able to "navigate easily in the white world" (Ellis 189) – lies thus within those fault-lines which, paradoxically, provide the context and condition of possibility for the writer's actions in what Appadurai terms a "diasporic public sphere" (*Modernity* 22). As Rushdie puts it in a 2008 interview, alluding to his at times controversial actions in that public sphere inhabited by the artist, "[n]othing of great interest for [him] is done sitting safely in the middle of the room. You want to push the boundaries as much as possible" (qtd. in Preston). This can well be read as an all-encompassing commentary on the circumstances of his own life and creative project thus far. Huggan questions whether the representativeness of postcolonial writers is "a function of their inscription in the margins, of the mainstream demand for an 'authentic', but readily translatable, marginal voice," but admits that this question "yield[s] no immediate or obvious answers" (26). The process the critic describes hints at the charges of self-exoticisation or gimmickification of South Asianness faced by artists who are seen as pandering to western reception. In this respect, he draws attention to the double coding involved in postcolonial self-fashioning "wherein space claimed for cultural expression becomes a constricted and restrained space within a wider system" (31). One of the main aims of this study has been to provide a tentative answer to Huggan's above quoted interrogation in relation to Rushdie's manifold roles as cultural broker and his concurrent desire to operate in multiple cultural spheres. In the pursuit of this purpose, this work has focused on the ways in which those roles are heavily coded as performance. Implicit in the many roles performed by Rushdie are valuable clues to the liminal position writers inhabit today. Because the answer offered by this book to Huggan's question is an undisguised attempt to instigate a redirection in Rushdie studies in the twenty-first century, this inquiry urgently requires alternative answers from other sources. These answers will provide a critique of the various institutional levels concurrently at work in the promotion of certain postcolonial figures as representatives of the cultural margins. Hopefully, the present research will open up space for additional interventions into the problematics of re-orientalisms today.

Foregrounding Rushdie's engagement with the above issues, in particular his development of a discourse of postcolonial cultural performativity and his enactment of a deconstructive politics of resistance through various platforms as a cultural broker, this study has attempted a critique taking on the very marketing

---

past as social cause or aesthetic precedent; it renews the past, refiguring it as a contingent 'in-between' space, that innovates and interrupts the performance of the present. The 'past-present' becomes part of the necessity, not the nostalgia, of living" (6).

of the exotic on which the writer's popularity nonetheless depends and in which it is very self-consciously situated. Notions of the exotic (whatever that may be supposed to entail and include) are ineradicably part of the "marketing story" (Squires, *Marketing Literature* 119–146) attached to Rushdie's narratives, a story with which the writer strategically engages rather than retreats from. Embedded within the fluidity of global culture, the term "Rushdie" acts as a brand name for a marketed cultural good with all the attendant complexities, including interpretations blinkered by preconceived expectations. Regimes of representation have a tendency to fix meanings in order to better manage and promote a cultural product. In the present case, the twin processes of cultural deterritorialisation (Rushdie as cosmopolitan diasporic writer) and reterritorialisation (Rushdie as an Indian writer) aid such categorisation. Self-irony, in particular the juggling with expectations of re-orientalisation, has definitely helped rupture such straitjackets. More than translating and mediating an authentic, exotic culture for his readers, the author suggests the possibility of an ironic, self-reflexive, if not metafictional, reading of postcolonial diasporic works. "I must say first of all that description is itself a political act," writes Rushdie in the essay "Imaginary Homelands" (13). Re-orientalist postcolonial narratives have destabilized the spectacle of otherness, morphing the display of the other to accommodate the representational shifts effected by those involved not only in cultural production, but also in cultural circulation and valuation. This inevitably leads to questions of power – by encouraging a metatextual awareness in their readers, re-orientalist works reinstate agency and foster empowerment in the face of an engulfing global literary marketplace.

Rushdie both parodies and slyly reroutes orientalism, opening the way for a re-examination of the expectations of his metropolitan readership. Such recourse to re-orientalism is not without its problems. The re-orientalist representational strategy adopted by the writer is one of appropriation and resistance though, like the use of stereotypes in general, it is a "complex, ambivalent, contradictory mode of representation, as anxious as it is assertive" (Bhabha, *Location* 70). Re-orientalism feeds on (and into) orientalism, while attempting to pre-empt its strength, insofar as it sustains the commodification of difference in an increasingly globalized market, but still maintains the potential to disrupt the systems within which that market operates. Probably one of the most disquieting characteristics of many postmodern analyses of power relations is their failure to effectively locate any kind of resistance in the strictly regulated world of social space, or acknowledge the existence of even a partial dismantling of the shifting power relations underlying cultural production, notwithstanding the repeated emphasis on opposition to that power. This sentiment, of an entire social space irredeemably shaped by "an implacable machine of power" (Hardt and Negri 323), recurs when one ponders the issue of whether or not Rushdie's writing reconstitutes the orientalist stereotypes that it attempts to destabilize. In effect, re-orientalist subversion is complicated by the powerful market forces undergirding orientalism, calling into question at times the success of re-orientalist experiments.

A critical engagement with the global brand "Rushdie" needs to explore its manifold reverberations. As stated in the introduction, this study wishes to extend current research on the writer and address a critical blind spot in Rushdie studies. It has attempted to do so not by disavowing Rushdie, the literary author, but by drawing him into a nuanced, multilayered picture composed of many other (at times paradoxical) Rushdies, in keeping with a postmodern emphasis on self-referentiality and cultural interplay. This study argues for an informed critique of the author's work across the intersections and conversations involving the "literary" and the "non-literary" Rushdies, labels which have unquestionably shaped the ways his oeuvre has been read. To scrutinise these complex intersections is, then, not to dislodge the relevance of the "literary" Rushdie in twenty-first-century Rushdie studies; rather, what this study has endeavoured is to re-texture our understanding of the writer from an angle of inquiry that seems as yet to be rather unexplored and, along the way, achieve a balance between the "literary" and the "non-literary" Rushdies.

Even though literary modes of analysis remain central to the discussion of Rushdie's works, this approach has allowed for the pursuing of a dialogic project by engaging with other narratives and has enabled new connections, thus bypassing notions of a single-authorial text and an exclusionary literature-centred approach. In unceasing dialogic tension, texts are in constant inevitable contact with other texts, irrespective of their high (in the sense of the preserve of an elite) or low cultural status. Rushdie's interleaved, palimpsestic texts point to the magpie tendency that permeates his writing, both fictional and non-fictional. In a way that prefigures major issues and paradoxes of current postcolonial studies, and also foregrounds the power relations underlying cultural production, this inclusive reading has stressed the parodic and subversive straddling of the high/low divide in Rushdie's oeuvre, while clearly marking the author's critical and self-reflexive position in regard to the circulation of his work within the global cultural economy, the latter constituting a "necessary evil."

It is worth recalling that the present work is grounded in the assumption that postcolonial authors necessarily inhabit a provisional position – though subject to metropolitan mediation, it is also prone to revision due to the dynamic interdependence between margins and centres. On the basis of that grounding, this study has striven to explore the commodification of ethnic difference without re-inscribing simple dichotomies and without falling prey to the limiting paradigms of totalising or essentialising binary logic. Besides, as Jane M. Jacobs reminds us, it is "a revisionary form of imperialist nostalgia that defines the colonized as always engaged in conscious work against the core" (15). Drawing on a concept of ethnicity not as a static, unchanging, or monolithic construct, but as a mobile, unstable, and polymorphous performative category, this study has attempted to contribute to the neutralising of the pernicious opposition between ethnically-defined individuals (e.g. Rushdie) and ethnically-unmarked individuals (the mainstream). In the process, it has focused on negotiations of heavily mediated power relations in a field of representation dominated by the logic of multinational capitalism.

Following this line of thought, one hopefully has been able to accommodate the complexities of the permeability of borders and of the fluidity of identification. Rushdie's own standing in the field of postcolonial cultural production cannot be adequately charted using the worn-out two-dimensional map which would rely on the endlessly repeated and renewed dichotomies of centre/periphery and left-wing/right-wing. The writer's fictional manifesto has shifted in response to the challenges of liquid modernity and has renewed itself as old constructs have failed to be productive. He eludes any easy classification of cultural politics. Besides, transnational cultural flows (including mass media's worldwide reach and globe-spanning migration) foster conditions for an increasingly complex identitarian cross-affiliation and for the rearticulation of overlapping cultural platforms. In this sense, Rushdie's work intersects with and cuts across the cultural industries and plainly illustrates that the opposition between high and low cultures as rigidly separate categories is today bound to be a futile (and false) one, not to mention that that opposition itself is non-operative in the context of the oeuvre under examination here. Rushdie's construction of an intertextual cultural web, within which multiple cultural referents circulate, conjoin, and alter one another, precludes the sustaining of a high/low divide. As well as tracing a complex network of globalisation processes, with its flows of images and cultural products, the debunking of the high/low divide is definitely part of the author's signature style. His depiction of a "global McCulture" ("Gandhi" 185) is attuned to the contradictions and complexities of late-era capitalism, in which literary works like his own rub shoulders with cultural products one might categorize as belonging to lower forms of cultural expression. Both may be vehicles for social critique and ideological subversion. Bringing us back full circle to one of the ideas sketched out in the introductory chapter, it is again a question of embracing the multiplicity of cultural points of identification, or the coexistence of Homer and Homer Simpson in the same sentence.

Works Cited

Works by Salman Rushdie

Novels

———. *Grimus*. 1975. London: Granada, 1985.
———. *Midnight's Children*. 1981. London: Vintage, 1995.
———. *Shame*. 1983. London: Vintage, 1995.
———. *The Satanic Verses*. 1988. New York and London: Viking, 1989.
———. *Haroun and the Sea of Stories*. 1990. London: Granta, 1991.
———. *The Moor's Last Sigh*. 1995. London: Vintage, 1996.
———. *The Ground Beneath Her Feet*. 1999. New York: Picador, 2000.
———. *Fury*. 2001. London: Vintage, 2002.
———. *Shalimar the Clown*. London: Jonathan Cape, 2005.
———. *The Enchantress of Florence*. London: Vintage, 2008.
———. *Luka and the Fire of Life*. London: Jonathan Cape, 2010.

Anthologies and Non-Fiction

———. *The Jaguar Smile: A Nicaraguan Journey*. London: Picador, 1987.
———. *Imaginary Homelands: Essays and Criticism 1981–1991*. London: Granta, 1991.
———. *The Wizard of Oz*. London: BFI, 1992.
———. (Co-ed.) *The Vintage Book of Indian Writing: 1947–1997*. London: Vintage, 1997.
———. *Step Across This Line: Collected Non-Fiction 1992–2002*. 2002. London: Vintage, 2003.
———. (Co-ed.) *The Best American Short Stories*. New York: Mariner, 2008.
———. *Joseph Anton: A Memoir*. London: Jonathan Cape, 2012.

Short Stories

———. "At the Auction of the Ruby Slippers." 1992. *East, West*. London: Vintage, 1995. 85–103.
———. "Chekov and Zulu." 1994. *East, West*. London: Vintage, 1995. 149–171.
———. "Christopher Columbus and Queen Isabella of Spain Consummate Their Relationship." 1994. *East, West*. London: Vintage, 1995. 105–119.
———. "The Courter." 1994. *East, West*. London: Vintage, 1995. 173–211.
———. "The Free Radio." 1994. *East, West*. London: Vintage, 1995. 17–32.
———. "Yorick." 1994. *East, West*. London: Vintage, 1995. 61–83.

Critical Texts (Essays, Articles, and Reviews)

———. "Imaginary Homelands." 1982. *Imaginary Homelands: Essays and Criticism 1981–1991.* London: Granta, 1991. 9–21.

———. "The New Empire Within Britain." 1982. *Imaginary Homelands: Essays and Criticism 1981–1991.* London: Granta, 1991. 129–138.

———. "'Commonwealth Literature' Does Not Exist." 1983. *Imaginary Homelands: Essays and Criticism 1981–1991.* London: Granta, 1991. 61–70.

———. "Günter Grass." 1984. *Imaginary Homelands: Essays and Criticism 1981–1991.* London: Granta, 1991. 273–281.

———. "Outside the Whale." 1984. *Imaginary Homelands: Essays and Criticism, 1981–1991,* London: Granta, 1991: 87–101.

———. "Dynasty." 1985. *Imaginary Homelands: Essays and Criticism 1981–1991.* London: Granta, 1991. 47–52.

———. "The Location of *Brazil*." 1985. *Imaginary Homelands: Essays and Criticism 1981–1991.* London: Granta, 1991. 118–125.

———. "In Good Faith." 1990. *Imaginary Homelands: Essays and Criticism 198–-1991.* London: Granta, 1991. 393–414.

———. "Is Nothing Sacred?" 1990. *Imaginary Homelands: Essays and Criticism, 1981–1991.* London: Granta, 1991. 415–429.

———. "Satyajit Ray." 1990. *Imaginary Homelands: Essays and Criticism 1981–1991.* London: Granta, 1991. 107–114.

———. "A Short Tale About Magic." *The Wizard of Oz.* London: BFI, 1992. 9–57.

———. "The Best of Young British Novelists." 1993. *Step Across This Line: Collected Non-Fiction 1992–2002.* London: Vintage, 2003. 34–39.

———. "On Being Photographed." 1995. *Step Across This Line: Collected Non-Fiction 1992–2002.* London: Vintage, 2003. 112–117.

———. (with Elizabeth West) "Biographical Notes." *The Vintage Book of Indian Writing: 1947–1997.* Eds Salman Rushdie and Elizabeth West. London: Vintage, 1997. 569–575.

———. "Damme, This Is the Oriental Scene for You." *The New Yorker* 23–30 Jun. 1997: 50–61.

———. "Damme, This Is the Oriental Scene for You." 1997. *Step Across This Line: Collected Non-Fiction 1992–2002.* London: Vintage, 2003. 159–173.

———. "Introduction." *The Vintage Book of Indian Writing: 1947–1997.* Eds Salman Rushdie and Elizabeth West. London: Vintage, 1997. ix–xxii.

———. "Notes on Writing and the Nation." 1997. *Step Across This Line: Collected Non-Fiction 1992–2002.* London: Vintage, 2003. 64–68.

———. "Gandhi, Now." 1998. *Step Across This Line: Collected Non-Fiction 1992–2002.* London: Vintage, 2003. 180–185.

———. "Edward Said." 1999. *Step Across This Line: Collected Non-Fiction 1992–2002.* London: Vintage, 2003. 317–319.

———. "Globalization." 1999. *Step Across This Line: Collected Non-Fiction 1992–2002.* London: Vintage, 2003. 296–298.

———. "Influence." 1999. *Step Across This Line: Collected Non-Fiction 1992–2002*. London: Vintage, 2003. 69–76.
———. "My Unfunny Valentine." *The New Yorker* 15 Feb. 1999: 28.
———. "The Taj Mahal." 1999. *Step Across This Line: Collected Non-Fiction 1992–2002*. London: Vintage, 2003. 186–187.
———. "A Dream of Glorious Return." 2000. *Step Across This Line: Collected Non-Fiction 1992–2002*. London: Vintage, 2003. 195–227.
———. "A Grand Coalition?" 2000. *Step Across This Line: Collected Non-Fiction 1992–2002*. London: Vintage, 2003. 359–361.
———. "The Attacks on America." 2001. *Step Across This Line: Collected Non-Fiction 1992–2002*. London: Vintage, 2003. 391–393.
———. "U2." 2001. *Step Across This Line: Collected Non-Fiction 1992–2002*. London: Vintage, 2003. 102–106.
———. "Anti-Americanism." 2002. *Step Across This Line: Collected Non-Fiction 1992–2002*. London: Vintage, 2003. 398–400.
———. "*The Baburnama*." 2002. *Step Across This Line: Collected Non-Fiction 1992–2002*. London: Vintage, 2003. 188–194.
———. "Step Across This Line." 2002. *Step Across This Line: Collected Non-Fiction 1992–2002*. London: Vintage, 2003. 405–442.
———. "The Half-Woman God." *Aids Sutra: Untold Stories from India*. Ed. Negar Akhavi. London: Vintage, 2008. 107–118.
———. "A Fine Pickle." *The Guardian* 28 Feb. 2009 <http://www.guardian.co.uk/books/2009/feb/28/salman-rushdie-novels-film-adaptations>.

Secondary Sources

Addley, Esther. "Literary World Applauds Rushdie Knighthood." *The Guardian* 16 Jun. 2007 <http://www.guardian.co.uk/society/2007/jun/16/books.politics>.
Adiga, Aravind. *The White Tiger*. London: Atlantic, 2008.
Adorno, Theodor. "On the Social Situation of Music." 1932. *Essays on Music*. Ed. Richard Leppert. Trans. Susan H. Gillespie et al. Berkeley: U of California P, 2002. 391–436.
———. "Letter to Walter Benjamin, London, 18 March 1936." 1936. *Aesthetics and Politics*. Eds Ernst Bloch et al. Trans. and ed. Rodney Taylor. London: Verso, 1977. 120–126.
———. "On the Fetish Character of Music and the Regression of Listening." 1938. *The Culture Industry: Selected Essays on Mass Culture*. Ed. J. M. Bernstein. London and New York: Routledge, 1991. 29–60.
———. "On Popular Music" (with George Simpson). *Studies in Philosophy and Social Science* IX (1941): 17–48.
———. "The Schema of Mass Culture." 1944–1947. *The Culture Industry: Selected Essays on Mass Culture*. Ed. J. M. Bernstein. London and New York: Routledge, 1991. 61–97.

———. "The Perennial Fashion – Jazz." 1953. *The Adorno Reader*. Ed. Brian O'Connor. Oxford: Blackwell, 2000. 267–279.

———. "Culture Industry Reconsidered." 1967. *The Culture Industry: Selected Essays on Mass Culture*. Ed. J. M. Bernstein. London and New York: Routledge, 1991. 98–106.

Ahmad, Aijaz. "The Politics of Literary Postcoloniality." 1995. *Contemporary Postcolonial Theory: A Reader*. Ed. Padmini Mongia. London and New York: Arnold, 1996. 276–293.

Ahmad, Hena. "Salman Rushdie." *Great World Writers: Twentieth Century*. Ed. Patrick M. O'Neil. New York: Marshall Cavendish, 2004. 1317–1332.

Anand, Mulk Raj. *Untouchable*. 1935. London: Penguin, 1986.

———. *Coolie*. 1936. London: Penguin, 1993.

Appadurai, Arjun. "Introduction: Commodities and the Politics of Value." *The Social Life of Things: Commodities in Cultural Perspective*. Ed. Arjun Appadurai. Cambridge: Cambridge UP, 1986. 3–63.

———. "How to Make a National Cuisine: Cookbooks in Contemporary India." *Comparative Studies in Society and History* 30.1 (1988): 3–24.

———. *Modernity at Large: Cultural Dimensions of Globalization*. Minneapolis: U of Minnesota P, 1996.

"Aravind Adiga: 'Life Goes on as Before.'" *themanbookerprize.com* 2008 <http://www.themanbookerprize.com/perspective/articles/1125>.

Armanet, François, and Gilles Anquetil. "Mes Lumières." *Le Nouvel Observateur* 21 Dec. 2006 <http://hebdo.nouvelobs.com/p2198/articles/a327856.html>.

Ashcroft, Bill, Gareth Griffiths, and Helen Tiffin, eds. *Key Concepts in Post-Colonial Studies*. London and New York: Routledge, 1998.

Auden, W.H. *W.H. Auden: A Selection by the Author*. Harmondsworth: Penguin, 1958.

Ball, John Clement. *Satire and the Postcolonial Novel: V.S. Naipaul, Chinua Achebe, Salman Rushdie*. New York and London: Routledge, 2003.

Banay, Sophia. "Knight on the Town." *Potfolio.com* Nov. 2008 <http://www.portfolio.com/culture-lifestyle/culture-inc/arts/2008/10/15/Rushdie-and-the-Ailing-Book-Industry>.

Banerjee, Mita. "Postethnicity and Postcommunism in Hanif Kureishi's *Gabriel's Gift* and Salman Rushdie's *Fury*." *Reconstructing Hybridity: Post-Colonial Studies in Transition*. Eds Joel Kuortti and Jopi Nyman. Amsterdam and New York: Rodopi, 2007. 309–324.

Bates, Daniel. "Four-times Married Salman Rushdie Vows Never to Get Hitched Again." *The Daily Mail* 3 Jan. 2009 <http://www.dailymail.co.uk/tvshowbiz/article-1104589/Four-times-married-Salman-Rushie-vows-hitched-again.html>.

Batty, David, and Peter Walker. "Rushdie Knighthood 'Justifies Suicide Attacks.'" *The Guardian* 18 Jun. 2007 <http://www.guardian.co.uk/world/2007/jun/18/books.religion>.

Bauman, Zygmunt. *Liquid Modernity*. Cambridge: Polity, 2000.

Behera, Smruti Ranjan. "The Literary Style of Mulk Raj Anand." *The Novels of Mulk Raj Anand: A Critical Study*. Eds Manmohan Krishna Bhatnagar and Rajeshwar Mittapalli. New Delhi: Atlantic, 2000. 88–123.

Benjamin, Walter. "Mickey Mouse." 1931. Trans. Rodney Livingstone. *Walter Benjamin: Selected Writings, Vol. 2: 1927–1934*. Eds Michael W. Jennings, Marcus Bullock, Howard Eiland, and Gary Smith. Cambridge, MA and London: The Belknap Press of Harvard UP, 1999. 545–546.

———. "The Work of Art in the Age of Its Technological Reproducibility." 1939 (third version). Trans. Howard Eiland. *Walter Benjamin: Selected Writings, Vol. 4: 1938–1940*. Eds Howard Eiland and Michael W. Jennings. Cambridge, MA: The Belknap Press of Harvard UP, 2003. 251–283.

Berger, John. *G*. 1972. London: Bloomsbury, 1996.

Berger, Mark. "Gandhi and the Guardians: Michael Edwardes and the Apologetics of Imperialism." *Bulletin of Concerned Asian Scholars* 23.3 (1991): 73–82.

Bernstein, J.M. "Introduction." *The Culture Industry: Selected Essays on Mass Culture*. Ed. J.M. Bernstein. London and New York: Routledge, 1991. 1–28.

Bhabha, Homi. "Introduction: Narrating the Nation." *Nation and Narration*. Ed. Homi Bhabha. London and New York: Routledge, 1990. 1–7.

———. *The Location of Culture*. London and New York: Routledge, 1994.

Bhatia, Nandi. *Acts of Authority/Acts of Resistance: Theatre and Politics in Colonial and Postcolonial India*. Ann Arbor: U of Michigan P, 2004.

Bhattacharyya, Gargi, and John Gabriel. "Gurinder Chadha and the *Apna* Generation: Black British Film in the 1990s." *Third Text* 27 (1994): 55–63.

Blake, Andrew. *Salman Rushdie: A Beginner's Guide*. London: Hodder and Stoughton, 2001.

Blaise, Claire. "A Novel of India's Coming of Age." *New York Times* 19 Apr. 1981: 1 <http://www.times.com/books/98/12/06/specials/rushdie-children.html>.

Blakely, Rhys. "Slum Tours Get *Slumdog Millionaire* Boost." *The Times* 21 Jan. 2009 <http://www.timesonline.co.uk/tol/news/world/asia/article5555635.ece>.

Bloom, Harold. *The Western Canon: The Books and School of the Ages*. New York: Harcourt Brace, 1994.

Bongie, Chris. "Exiles on Main Stream: Valuing the Popularity of Postcolonial Literature." *Postmodern Culture* 14.1 (2003): 66 paragraphs. 24 Oct. 2007 <http://www3.iath.virginia.edu/pmc/issue.903/14.1bongie.html>.

Boorstin, Daniel. *The Image, or What Happened to the American Dream*. New York: Atheneum, 1962.

Bosman, Julie. "Booker Prize Shortlist Is Announced." *The Times* 9 Sep. 2008 <http://www.nytimes.com/2008/09/10/books/10book.html?_r=1&em>.

Bourdieu, Pierre. *The Field of Cultural Production: Essays on Art and Literature*. Ed. Randal Johnson. New York: Columbia UP, 1993.

Boyagoda, Randy. "Postmodern Chutney." *First Things: A Monthly Journal of Religion and Public Life* 1 Feb. 2003: 47–49.

Brah, Avtar. *Cartographies of Diaspora: Contesting Identities*. London and New York: Routledge, 1996.

Braudy, Leo. *The Frenzy of Renown: Fame and Its History*. Oxford: Oxford UP, 1986.

Brennan. Timothy. *Wars of Position: The Cultural Politics of Left and Right*. New York: Columbia UP, 2006.

Brouillette, Sarah. *Postcolonial Writers in the Global Literary Marketplace*. New York: Palgrave, 2007.

Burke, Rupalee. "Mulk Raj Anand's *Coolie*: A Story of Human Relationships." *Critical Response to V.S. Naipaul and Mulk Raj Anand*. Ed. Amar Nath Prasad. New Delhi: Sarup & Sons, 2003. 170–178.

Busby, Graham, and Julia Klug. "Movie Induced Tourism: The Challenge of Measurement and Other Issues." *Journal of Vacation Marketing* 7.4 (2001): 316–332.

Carey, Peter. *Oscar and Lucinda*. 1988. London: Faber and Faber, 2008.

Cartelli, Thomas. *Repositioning Shakespeare: National Formations, Postcolonial Appropriations*. London and New York: Routledge, 1999.

Cashmore, Ellis. *The Black Culture Industry*. London and New York: Routledge, 1997.

Chandra, Vikram. *Love and Longing in Bombay*. 1997. London: Faber and Faber, 2007.

———. "The Cult of Authenticity: India's Cultural Commissars Worship 'Indianness' Instead of Art." *Boston Review* Feb./Mar. 2000 <http://bostonreview.net/BR25.1/chandra.html>.

———. *Sacred Games*. 2006. London: Faber and Faber, 2007.

Chaudhry, Lubna, and Saba Khattak. "Images of White Women and Indian Nationalism: Ambivalent Representations in *Shakespeare Wallah* and *Junoon*." *Gender and Culture in Literature and Film East and West: Issues of Perception and Interpretation*. Eds Nitaya Masavisut, George Simson, and Larry E. Smith. Honolulu: U of Hawaii P, 1994. 19–25.

Chaudhuri, Amit. "Modernity and the Vernacular." 1997. *The Picador Book of Modern Indian Literature*. Ed. Amit Chaudhuri. London: Picador, 2001. xvii–xxii.

———. "The Construction of the Indian Novel in English." 1999. *The Picador Book of Modern Indian Literature*. Ed. Amit Chaudhuri. London: Picador, 2001. xxiii–xxxi.

———. *A New World*. 2000. London: Picador, 2001.

———. "A Note on the Selection." *The Picador Book of Modern Indian Literature*. Ed. Amit Chaudhuri. London: Picador, 2001. xxxii–xxxiv.

———. "Travels in the Subculture of Modernity." *Clearing a Space: Reflections on India, Literature and Culture*. Oxford: Peter Lang, 2008. 140–159.

Chaudhuri, Nirad C. *The Autobiography of an Unknown Indian*. 1951. New York: New York Review of Books, 2001.

Chaudhuri, Una. "Imaginative Maps: Excerpts from a Conversation With Salman Rushdie." 1983. *Salman Rushdie Interviews: A Sourcebook of His Ideas*. Ed. Pradyumna S. Chauhan. Westport, CT: Greenwood, 2001. 21–31.

Chaudhury, Shoma. "Success Devastated My Life. It Changed All the Equations." *Tehelka* 5.9 8 Mar. 2008 <http://www.tehelka.com/story_main38.asp?filename=hub080308success_devastated.asp#>.
Chhabra, Aseem. "Chadha's Newest Wows Sundance Fest." *Rediff.com* 2 Feb. 2000 <http://www.rediff.com/news/2000/feb/02us4.htm>.
Chin, Frank. *The Chickencoop Chinaman/The Year of the Dragon*. 1981. Seattle, WA: U of Washington P.
Chordiya, Deepa. "'Taking on the Tone of a Bombay Talkie': The Function of Bombay Cinema in Salman Rushdie's *Midnight's Children*." *ARIEL* 38. 4 (2007): 97–121.
Coetzee, J.M. *Life and Times of Michael K*. London: Vintage, 2004.
Cohen, Margaret. "Walter Benjamin's Phantasmagoria." *New German Critique* 48 (1989): 87–107.
Cohen, Patricia. "Now He's Only Hunted by Cameras." *New York Times* 25 May 2008 <http://www.nytimes.com/2008/05/25/books/25cohe.html>.
Collett-White, Mike. "For Salman Rushdie, Celebrity Is a Curse." *New Zealand Herald* 6 Sep. 2005 <http://www.nzherald.co.nz/lifestyle/news/article.cfm?c_id=6&objectid=10344150>.
Concilio, Carmen. "The City as Text(ure): Bombay in Salman Rushdie's *The Ground Beneath Her Feet*." *The Great Work of Making Real: Salman Rushdie's The Ground Beneath Her Feet*. Eds Elsa Linguanti and Viktoria Tchernichova. Pisa: Edizioni ETS, 2003. 129–149.
Cook, Deborah. *The Culture Industry Revisited: Theodor W. Adorno on Mass Culture*. Lanham, Maryland and London: Rowman & Littlefield, 1996.
Coombes, Annie E., and Avtar Brah. "Introduction: The Conundrum of 'Mixing.'" *Hybridity and Its Discontents: Politics, Science, Culture*. Eds Avtar Brah and Annie E. Coombes. London: Routledge, 2000. 1–16.
Cooper, Darius. *The Cinema of Satyajit Ray: Between Tradition and Modernity*. Cambridge: Cambridge UP, 2000.
Corner, John, and Sylvia Harvey, eds. *Enterprise and Heritage: Crosscurrents of National Culture*. London: Routledge, 1991.
Cowley, Jason. "Guest Column." *India Today International* 27 Oct. 1997: 23.
Craig, Cairns. "Rooms Without a View." 1991. *Film/Literature/Heritage: A Sight and Sound Reader*. Ed. Ginette Vincendeau. London: BFI, 2001. 3–6.
Cronenberg, David. "Cronenberg Interview." 1995. *Salman Rushdie Interviews: A Sourcebook of His Ideas*. Ed. Pradyumna S. Chauhan. Westport, CT: Greenwood, 2001. 167–178.
Crow, Jonathan. "Six Secrets of 'Slumdog' Success." *Movies.yahoo.com* 13 Jan. 2009 <http://movies.yahoo.com/feature/slumdog-millionaire-blog.html>.
Daiya, Kavita. *Violent Belongings: Partition, Gender, and Postcolonial Nationalism in India*. Philadelphia: Temple UP, 2008.
Dalrymple, William. "The Lost Sub-continent." *The Observer* 13 Aug. 2005 <http://books.guardian.co.uk/review/story/0,12084,1547816,00.html>.

Damrosch, David. "World Literature in a Postcanonical, Hypercanonical Age." *Comparative Literature in an Age of Globalization*. Ed. Haun Saussy. Baltimore: Johns Hopkins UP, 2006. 43–53.

Damrosch, David, et al, eds. *Longman Anthology of World Literature: The Twentieth Century*. Vol. F. London: Longman, 2003.

Damrosch, David, Kevin J. H. Dettmar, and Jennifer Wicke, eds. *The Longman Anthology of British Literature: The Twentieth Century*. Vol. 2C. London: Longman, 2005.

Datta, Sudipta. "South Asian Writing Is Very Vibrant Right Now." *The Financial Express* 19 Oct. 2008 <http://www.financialexpress.com/news/--South-Asian-writing-is-very-vibrant-right-now--/375110/>.

Debord, Guy. *Society of the Spectacle*. 1967. Trans. Fredy Perlman and Jon Supak. Detroit: Black & Red, 1977.

Deleuze, Gilles, and Félix Guattari. *A Thousand Plateaus. Capitalism and Schizophrenia*. Trans. Brian Massumi. Minneapolis: U of Minnesota P, 1987.

DeLillo, Don. *Falling Man*. 2007. New York: Picador, 2008.

Desai, Anita. *Clear Light of Day*. 1980. London: Vintage, 2001.

———. *In Custody*. 1984. London: Vintage, 2001.

———. *Fasting, Feasting*. 1999. London: Vintage, 2000.

———. "One Rip Van Winkle Sleep And…" *Outlook India* 6 Oct. 2008 <http://www.outlookindia.com/full.asp?fodname=20081006&fname=Anita+Desai+%28F%29&sid=1&pn=1>.

Desai, Jigna. *Beyond Bollywood: The Cultural Politics of South Asian Diasporic Film*. New York: Routledge, 2004.

Desai, Kiran. "The Sermon in the Guava Tree." *The New Yorker* 23–30 Jun. 1997: 90–100.

———. "Strange Happenings in the Guava Orchard". *The Vintage Book of Indian Writing: 1947–1997*. Eds Salman Rushdie and Elizabeth West. London: Vintage, 1997. 559–568.

———. *Hullabaloo in the Guava Orchard*. London: Faber, 1998.

———. *The Inheritance of Loss*. London: Hamish Hamilton, 2006.

Dharker, Rani. "An Interview With Salman Rushdie." 1983. *Salman Rushdie Interviews: A Sourcebook of His Ideas*. Ed. Pradyumna S. Chauhan. Westport, CT: Greenwood, 2001. 47–61.

Di Leo, Jeffrey. *On Anthologies: Politics and Pedagogy*. Lincoln: U of Nebraska P, 2004.

Divakaruni, Chitra Banerjee. *The Mistress of Spices*. London: Black Swan, 1997.

Donnell, Alison, ed. *Companion to Contemporary Black British Culture*. London: Routledge, 2002.

Dube, Rani. "Salman Rushdie." 1982. *Salman Rushdie Interviews: A Sourcebook of His Ideas*. Ed. Pradyumna S. Chauhan. Westport, CT: Greenwood, 2001. 7–19.

Dugan, Emily. "Queen's Birthday Honours Recognise Famous Names and Private Deeds." *The Independent on Sunday* 16 Jun. 2007 <http://news.independent.co.uk/uk/this_britain/article2663239.ece>.

Dyer, Richard. *Stars*. London: BFI, 1979.

Ellis, Trey. "The New Black Aesthetic." *Callaloo* 12 (1989): 233–243.

English, James F. "Winning the Culture Game: Prizes, Awards, and the Rules of Art." *New Literary History* 33.1 (2002): 109–135.

———. *The Economy of Prestige: Prizes, Awards, and the Circulation of Cultural Value*. Cambridge, MA: Harvard UP, 2005.

English, James F., and John Frow. "Literary Authorship and Celebrity Culture." *A Concise Companion to Contemporary British Fiction*. Ed. James F. English. Malden, MA: Blackwell, 2006. 39–57.

Esquivel, Laura. *Like Water for Chocolate*. 1989. London: Black Swan, 1993.

Fairclough, Norman. *Discourse and Social Change*. 1992. Cambridge: Polity, 1993.

Farrell, J.G. *The Siege of Krishnapur*. 1973. London: Phoenix, 1996.

Fielding, Helen. *Bridget Jones's Diary*. 1996. London: Picador, 2001.

Fischer, Michael M.J., and Mehdi Abedi. *Debating Muslims: Cultural Dialogues in Postmodernity and Tradition*. Madison, Wisconsin: U of Wisconsin P, 1990.

Fiske, John. *Television Culture*. London: Routledge, 1988.

Fletcher, M.D. "Salman Rushdie: An Annotated Bibliography." *Journal of Indian Writing in English* 19.1 (1991): 15–23.

Foer, Jonathan Safran. *Extremely Loud and Incredibly Close*. 2005. London: Penguin, 2006.

Forster, E.M. *A Passage to India*. 1924. London: Penguin, 2005.

———. "Preface." *Untouchable*. By Mulk Raj Anand. 1935. London: Penguin, 1986. v–viii.

Freeman, John. "Hay Festival: Rushdie's Return to Magical Thinking." *The Guardian* 26 May 2008 <http://blogs.guardian.co.uk/books/2008/05/hay_festival_rushdies_return_t.html>.

Friedberg, Anne. *Window Shopping: Cinema and the Postmodern*. Berkeley: U of California P, 1994.

Frow, John. *Cultural Studies and Cultural Value*. Oxford: Clarendon, 1995.

———. "Economies of Value." *Multicultural States: Rethinking Difference and Identity*. Ed. David Bennett. London: Routledge, 1998. 53–68.

Ganapathy-Doré, Geetha. "An Orphic Journey to the Disorient: Salman Rushdie's *The Ground Beneath Her Feet*." *Journal of Postcolonial Writing* 38.2 (2000): 17–27.

———. "Shakespeare in Rushdie/Shakespearean Rushdie." *ATLANTIS: Journal of the Spanish Association of Anglo-American Studies* 31.2 (2009): 9–22.

Gandhi, Leela. *Postcolonial Theory: A Critical Introduction*. St. Leonards, N.S.W.: Allen & Unwin, 1998.

Ghosh, Amitav. "India's Untold War of Independence." *The New Yorker* 23–30 Jun. 1997: 104–121.

———. *The Glass Palace*. 2000. London: Flamingo, 2002.

———. "Commonwealth: Misnomer, Not an Award." *The Times of India* 21 Mar. 2001 <http://timesofindia.indiatimes.com/articleshow/34944899.cms>.

———. *Sea of Poppies*. 2008. London: John Murray, 2009.
Ghoshal, Somak. "Booker for the Billion." *The Telegraph* 23 Oct. 2008 <http://epaper.telegraphindia.com/TT/TT/2008/10/23/ArticleHtmls/23_10_2008_008_019.shtml>.
Gikandi, Simon. *Maps of Englishness: Writing Identity in the Culture of Colonialism*. New York: Columbia UP, 1996.
Gilroy, Paul. *After Empire: Melancholia or Convivial Culture?* London: Routledge, 2004.
Godeau, Rémi. "Lord Ahmed: 'Son Titre Doit Lui Être Retiré.'" *Le Figaro* 14 Oct. 2007 <http://www.lefigaro.fr/international/2007/06/21/01003-20070621ARTWWW90263-lord_ahmed_son_titre_doit_lui_etre_retire.php>.
Gonzalez, Madelena. *Fiction After the Fatwa: Salman Rushdie and the Charm of Catastrophe.* Amsterdam: Rodopi, 2005.
Gopal, Priyamvada. "Sir Salman's Long Journey." *The Guardian* 18 Jun. 2007 <http://books.guardian.co.uk/comment/story/0,,2105445,00.html>.
Gopinath, Gayatri. "Bollywood Spectacles: Queer Diasporic Critique in the Aftermath of 9/11." *Social Text* 84–85, 23.3–4 (2005): 157–169.
Gordimer, Nadine. *The Conservationist*. 1974. London: Bloomsbury, 2005.
Gould, Phil. "Goodness Gracious, It's All Go for Meera; TV's *Goodness Gracious Me* Star Meera Syal Talks to Phil Gould about Her Flourishing Career." *The Birmingham Post* 22 Feb. 2000. 15.
Guest, Katy. "Beauty and the Brain: So, What Attracted You to a Short, Balding Egomaniac?" *The Independent* 25 Oct. 2009 <http://www.independent.co.uk/news/people/news/beauty-and-the-brain-so-what-attracted-you-to-a-short-balding-egomaniac-1808973.html>.
Gunster, Shane. *Capitalizing on Culture: Critical Theory for Cultural Studies*. Toronto: U of Toronto P, 2004.
Gupta, Kanchan. "*Slumdog* Is About Defaming Hindus." *The Daily Pioneer* 25 Jan. 2009 <http://dailypioneer.com/152164/Slumdog-is-about-defaming-Hindus.html>.
Gurnah, Abdulrazak. "Introduction." *The Cambridge Companion to Salman Rushdie*. Ed. Abdulrazak Gurnah. Cambridge: Cambridge UP, 2007. 1–8.
Gussow, Mel. "Another Bend in the River for Naipaul: He Tests the Water for Nobel Prize Speech." *New York Times* 15 Nov. 2001 <http://query.nytimes.com/gst/fullpage.html?res=9F01EED71F38F936A25752C1A9679C8B63>.
Hall, Stuart. "New Ethnicities." 1988. *Stuart Hall: Critical Dialogues in Cultural Studies*. Eds David Morley and Kuan-Hsing Chen. London: Routledge, 1996. 442–451.
———. "The Local and the Global: Globalization and Ethnicity." *Dangerous Liaisons: Gender, Nation, and Postcolonial Perspectives*. Eds Anne McClintock, Aamir Mufti, and Ella Shohat. Minneapolis: U of Minnesota P, 1997. 173–187.
———. "Cultural Identity and Diaspora." *Theorizing Diaspora: A Reader*. Eds Jana Evans Braziel and Anita Mannur. Oxford: Blackwell, 2003. 233–246.

Hamid, Mohsin. *The Reluctant Fundamentalist*. Orlando: Harcourt, 2007.
Hanif. Mohammed. *A Case of Exploding Mangoes*. 2008. London: Vintage, 2009.
Hardt, Michael, and Antonio Negri. *Empire*. Cambridge, MA: Harvard UP, 2000.
Hassumani, Sabrina. *Salman Rushdie: A Postmodern Reading of His Major Works*. Cranbury: Fairleigh Dickinson, 2002.
Hesmondhalgh, David. *The Cultural Industries*. London: Sage, 2002.
Higgins, Charlotte. "Out of the Darkness: Adiga's *White Tiger* Rides to Booker Victory Against the Odds." *The Guardian* 14 Oct. 2008 <http://www.guardian.co.uk/books/2008/oct/14/booker-prize-adiga-white-tiger>.
Higson, Andrew. "The Instability of the National." *British Cinema: Past and Present*. Eds Andrew Higson and Justine Ashby. London: Routledge, 2000. 35–47.
———. *English Heritage, English Cinema: Costume Drama Since 1980*. Oxford: Oxford UP, 2003.
———, ed. *Dissolving Views: Key Writings on British Cinema*. London: Cassell, 1996.
Hill, John. *British Cinema in the 1980's: Issues and Themes*. Oxford: Clarendon, 1999.
Hipsky, Martin. "Anglophil(m)ia: Why Does America Watch Merchant-Ivory Movies?" *Journal of Popular Film and Television* 22.3 (1994) 98–107.
"His Master's Voice." *The Economist* 11 Sep. 2008 <http://www.economist.com/books/displaystory.cfm?story_id=12202501>.
Hohendahl, Peter Uwe. *Prismatic Thought: Theodor W. Adorno*. Lincoln, NE: U of Nebraska P, 1995.
Horkheimer, Max, and Theodor Adorno. *Dialectic of Enlightenment*. 1972. Trans. John Cumming. New York: Continuum, 2001.
Hornaday, Ann. "From 'Slumdog' to Riches in a Crowd-Pleasing Fable." *Washington Post*. 12 Nov. 2008 <http://www.washingtonpost.com/wpdyn/content/article/2008/11/11/AR2008111102775.html>.
Huggan, Graham. *The Postcolonial Exotic: Marketing the Margins*. London: Routledge, 2001.
———. *Interdisciplinary Measures: Literature and the Future of Postcolonial Studies*. Liverpool: Liverpool UP, 2008.
Hulme, Keri. *The Bone People*. 1985. London: Picador, 2001.
Huq, Rupa. "Global Youth Cultures in Localized Spaces: The Case of the UK New Asian Dance Music and French Rap." *The Post-Subcultures Reader*. Eds David Muggleton and Rupert Weinzierl. New York: Berg, 2003. 195–208.
———. *Beyond Subculture: Pop, Youth and Identity in a Postcolonial World*. London: Routledge, 2006.
Hutcheon, Linda. *The Politics of Postmodernism*. London: Routledge, 1989.
Hutnyk, John. *Critique of Exotica: Music, Politics and the Culture Industry*. London: Pluto, 2000.
Iftekharuddin, Farhat. "Salman Rushdie." *A Reader's Companion to the Short Story in English*. Eds Erin Fallon, R.C. Feddersen, James Kurtzleben, Maurice A. Lee, and Susan Rochette-Crawley. Westport, CT: Greenwood, 2001. 364–374.

"I Highlighted India's Brutal Injustices: Adiga." *Rediff.com* 16 Oct. 2008 <http://www.rediff.com/news/2008/oct/16adiga.htm>.

"India Uses Gun License as Sterilization Incentive." *The Washington Times* 29 Mar. 2008 <http://www.washingtontimes.com/news/2008/mar/29/india-uses-gun-license-as-sterilization-incentive/>.

Ishiguro, Kazuo. *The Remains of the Day*. 1989. London: Faber and Faber, 2005.

Ivory, James. *Savages, Shakespeare Wallah: Two Films by James Ivory*. New York: Grove, 1973.

Iyer, Meena, and Anubha Sawhney Joshi. "Whats and Whys of a Film Shot in Mumbai." *The Times of India* 13 Jan. 2009 <http://timesofindia.indiatimes.com/Sunday_TOI/Deep_Focus/Whats_and_whys_of_a_film_shot_in_Mumbai/articleshow/3970141.cms>.

Jacobs, Jane M. *Edge of Empire: Postcolonialism and the City*. London: Routledge, 1996.

Jameson, Frederic. "Third World Literature and National Allegory." *Social Text* 15 (1986): 69–88.

Jeffries, Stuart. "'I'm the Luckiest Novelist in the World.'" *The Guardian* 16 Jan 2009 <http://www.guardian.co.uk/books/2009/jan/16/danny-boyle-india>.

Jhabvala, Ruth Prawer. *Heat and Dust*. 1975. New York: Counterpoint, 2003.

Jury, Louise. "Outsider Desai Is Youngest Woman to Win Man Booker." *The Independent* 11 Oct. 2006 <http://www.independent.co.uk/arts-entertainment/books/news/outsider-desai-is-youngest-woman-to-win-man-booker-419525.html>.

Kadzis, Peter. "Rushdie Rocks." *weeklywire.com* 10 May 1999 <http://weeklywire.com/ww/05-10-99/boston_books_3.html>.

———. "Salman Speaks." *Conversations With Salman Rushdie*. Ed. Michael R. Reder. Jackson: U of Mississippi P, 2000. 216–227.

Kalfus, Ken. *A Disorder Peculiar to the Country*. 2006. London: Pocket, 2007.

Kapadia, Parmita. "Shakespeare Transposed: The British Stage on the Post-Colonial Screen." *Almost Shakespeare: Reinventing His Works for Cinema and Television*. Eds James R. Keller and Leslie Stratyne. Jefferson, NC: McFarland & Company, 2004. 42–56.

———. "Transnational Shakespeare: Salman Rushdie and Intertextual Appropriation." *Borrowers and Lenders: The Journal of Shakespeare and Appropriation* 3.2 (2008): 1–21 <http://www.borrowers.uga.edu/cocoon/borrowers/pdf?id=781652>.

Kapur, Akash. "The Secret of His Success." *New York Times* 7 Nov. 2008 <http://www.nytimes.com/2008/11/09/books/review/Kapur-t.html?_r=1>.

Kaur, Raminder, and Virinder S. Kalra. "New Paths for South Asian Identity and Musical Creativity." *Dis-Orienting Rhythms: The Politics of the New Asian Dance Music*. Eds Sanjay Sharma, John Hutnyk, and Ashwani Sharma. London: Zed, 1996. 217–231.

Kendal, Geoffrey, and Clare Colvin. *The Shakespeare Wallah*. London: Sidgwick & Jackson, 1986.

"Kiran Desai: Exclusive Interview." *themanbookerprize.com* n.d. <http://www.themanbookerprize.com/perspective/qanda/40>.
Kortenaar, Neil. *Self, Nation, Text in Salman Rushdie's* Midnight's Children. Montreal: McGill-Queen's UP, 2004.
Krasny, Michael. "A Conversation With Salman Rushdie." *FORA.tv* 18 Jun. 2008 <http://fora.tv/2008/06/18/A_Conversation_with_Salman_Rushdie>.
Kumar, Amitava. "Is Salman Rushdie God?" *Tehelka* 6 Aug. 2005 <http://www.amitavakumar.com/articles/rushdie2.html>.
———. "*Slumdog Millionaire*'s Bollywood Ancestors." *Vanity Fair* 23 Dec. 2008 <http://www.vanityfair.com/online/oscars/2008/12/slumdog-millionaires-bollywood-ancestors.html>.
Kuortti, Joel. *The Salman Rushdie Bibliography: A Bibliography of Salman Rushdie's Work and Rushdie Criticism.* Frankfurt: Peter Lang, 1997.
Kureishi, Hanif. *Gabriel's Gift.* London: Faber and Faber, 2001.
Lakshman, Nirmala. "A Columbus of the Near-at-Hand." 1999. *Salman Rushdie Interviews: A Sourcebook of His Ideas.* Ed. Pradyumna S. Chauhan. Westport, CT: Greenwood, 2001. 279–289.
Lakshmi, Padma. *Easy Exotic: Low-Fat Recipes from Around the World.* New York: Hyperion, 1999.
Lanier, Douglas. *Shakespeare and Modern Popular Culture.* New York: Oxford UP, 2002.
Lash, Scott, and John Urry. *Economies of Signs and Space.* Thousand Oaks, CA: Sage, 1994.
Lau, Lisa. "Re-Orientalism: The Perpetation and Development of Orientalism by Orientals." *Modern Asian Studies* 43. 2 (2009): 571–590.
Lau, Lisa and Ana Mendes, eds. *Re-Orientalism and South Asian Identity Politics: The Oriental Other Within.* London: Routledge, 2011.
Law, Lisa, Tim Bunnell, and Chin-Ee Ong. "*The Beach*, The Gaze and Film Tourism." *Tourist Studies* 7.2 (2007): 141–164.
Lim, Dennis. "What, Exactly, Is *Slumdog Millionaire*?" *Slate* 26 Jan. 2009 <http://www.slate.com/id/2209783/>.
Loomba, Ania. *Gender, Race, Renaissance Drama.* Manchester: Manchester UP, 1989.
Loshitzky, Yosefa. "Travelling Culture/Travelling Television" *Screen* 37.4 (1996): 323–335.
Luckett, Moya. "Postnational Television? *Goodness Gracious Me* and the Britasian Diaspora." *Planet TV: A Global Television Reader.* Eds Lisa Parks and Shanti Kumar. New York: New York UP, 2003. 402–422.
MacCabe, Colin. "Salman Rushdie Talks to the London Consortium About *The Satanic Verses.*" 1996. *Salman Rushdie Interviews: A Sourcebook of His Ideas.* Ed. Pradyumna S. Chauhan. Westport, CT: Greenwood, 2001. 213–229.
Magnier, Mark. "Now Playing in India, 'Slumdog' Dismays Some." *Los Angeles Times* 25 Jan. 2009 <http://www.boston.com/news/world/asia/articles/2009/01/25/now_playing_in_india_slumdog_dismays_some/>.

Malik, Sarita. *Representing Black Britain: Black and Asian Images on Television.* London: Sage, 2002.

Mannur, Anita. "Culinary Fictions: Immigrant Foodways and Race in Indian American Literature." *Asian American Studies After Critical Mass.* Ed. Kent A. Ono. Malden, MA: Blackwell, 2004. 56–70.

Manus, Willard. "A Talk With Salman Rushdie." *Lively Arts: An Internet Cultural Magazine.* Nov./Dec. 2002 <http://www.lively-arts.com/books/2002/0211/salman_rushdie.htm>.

Marrouchi, Mustapha. "Fear of the *Other*, Loathing the Similar." *College Literature* 26.3 (1999): 17–58.

Marshall, P. David. *Celebrity and Power: Fame in Contemporary Culture.* Minneapolis: U of Minnesota P, 1997.

Marx, John. "Postcolonial Literature and the Western Literary Canon." *The Cambridge Companion to Postcolonial Literary Studies.* Ed. Neil Lazarus. Cambridge: Cambridge UP, 2004. 83–96.

Marzorati, Gerald. "Salman Rushdie: Fiction's Embattled Infidel." *New York Times* 29 Jan. 1989 <http://query.nytimes.com/gst/fullpage.html?res=950DE6DD1F39F93AA15752C0A96F948260&sec=&spon=&pagewanted=6>.

Mattin, David. "*The White Tiger*, by Aravind Adiga." *The Independent* 11 May 2008 <http://www.independent.co.uk/arts-entertainment/books/reviews/the-white-tiger-by-aravind-adiga-823472.html>.

McCrum, Robert. "Eight Oscars: Not Bad for a Debut Novelist." *The Observer* 1 Mar. 2009 <http://www.guardian.co.uk/books/2009/mar/01/fiction>.

McEwan, Ian. *Saturday.* 2005. London: Vintage, 2006.

McInerney, Jay. *The Good Life.* London: Bloomsbury, 2007.

Mehta, Suketu. *Maximum City: Bombay Lost and Found.* London: Vintage, 2005.

Mercer, Kobena. *Welcome to the Jungle: New Positions in Black Cultural Studies.* London: Routledge, 1994.

Meyer, Michael. "Swift and Sterne Revisited: Postcolonial Parodies in Salman Rushdie and Singh-Toor." *Cheeky Fictions: Laughter and the Postcolonial.* Eds Susanne Reichl and Mark Stein. Amsterdam and New York: Rodopi, 2005. 117–130.

"Middle Youth Alert." *The Sunday Times* 11 May 2008 <http://www.timesonline.co.uk/tol/life_and_style/men/article3883104.ece>.

Mignolo, Walter. *Local Histories/Global Designs: Coloniality, Subaltern Knowledges, and Border Thinking.* Princeton: Princeton UP, 2000.

Miller, Laura. "*Shalimar the Clown*: An Assassin Prepares." *New York Times* 23 Oct. 2005 <http://www.nytimes.com/2005/10/23/books/review/23miller.html>.

Mirchandani, Raakhee, and Danica Lo. "Haute List: Yay Bombay." *The New York Post.* 3 Apr. 2008 <http://www.nypost.com/seven/04032008/entertainment/fashion/haute_list_104762.htm>.

Mishra, Pankaj. *The Romantics.* 2000. London: Picador, 2001.

Mishra, Vijay. "Salman Rushdie and Bollywood Cinema." *The Cambridge Companion to Salman Rushdie.* Ed. Abdulrazak Gurnah. Cambridge: Cambridge UP, 2007. 11–28.

Mistry, Rohinton. *Such a Long Journey.* 1991. London: Faber and Faber, 2006.

———. *A Fine Balance.* 1995. New York: Knopf, 2001.

———. *Family Matters.* 2002. London: Faber and Faber, 2006.

Mitchell, W.J.T. *What Do Pictures Want?: The Lives and Loves of Images.* Chicago: U of Chicago P, 2005.

Mitchinson, John. "Between God and Evil." 1988. *Salman Rushdie Interviews: A Sourcebook of His Ideas.* Ed. Pradyumna S. Chauhan. Westport, CT: Greenwood, 2001. 93–97.

Mittapalli, Rajeshwar, and Joel Kuortti, eds. *Salman Rushdie: New Critical Insights.* 2 vols. New Delhi: Atlantic, 2003.

Mondal, Anshuman A. "*The Ground Beneath Her Feet* and *Fury*: The Reinvention of Location." *The Cambridge Companion to Salman Rushdie.* Ed. Abdulrazak Gurnah. Cambridge: Cambridge UP, 2007. 169–183.

Moran, Joe. *Star Authors: Literary Celebrity in America.* London: Pluto, 2000.

Morley, David, and Kevin Robbins. *Spaces of Identity: Global Media, Electronic Landscapes, and Cultural Boundaries.* London: Routledge, 1995.

Morton, Stephen. *Salman Rushdie: Fictions of Postcolonial Modernity.* Basingstoke: Palgrave, 2008.

Muir, Kate. "Exclusive Interview With Salman Rushdie." *The Times* 4 Apr. 2008 <http://entertainment.timesonline.co.uk/tol/arts_and_entertainment/books/article3681048.ece>.

Mukherjee, Meenakshi. *The Perishable Empire: Essays on Indian Writing in English.* New York: Oxford UP, 2000.

Muraleedharan, T. "Imperial Migrations: Reading the Raj Cinema of the 1980s." *British Historical Cinema: The History, Heritage and Costume Film.* Eds Claire Monk and Amy Sargeant. London: Routledge, 2002. 144–162.

Nagarajan, Vijaya. "Salman Rushdie on Bombay, Rock N' Roll, and *The Satanic Verses.*" *Whole Earth Review* Fall 1999 <http://wholeearth.com/issue/98/article/90/salman.rushdie.on.bombay.rock.n'.roll.and.the.satanic.verses>.

Nagra, Daljit. *Look We Have Coming to Dover!.* London: Faber and Faber, 2007.

Naipaul, V.S. *An Area of Darkness.* 1964. London: Vintage, 2002.

———. *In A Free State.* 1971. London: Picador, 2002.

Naravane, Vaiju. "Eyes Wide Open." *The Hindu* 07 Oct. 2007 <http://www.thehindu.com/thehindu/lr/2007/10/07/stories/2007100750110100.htm>.

Narayan, R.K. *The Guide.* 1958. London: Penguin, 2006.

Narayan, Shoba. *Monsoon Diary: A Memoir With Recipes.* New York: Random House, 2004.

"'Narcopolis': Inside India's Dark Underbelly." *NPR* 08 Apr. 2012 <http://m.npr.org/story/150003126?url=/2012/04/08/150003126/wesun-narcopolis-shell>.

Nogueira, Adelaine. "Shakespeare's *Hamlet*, Salman Rushdie's 'Yorick,' and the Dilemmas of Tradition." *Foreign Accents: Brazilian Readings of Shakespeare.* Eds Thomas LaBorie Burns and Aimara da Cunha Resende. Newark: U of Delaware P, 2002. 138–153.
Ommundsen, Wenche. "Sex, Soap and Sainthood: Beginning to Theorise Literary Celebrity." *JASAL* 3 (2004): 45–56.
O'Neill, Joseph. *Netherland.* London: Fourth Estate, 2008.
O'Regan, Tom. "A National Cinema." *The Film Cultures Reader.* Ed. Graeme Turner. London: Routledge, 2002. 139–164.
Orsini, Francesca. "India in the Mirror of World Fiction." *Debating World Literature.* Ed. Christopher Prendergast. London: Verso, 2004. 319–333.
Osaka, Chika. "*Slumdog* Author Says Film Gained From India Setting." *Reuters India* 14 Mar. 2009 <http://in.reuters.com/article/topNews/idINIndia-38501320090313>.
Parry, Benita. *Postcolonial Studies: A Materialist Critique.* New York: Routledge, 2004.
Pipes, Daniel. *The Rushdie Affair: The Novel, the Ayatollah, and the West.* 1990. 2nd ed. New Brunswick, NJ: Transaction, 2003.
Pirbhai, Mariam. "The Paradox of Globalization as an 'Untotalizable Totality' in Salman Rushdie's *The Ground Beneath Her Feet.*" *International Fiction Review* 28 (2001): 54–66.
Ponzanesi, Sandra. "Boutique Postcolonialism: Literary Awards, Cultural Value and the Canon." *Fiction and Literary Prizes in Great Britain.* Eds Holger Klein and Wolfgang Görtschacher. Vienna: Praesens Verlag, 2006. 107–134.
Prashad, Vijay. *The Karma of Brown Folk.* Minneapolis: U of Minnesota P, 2000.
Preston, John. "Salman Rushdie: Provoking People Is in My DNA." *The Daily Telegraph* 29 Dec. 2008 <http://www.telegraph.co.uk/culture/books/4015303/Salman-Rushdie-provoking-people-is-in-my-DNA.html>.
Price, Leah. *The Anthology and the Rise of the Novel.* Cambridge: Cambridge UP, 2000.
Procter, James. *Dwelling Places: Postwar Black British Writing.* Manchester: Manchester UP, 2003.
———. "New Ethnicities, the Novel, and the Burdens of Representation." *A Concise Companion to Contemporary British Fiction.* Ed. James F. English. Oxford: Blackwell, 2006. 101–120.
"Q&A With Indra Sinha." *sepiamutiny.com* 13 Mar. 2008 <http://www.sepiamutiny.com/sepia/archives/005088.html>.
Rajan, Rajeswari. "Writing in English in India, Again." *The Hindu* 18 Feb. 2001 <http://www.hindu.com/2001/02/18/stories/1318067m.htm>.
Ramachandran, Hema. "Salman Rushdie's *The Satanic Verses*: Hearing the Postcolonial Cinematic Novel." *The Journal of Commonwealth Literature* 40.3 (2005): 102–117.
Ranasinha, Ruvani. *South Asian Writers in Twentieth-Century Britain: Culture in Translation.* Oxford: Oxford UP, 2007.

Rao, Raja. *Kanthapura*. 1938. Bombay: Oxford UP, 1963.
ReVelle, Penelope, and Charles ReVelle. *The Global Environment: Securing a Sustainable Future*. Boston: Jones & Bartlett, 1992.
Robinson, Andrew. *Satyajit Ray: The Inner Eye: The Biography of a Master Film-Maker*. London: I. B. Tauris, 2004.
Rollason, Christopher. "Rushdie's Un-Indian Music: *The Ground Beneath Her Feet*." *Salman Rushdie: New Critical Insights*. Vol. 2. Eds Rajeshwar Mittapalli and Joel Kuortti. New Delhi: Atlantic, 2003. 89–125. Updated version, 2006: <http://yatrarollason.info/files/RushdieGFupdated.pdf>.
Rombes, Nicholas D. "*The Satanic Verses* as a Cinematic Narrative." *Literature-Film Quarterly* 21.1 (1993): 47–53.
Rose, Charlie. "The Moor's Last Sigh." *Conversations With Salman Rushdie*. Ed. Michael R. Reder. Jackson: U of Mississippi P, 2000. 199–215.
Ross, Jean W. "*Contemporary Authors* Interview: Salman Rushdie." *Conversations With Salman Rushdie*. Ed. Michael R. Reder. Jackson: U of Mississippi P, 2000, 1–7.
Roy, Arundhati. *The God of Small Things*. 1997. London: Harper Perennial, 2004.
———. "Caught on Film: India 'Not Shining.'" *Dawn.com* 2 Mar. 2009 <http://www.dawn.com/wps/wcm/connect/dawn-content-library/dawn/news/entertainment/caught-on-film-india-not-shining-ss>.
"The Rushdies: Babe Magnets?" *The New York Post* 12 Dec. 2006 <http://www.nypost.com/seven/12122006/gossip/pagesix/pagesix.htm>.
Rutherford, Jonathan. "A Place Called Home: Identity and the Cultural Politics of Difference." *Identity: Community, Culture, Difference*. Ed. Jonathan Rutherford. London: Lawrence and Wishart, 1990. 9–27.
———. "The Third Space: Interview With Homi Bhabha." *Identity: Community, Culture, Difference*. Ed. Jonathan Rutherford. London: Lawrence and Wishart, 1990. 207–221.
Said, Edward. *The World, the Text, and the Critic*. Cambridge, MA: Harvard UP, 1983.
———. *Culture and Imperialism*. London: Vintage, 1993.
———. *Representations of the Intellectual: The 1993 Reith Lectures*. London: Vintage, 1994.
———. *Out of Place: A Memoir*. New York: Vintage, 1999.
———. "The Public Role of Writers and Intellectuals." *The Public Intellectual*. Ed. Helen Small. Oxford: Blackwell, 2002. 19–39.
Saltzman, Paul. *The Beatles at Rishikesh*. New York: Viking, 2001.
Salvatore, Armando. "The Problem of the Ingraining of Civilizing Traditions into Social Governance." *Muslim Traditions and Modern Techniques of Power*. Ed. Armando Salvatore. Hamburg: LIT, 2001. 9–44.
Sanga, Jaina. *Salman Rushdie's Postcolonial Metaphors: Migration, Translation, Hybridity, Blasphemy, and Globalization*. Westport, CT: Greenwood, 2001.
Sardar, Ziauddin. "Welcome to Planet Blitcon." *New Statesman* 11 Dec. 2006 <http://www.newstatesman.com/200612110045>.

Sawhney, Anubha. "An Indian is Not a Freak in London: Rushdie." *The Times of India* 21 Jan. 2007 <http://timesofindia.indiatimes.com/articleshow/msid-1343391,prtpage-1.cms>.

Sawhney, Sabina, and Simona Sawhney. "Reading Rushdie After September 11, 2001." *Twentieth Century Literature* 47.4 (2001): 431–444.

Schürer, Norbert. *Salman Rushdie's* Midnight's Children*: A Reader's Guide*. New York: Continuum, 2004.

Scott, Paul. *Staying On*. 1977. London: Arrow, 1999.

Seabrook, John. *Nobrow: The Culture of Marketing, The Marketing of Culture*. New York: Knopf, 2000.

Self, Will. "If the Veil Sucks, So Does the Extremism of Its Foes." *The Evening Standard* 12 Oct. 2006 <http://www.encyclopedia.com/doc/1G1-152709631.html>.

Seth, Vikram. *A Suitable Boy*. London: Orion, 1994.

Sexton, David. "A Scathing, Abusively Satirical Antidote to the Romance of Rushdie." *Evening Standard* 15 Oct. 2008 <http://www.thisislondon.co.uk/standard/article-23572936-details/A+scathing,+abusively+satirical+antidote+to+the+romance+of+Rushdie/article.do>.

Sharma, Purnima. "Hot Write Now." *The Times of India* 8 Dec. 2008 <http://timesofindia.indiatimes.com/Potpourri/Hot_write_now/articleshow/3804469.cms>.

Sharma, Shailja. "Citizens of the Empire: Revisionist History and the Social Imaginary in *Gandhi*." *Velvet Light Trap* 35 (1995): 61–68.

Sharma, Sanjay. "Noisy Asians or 'Asian Noise'?" *Dis-Orienting Rhythms: The Politics of the New Asian Dance Music*. Eds Sanjay Sharma, John Hutnyk, and Ashwani Sharma. London: Zed, 1996. 32–57.

Sharma, Sanjay, John Hutnyk, and Ashwani Sharma. "Introduction." *Dis-Orienting Rhythms: The Politics of the New Asian Dance Music*. Eds Sanjay Sharma, John Hutnyk, and Ashwani Sharma. London: Zed, 1996. 1–11.

Sheth, Ketaki. *Bombay Mix: Street Photographs*. Stockport: Dewi Lewis and Sepia International, 2007.

Shivani, Anis. "Indo-Anglian Fiction: The New Orientalism." *Race & Class* 47.4 (2006): 1–25.

Siddiqi, Yumna. "'Power Smashes into Private Lives': Violence, Globalization and Cosmopolitanism in Salman Rushdie's *Shalimar the Clown*." *South Asia Research* 27.3 (2007): 293–309.

Silverblatt, Michael. "*Bookworm With Michael Silverblatt*, Guest: Salman Rushdie." 1996. *Salman Rushdie Interviews: A Sourcebook of His Ideas*. Ed. Pradyumna S. Chauhan. Westport, CT: Greenwood, 2001. 199–208.

Simon, Taryn. *An American Index of the Hidden and Unfamiliar*. Göttingen: Steidl, 2007.

Singh, Charu. *Spectrum History of Indian Literature in English*. New Delhi: Atlantic, 1997.

Singh, Jyotsna. "Different Shakespeares: The Bard in Colonial/Postcolonial India." *Theatre Journal* 41 (1989): 445–458.

Sinha, Indra. *Animal's People*. 2007. London: Simon & Schuster, 2008.
Smale, David, ed. *Salman Rushdie:* Midnight's Children/The Satanic Verses: *A Reader's Guide to Essential Criticism*. Hampshire: Palgrave, 2001.
Smith, Zadie. *White Teeth*, London: Hamish Hamilton, 2000.
———. *On Beauty*. 2005. London: Penguin, 2006.
Solomons, Jason. "Mumbai Millionaire Makes a Fabulous Finale." *The Observer* 2 Nov. 2008 <http://www.guardian.co.uk/film/2008/nov/02/londonfilmfestival>.
Spencer, Robert. "Death to Rushdie, Again." *FrontPageMagazine.com* 20 Jun. 2007 <http://frontpagemagazine.com/Articles/Read.aspx?GUID=A81DD5BC-CAA8-4E1F-A867-4DF059F2B3DF>.
Squires, Claire. "A Common Ground? Book Prize Culture in Europe." *The Public* 11.4 (2004): 37–48.
———. *Marketing Literature: The Making of Contemporary Writing in Britain*. London: Palgrave, 2007.
Street, John. "'Showbusiness of a Serious Kind': a Cultural Politics of the Arts Prize." *Media, Culture & Society* 27.6 (2005): 819–840.
Street, Sarah. *British National Cinema*. London: Routledge, 1997.
Strongman, Luke. *The Booker Prize and the Legacy of Empire*. Amsterdam and New York: Rodopi, 2002.
Subrahmanyam, Sanjay. "Diary." *London Review of Books* 6 Nov. 2008 <http://www.lrb.co.uk/v30/n21/subr01_.html>
———. "The Angel and the Toady." *The Guardian* 14 Feb. 2009 <http://www.guardian.co.uk/books/2009/feb/14/salman-rushdie-ayatollah-khomeini-fatwa>.
Sutherland, John. "The Sound and the Fury." *The Guardian* 25 Aug. 2001 <http://www.guardian.co.uk/books/2001/aug/25/fiction.salmanrushdie>.
Swarup, Vikas. *Q & A*. 2005. London: Black Swan, 2006.
Syal, Meera. *Anita and Me*. London: HarperCollins, 1996.
———. "Last Laugh." *redhotcurry.com* n.d. <http://www.redhotcurry.com/pdfs/multicultural_essay_syal.pdf>.
Tagore, Rabindranath. "Letter from Rabindranath Tagore to Lord Chelmsford, Viceroy of India." 1919. 2001. <http://www.calcuttaweb.com/tagore/knighthoodrej.shtml>.
Tejpal, Tarun. "Rushdie and the Sea of Prejudice." *Outlookindia.com* 16 Jul. 1997 <http://www.outlookindia.com/article.aspx?203839>.
———. "The Missionary Position." *Tehelka* 6.9 7 Mar. 2009 <http://www.tehelka.com/story_main41.asp?filename=hub070309the_missionary.asp>.
Teverson, Andrew. *Salman Rushdie*. Manchester: Manchester UP, 2007.
Thakraney, Anil. "Bhopal's Angel." 22 Sep. 2007 <http://anilthakraneyonsunday.blogspot.com/2007/09/bhopals-angel.html>.
Thieme, John. "'So Few Rainbows Any More'? Cinema, Nostalgia and the Concept of 'Home' in Salman Rushdie's Fiction." *Le Simplegadi: Rivista Internazionale On-line di Lingue e Letterature Moderne* 2 (2004) <http://web.uniud.it/all/simplegadi/>

Thomson, Alex. *Adorno: A Guide for the Perplexed*. London: Continuum, 2006.
Thomson, Alice, and Rachel Sylvester. "Saturday Interview: Salman Rushdie." *The Times* 3 Jan. 2009 <http://entertainment.timesonline.co.uk/tol/arts_and_entertainment/books/article5434968.ece>.
Todd, Richard. *Consuming Fictions: The Booker Prize and Fiction in Britain Today*. London: Bloomsbury, 1996.
Tolkien, J.R.R. *The Lord of the Rings*. 1937–1949. 3 vols. London: HarperCollins, 2007.
Tonkin, Boyd. "Salman Rushdie: 'Fiction Saved My Life.'" *The Independent* 11 Apr. 2008 <http://www.independent.co.uk/arts-entertainment/books/features/salman-rushdie-fiction-saved-my-life-807501.html>.
———. "General Fiction: Wizards of Oz Surf into Fiction's Front Rank." *The Independent* 28 Nov. 2008 <http://www.independent.co.uk/arts-entertainment/books/features/general-fiction-wizards-of-oz-surf-into-fictions-front-rank-1037794.html>.
Tripathi, Salil. "Unconvincing Dehumanization." *The Philadelphia Inquirer* 16 Nov. 2008 <http://www.philly.com/inquirer/entertainment/books/20081116_Unconvincing_dehumanization.html>.
Updike, John. "Paradises Lost: Rushdie's *Shalimar the Clown*." *The New Yorker* 5 Sep. 2005 <http://www.newyorker.com/archive/2005/09/05/050905crbo_books?currentPage=all>.
———. *Terrorist*. 2006. London: Penguin, 2007.
Urry, John. *The Tourist Gaze*. London: Sage, 2002.
Usha, K.R. "Two Destinies." *Phalanx* n.d. <http://www.phalanx.in/pages/review_current_2.html>.
Varma, Rashmi. "Provincializing the Global City: From Bombay to Mumbai." *Social Text* 81 22. 4 (2004): 65–89.
Vohra, Meera. "No Small Talk: Arundhati Slams *Slumdog*." *The Times of India* 11 Feb. 2009 <http://timesofindia.indiatimes.com/articleshow/4112989.cms>.
Wachinger, Tobias. "Spicy Pleasures: Postcolonial India's Literary Celebrities and the Politics of Consumption." *Ariel* 34.2–3 (2003): 71–94.
Wagner, Erica. "Aravind Adiga Wins Man Booker Prize With *The White Tiger*." *The Times* 15 Oct. 2008 <http://entertainment.timesonline.co.uk/tol/arts_and_entertainment/books/article4944850.ece>.
Wagner, Tamara S. "Boutique Multiculturalism and the Consumption of Repulsion: Re-Disseminating Food Fictions in Malaysian and Singaporean Diasporic Novels." *The Journal of Commonwealth Literature* 42 (2007): 31–46.
Walia, Nona. "Our Sheikhspeare?" *The Times of India* 8 Jul. 2005 <http://timesofindia.indiatimes.com/articleshow/1165634.cms>.
———. "Women Prefer Nerds!" *The Times of India* 15 Nov. 2009 <http://timesofindia.indiatimes.com/life/relationships/man-woman/Women-prefer-nerds/articleshow/5226726.cms>.

Wayne, Valerie. "*Shakespeare Wallah* and Colonial Specularity." *Shakespeare, the Movie: Popularizing the Plays on Film, TV, and Video*. Eds Lynda E. Boose and Richard Burt. London: Routledge, 1997. 95–102.

Webb, W.L. "Salman Rushdie: *Satanic Verses*." *Conversations With Salman Rushdie*. Ed. Michael R. Reder. Jackson: U of Mississippi P, 2000. 87–100.

Weedon, Chris. "*Goodness Gracious Me*: Comedy as a Tool for Contesting Racism and Ethnocentrism." *Culture and Power: Challenging Discourses*. Ed. Maria José Coperías Aguilar. Valencia: University of Valencia, Servei de Publicaciones, 2000. 261–269.

Weich, Dave. "Salman Rushdie, Out and About." *Powells.com* 25 Sep. 2002 <http://www.powells.com/authors/rushdie.html>.

Werbner, Pnina. "Theorising Complex Diasporas: Purity and Hybridity in the South Asian Public Sphere in Britain." *Journal of Ethnic and Migration Studies* 30.5 (2004): 895–911.

White, Michael. "Why Did Rushdie Even Accept a Knighthood?" *The Guardian* 20 Jun. 2007 <http://blogs.guardian.co.uk/books/2007/06/why_did_rushdie_even_accept_a.html>

Wilson, A.N. "Why the Prize for Pomposity, Titanic Conceit and Turgid Novels Should Go to Salman Rushdie Every Year." *The Daily Mail* 31 Jul. 2008 <http://www.dailymail.co.uk/news/article-1039995/Why-prize-pomposity-titanic-conceit-turgid-novels-Salman-Rushdie-year.html>.

Witkin, Robert W. *Adorno on Popular Culture*. London: Routledge, 2003.

Wollen, Tana. "Over Our Shoulders: Nostalgic Screen Fictions for the 1980s." *Enterprise and Heritage*. Eds John Corner and Sylvia Harvey. London: Routledge, 1991. 178–193.

Womack, Sarah. "Rushdie Does Not Need Police Guard Say Asian Peers." *The Daily Telegraph* 19 Jun. 2001 <http://www.telegraph.co.uk/news/uknews/1372442/Rushdie-does-not-need-police-guard-say-Asian-peers.html>.

Wong, Sau-ling Cynthia. *Reading Asian American Literature: From Necessity to Extravagance*. Princeton: Princeton UP, 1993.

Zephaniah, Benjamin. "'Me? I Thought, OBE Me? Up Yours, I Thought.'" *The Guardian* 27 Nov. 2003 <http://www.guardian.co.uk/books/2003/nov/27/poetry.monarchy>.

Index

Achebe, Chinua 5, 101
Adiga, Aravind 34–35, 37, 47–50, 53–64, 106–108, 114
Adorno, Theodor W. 2, 7, 10–12, 27, 35, 45, 47, 49, 71, 73, 116, 127–129, 133–134, 137
Ahmad, Aijaz 34, 159
Amis, Martin 70, 149–150
Anand, Mulk Raj 48, 53, 60–61, 92
Attenborough, Richard 114, 163
Avedon, Richard 6
Ayatollah Khomeini 69, 151, 161, 166

Bachchan, Amitabh 106
Baudrillard, Jean 141
Baum, L. Frank 103
Benjamin, Walter 12, 18, 73, 104, 111, 163
Berger, John 39
Bhabha, Homi K. 4, 78–79, 83, 86–87, 95, 169, 171
Blair, Tony 124, 163–164
Bloom, Harold 99, 101
Bollywood 6, 9, 23, 58, 80–82, 104–106, 108–109, 116–118, 131
Booker (Prize) 31, 34, 37–42, 44–48, 54–56, 58, 60–64, 67–69, 71, 80, 98–100, 113
Bourdieu, Pierre 2, 38
Boyle, Danny 35, 104–108, 112, 114–118, 130
Brennan, Timothy 8–9, 70, 151
Brown, Gordon 160
Bush, George W. 151–152

Carey, Peter 80
Chadha, Gurinder 23, 117, 129–131
Chandra, Vikram 41, 48, 60–64, 95–96, 100
Chaudhuri, Amit 43, 77, 88–92, 94–95, 97–98, 100–101
Chaudhuri, Nirad C. 52, 92
Chopra, Deepak 26

Coetzee, J.M. 80, 84
Commonwealth Writers Prize 59–60
Cronenberg, David 58, 103

Dalrymple, William 41
Damrosch, David 77, 88, 101
DeLillo, Don 24, 37, 156
Desai, Anita 65, 100
Desai, Kiran 7, 34, 37, 39–45, 47, 55–56, 100
Dickens, Charles 53–54, 107
Divakaruni, Chitra Banerjee 22–26, 28–31, 98
Dutt, Michael Madhusudhan 95
Dutt, Nargis 109
Dylan, Bob 1, 135, 138

Emory University 68, 84

Fanon, Frantz 169
The Far Pavilions 119, 122
Farrell, J.G. 78–80
fatwa 4, 15–16, 35, 37, 55, 65, 67–71, 73, 75, 141, 158–159, 161, 165–167
film tourism 111–112, 115
Forman, Miloš 75
Forster, E.M. 61, 97, 113
Frankfurt School 11, 128
Frears, Stephen 130

Gandhi, Indira 8, 56–57
Gandhi, Mohandas K. (Mahatma) 43, 114, 123
Gandhi, Rajiv 9
Ghosh, Amitav 44, 47–48, 56, 59–60, 62–63, 77, 99–100
Gilroy, Paul 119, 123, 129, 162
globalization 135, 147, 152, 154
Goodness Gracious Me 40–42, 118–119, 121–124
Gopal, Priyamvada 166–167

Gordimer, Nadine 80, 84
Gunesekera, Romesh 100
Gurnah, Abdulrazak 84, 152

Hall, Stuart 6, 132
Hamid, Mohsin 154
Handsworth Songs 6
Hanif, Mohammed 47
Hollywood 11, 15, 23, 49, 65, 108, 130–131
Howe, Darcus 6
Hulme, Keri 80

The Iliad 7–8
independence (Indian) 40, 52, 80–82, 89–90, 92, 94, 97–98, 100, 110
International Guerrillas 7, 72
Iraq 152, 163, 165
Ishiguro, Kazuo 80
Ivory, James 34, 81

Jackson, Michael 128
Jameson, Frederic 159
The Jewel in the Crown 113, 119, 122–124
Jhabvala, Ruth Prawer 44, 80–81, 99, 113

Kalirai, Harmage Singh 122
Kashmir 147–148, 156–157
Kendal, Geoffrey 81
Khakhar, Bhupen 14
Khan, Mehboob 109
knighthood 35, 65, 160–168
Kumar, Amitava 30, 43, 45–46, 55, 117
Kureishi, Hanif 3–4, 7, 46, 150

Lakshmi, Padma 23–24, 55, 65–66, 69, 73, 165
Lean, David 113, 119
The Lord of the Rings 8
Luhrmann, Baz 117

Madonna 129, 138
magical realism 23, 26
Manto, Saadat Hassan 94–95
McEwan, Ian 149–150, 156
McInerney, Jay 69, 156
Mehta, Deepa 6
Mehta, Suketu 46

Mercer, Kobena 24
Merchant-Ivory 34, 80–83, 113
M.I.A. 110–111
migrancy 5–6, 14, 19, 21, 147–148
Mill, John Stuart 151
mimicry 4, 79, 87
Mishra, Pankaj 27, 77, 100–101
The Mistress of Spices 22–23, 24–27, 29–31, 98
Mistry, Rohinton 44, 48, 56–58, 77, 91, 100
Monroe, Marilyn 10, 117
Mukherjee, Bharati 60–61, 95–96
Mukherjee, Meenakshi 91

Nagarkar, Kiran 91
Nagra, Daljit 48, 55
Naipaul, V.S. 3–5, 43, 69, 80, 89
Nair, Mira 30, 41, 109
Narayan, R.K. 60, 99, 101
Narayan, Shoba 30–31
Nehru, Jawaharlal 110
New York 6, 15, 41, 45, 63, 98, 140, 147, 151–154

Ophüls, Max 75
Orwell, George 159

Pakistan 14, 16, 138, 147, 153, 160
parody 2, 35, 52, 87, 123
pastiche 2, 78, 87, 117–118, 129
photography 6, 24, 35
Prashad, Vijay 26
Presley, Elvis 135, 138
Pussycat Dolls 118

Rahman, A.R. 110–111, 118
Raj revival 35, 103–104, 113–114, 119–120, 122–123
Rao, Raja 60, 92–93
Ray, Satyajit 82, 109
re-orientalism 3, 13, 22, 28–30, 37, 64, 140, 170–171
Richard, Cliff 117
Roy, Arundhati 35, 40, 44, 91, 100, 104–105
Rugby School 8, 14, 167–168
Rushdie, Salman
    "At the Auction of the Ruby Slippers" 13–15, 17, 19–22, 25

"Chekov and Zulu" 8–9, 84
"Christopher Columbus and Queen Isabella of Spain Consummate Their Relationship" 84
"Commonwealth Literature Does Not Exist" 59–60, 64, 92–97, 147
"The Courter" 10
"A Dream of Glorious Return" 15, 70, 72, 75, 98
"Dynasty" 57
The Enchantress of Florence 33, 44, 47, 55, 75, 155, 158
"A Fine Pickle" 113–114, 116–117
"The Free Radio" 34, 56–58, 106, 108
Fury 10, 16, 49, 68–70, 85, 145–146, 152–153, 155, 158
"Globalization" 151–152, 154
Grimus 5, 19
The Ground Beneath Her Feet 8, 10, 14, 16–17, 22, 35, 68, 71–72, 75, 127, 134–138, 142–143, 145
Haroun and the Sea of Stories 6, 97, 155
Imaginary Homelands 13, 149
"Imaginary Homelands" 17, 19, 88, 171
"In Good Faith" 9, 21, 70, 75
"Is Nothing Sacred" 155
The Jaguar Smile 149, 151, 153
Joseph Anton 4, 8, 19, 33, 158–159
"The Location of *Brazil*" 148
Luka and the Fire of Life 33
Midnight's Children 3–6, 9, 16, 19, 22, 26–28, 31–32, 42–45, 51, 53, 56–57, 59, 62, 68, 72, 93, 99–101, 150, 153, 158
The Moor's Last Sigh 1, 22, 26, 30, 42, 44
"Notes on Writing and the Nation" 155, 169
"Outside the Whale" 104, 119, 121–124, 145–146, 155, 159
The Satanic Verses 1, 5, 7, 9, 16, 26, 44, 67, 69, 72, 81, 85, 96–97, 142, 145, 149–150, 153–154, 158, 160–162, 165–167
Shalimar The Clown 33, 44, 75, 145–146, 148, 150, 156–157
"A Short Tale About Magic" 15, 18–20, 57, 103
Step Across This Line 9, 15, 44, 145–146, 149

"Step Across This Line" 16, 147–148, 151, 154, 159
The Vintage Book of Indian Writing 7, 35, 43–44, 77, 88–90, 92, 94–95, 97–99, 101, 169
"Yorick" 34, 77–78, 80, 83, 85–87
Rushdie, Zafar 66
"Rushdie's Children" 43, 77, 100

Said, Edward 9, 14, 78, 86, 136–138, 146, 148–149, 169
Scott, Paul 80, 122
Seinfeld 72
Self, Will 44, 46
Seth, Vikram 40, 48, 77, 100
Shakespeare, William 34–35, 77–83, 85–87
Shakespeare Wallah 34–35, 80–83, 123
Sheth, Ketaki 46
Simon, Taryn 6
The Simpsons 7–8
Sinha, Indra 40, 55
Slumdog Millionaire 35, 104–108, 110–112, 114–115, 117–118
Smith, Zadie 7, 24, 37, 122
Soyinka, Wole 84
Star Trek 8–9
Syal, Meera 40, 121, 129
Swarup, Vikas 105, 116–117

Tagore, Rabindranath 95, 163, 166
terrorism 8, 151–152, 156–157
Thatcher, Margaret 119–120, 165
Thayil, Jeet 47, 54
Tharoor, Shashi 77, 99
Thompson, E.P. 162

Updike, John 70, 156
Usha, K.R. 50, 62

Vakil, Ardashir 46, 100
Vidal, Gore 72

Walcott, Derek 84, 101
Wenders, Wim 73
West, Elizabeth 35, 69
The Wizard of Oz 15, 17–20, 57, 103
"writing back" 6, 80, 87

Zephaniah, Benjamin 163–164, 166

For Product Safety Concerns and Information please contact our EU
representative GPSR@taylorandfrancis.com
Taylor & Francis Verlag GmbH, Kaufingerstraße 24, 80331 München, Germany

www.ingramcontent.com/pod-product-compliance
Lightning Source LLC
Chambersburg PA
CBHW071356290426
44108CB00014B/1569